Antonia Cl

speakout

2ND EDITION

Pre-intermediate
Flexi Course Book 1

with DVD-ROM

Pearson Education Limited
Edinburgh Gate
Harlow
Essex CM20 2JE
England
and Associated Companies throughout the world.

www.pearsonelt.com

© Pearson Education Limited 2015

The right of Antonia Clare and JJ Wilson to be identified as authors of this Work have been asserted by them in accordance with the Copyright, Designs and Patents Act 1988.

First published 2015
This edition published 2016
ISBN: 978-1-292-14933-2
Set in Aptifer sans 10/12 pt

Acknowledgements

The Publisher and authors would like to thank the following people and institutions for their feedback and comments during the development of the material:
Hungary: Tom Boyle; Japan: Will Pearson; Poland: Lech Wojciech Krzeminski, Piotr Święcicki; UK: Ben Hodge, Joelle Finck, John Barron, Prakash Parmer.

Text acknowledgements

We are grateful to the following for permission to reproduce copyright material:
Extract on page 172 from Outlook, Matthew Bannister interviewing Jessica Fox, 31/01/2013, http://jessicafox.info/wp-content/uploads/2013/01/BBCWorld-Service-Interview-1_21_2013.mp3, copyright © BBC Worldwide Learning.

Audio acknowledgements

Extract from Outlook, Matthew Bannister interviewing Jessica Fox, 31/01/2013, http://jessicafox.info/wp-content/uploads/2013/01/BBCWorld-Service-Interview-1_21_2013.mp3, copyright © BBC Worldwide Learning.

Illustration acknowledgements

Fred Blunt pgs 9, 11, 39, 43, 56, 66, 76, 86, 91, 106, 109, 126, 133, 138, 141, 145, 148; Stephen Cheetham (Handsome Frank) pgs 80; Matt Herring pgs 159; Infomen pgs 161, 163; Joanna Kerr pgs 60; Andrew Lyons pgs 90; Harry Malt pgs 165, 166; Vicky Woodgate pgs 18, 39, 80; Jurgen Ziewe pgs 103; In house pgs 16, 46, 52, 53, 56, 7 8, 136.

Photo acknowledgements

The Publisher would like to thank the following for their kind permission to reproduce their photographs:

(Key: b-bottom; c-centre; l-left; r-right; t-top)

123RF.com: Cathy Yeulet 152 (j), Seanjoh 93 (g), Andrei Shumskiy 7b (icon), 17b (icon), 27b (icon), 37b (icon), 47b (icon), 57b (icon), 67b (icon), 77b (icon), 87b (icon), 97b (icon), 107b (icon), 117b (icon), Hieng Ling Tie 157 (soya); 4Corners Images: Antonino Bartuccio / Sime 27r, 34-35; Alamy Images: Age Fotostock / Caroline Webber 52cr, Alvey & Towers Picture Library 20 (c), Ammentorp Photography 37cr, 43b, Blend Images 37l, BriggsMorris 153 (o), Paul Brown 102 (c), Viktor Cap 50bl, Cultura Creative (RF) 12l, 17cr, Cyrille Gibot 162, Ian Dagnall 87cr, dbimages 88 (c), Dbimages / Allen Brown 32, Eagle Visions Photography / Craig Lovell 93 (f), EpicStockMedia 58tr, Jose Pedro Fernandes 155 (travel guide), Andrew Fox 103t, Kevin Foy 100 (b), fStop / Andreas Stamm 43t, Manfred Grebler 156 (m), H. Mark Weidman Photography 154 (13), Hi Brow Arabia 38c, ICIMAGE 77t, Image Source 83 (e), Image Source Salsa 57r, 64-65, imageBROKER 20 (b), 113, Mark Jordan 102 (b), Juice Images 38cr, Mikael Karlsson 92c, Lucie Lang

110-111tc, Freer Law 63l, Cro Magnon 52tr, Steven May 158 (f), Mediacolor's 47r, New York City 30-31b, PhotoAlto / Frederic Cirou 42tr, Prisma Bildagentur AG 29t, Purepix 7t, Sabena Jane Blackbird 85r, Alex Segre 28tl, Adrian Sherratt 41tl, Paul Springett 08 23 (c), Anna Stowe 12tr, Tetra Images 81 (a), 153 (e), Eniz Umuler 122 (c), Gregg Vignal 153 (n), Jonny White 154 (12), XiXinXing 17l, ZUMA Press Inc 58c; BBC Photo Library: Gary Moyes 7r, 14-15; BBC Worldwide Ltd: 14l, 24l, 34l, 44, 44cl, 64l, 67r, 74l, 94l, 114bl; Camera Press Ltd: Telegraph / Martin Pope 121; Corbis: Aflo / Naho Yoshizawa 41tr, Tim Clayton 28bl, Crave / Hbss 122 (b), Flame / Simon Marcus 30-31t, Hello Lovely 160, Image Source 38bl, 156 (f), Jabruson / Nature Picture Library 67t, Karen Kasmauski 79b, Move Art Management 102 (a), Ocean 27cl, Redchopsticks 59t, Sopa / Antonino Bartuccio 52tl, Tetra Images 57cr, Tetra Images / Mike Kemp 107r, 114-115, Silke Woweries 109cl, Arman Zhenikeyev 117l; Datacraft Co Ltd: 41b, 154 (5); DK Images: 155 (first aid kit), Steve Baxter 60cr, Dave King 77l, Mockford and Bonetti 155 (b), Rough Guides / Nelson Hancock 29b, 83 (d), Rough Guides / Victor Borg 155 (d), William Shaw 157 (lamb), Lorenzo Vecchia 157 (grapefruit); Fotolia: Amax 51tr, barneyboogles 82b, Belman 80br, Mariusz Blach 157 (garlic), Calado 155 (g), CandyBox Images 13br, courtyardpix 97l, drx 153 (l), EpicStockMedia 48, eurobanks 20 (g), fovito 67cr, goodluz 10b, Joe Gough 157 (steak), grafikplusfoto 71, Guido Grochowski 78br, imagedb.com 156 (e), Kletr 70tr, lowonconcept 155 (souvenir), M.studio 57cl, Maksud 60cl, mangostock 152 (n), Marek 154 (7), margo555 157 (peas), mates 157 (cucumber), Monart Design 61, natalyka 157 (courgette), Natika 157 (carrots), Sergey Nivens 87l, Igor Normann 93 (c), Oleg_Zabielin 81 (f), PR 92t, Franz Pfluegl 20 (d), PhotoSG 158, pressmaster 153 (m), Route66 158 (a), runique 93 (b), Spinetta 70cr, stockphoto-graf 157 (ice cream), Syda Productions 153 (j), Taboga 93 (d), Thegoatman 93 (a), Nicola Vernizzi 93 (e), Vicgmyr 70tl, Swetlana Wall 157 (duck), whitelook 17r, 24b, Maksym Yemelyanov 70bl, yvdavid 157 (shrimps), Zharastudio 98b; Getty Images: AFP / Calle Toernstroem 21, AFP / Stringer 77r, 84l, Altrendo Images 153 (k), Andersen Ross 13bl, Blend Images / Tom Grill 153 (c), Shaun Botterill 124l, Caiaimage / Chris Ryan 153 (b), China Span / Keren Su 47cl, Robert Cianflone 97t, Connie Coleman 51bl, Cultura RM / Nancy Honey 154 (10), Mary Kate Denny 52b, Digital Vision 20 (f), E+ / Ilbusca 100 (a), E+ / Mark Bowden 97cr, Hulton Archive 45b, Image Source 111c, iStock / Pixdeluxe 156 (c), iStock / 360 / Jacob Wackerhausen 153 (h), iStock / Hadynyah 54b, iStock / Helena Lovincic 97cl, Jean-Erick PASQUIER / Contributor 17t, Christopher Kimmel 96, Dan Kitwood 107cl, Shaun Lombard / Vetta 27t, Maskot 62, Moment 84-85 (background), PhotoAlto / James Hardy 77cr, Javier Pierini 18, Oli Scarff 58tl, The Image Bank 102 (d), The Image Gate 107t, Travel Ink 104b, Betsie Van Der Meer 7cr, WireImage / Amanda Edwards 120tl, www. ExtremeSportsPhoto.com / David Spurdens 51br, Daniel Zuchnik 117cl, 120tr; Hug it forward: 88 (a); Imagemore Co., Ltd: 156 (b); John Foxx Images: Imagestate 92l, 159t (g), 159t (r); Masterfile UK Ltd: Thomas Dannenberg 47cr; Nature Picture Library: Edwin Giesbers 87t; Pearson Education Ltd: Gareth Boden 81 (c), 81 (d), 153 (a), Jules Selmes 23 (b), Tudor Photography 155 (walking boots), Coleman Yuen 155 (h); Pearson Education Ltd: 155 (dictionary); Alan Peebles: alanpeebles.com 67l, 68; Plainpicture Ltd: Kniel Synnatzschke 33; Press Association Images: AP / Denis Farrell 79tl, Zak Hussein 89 (b), PA Archive / Andrew Milligan 97r, 104l; Reuters: Claudia Daut (CUBA) 57t; Rex Features: 31cl, Associated Newspapers 67cl, 70c, Peter Brooker 79tr, Duncan Bryceland 54l, Csu Archv / Everett 37r, 44-45, Image Broker 47t, Most Wanted 78b, Robert Harding / David C Poole 104-105, Staley / Lat 124-125b, Crispin Thruston 117r, 125b, Dan Tuffs 100 (c); Robert Harding World Imagery: 28tr; Shutterstock.com: Africa Studio 157 (tea), Alexander Raths 152 (l), Andrey Burmakin 152 (i), antb 152 (f), Jim Barber 158 (h), Stephane Bidouze 159t (t), bikeriderlondon 156 (i), Ruth Black 157 (cupcake), BlueOrange Studio 82 (a), Bochkarev Photography 157 (fish), Christopher Boswell 158 (g), bullet74 155 (e), Diego Cervo 153 (f), Jacek Chabraszewski 156 (a), Konstantin Chagin 37cl, claffra 159t (k), James Clarke 155 (binoculars), Coprid 155 (hat), Corepics VOF 87r,

Tiago Jorge da Silva Estima 159t (f), davidpstephens 159t (a), Deklofenak 153 (i), design56 155 (soap), Dionisvera 157 (apple), 157 (spinach), Goran Djukanovic 122 (a), Pichugin Dmitry 158 (desert), dotshock 156 (d), Denis Dryashkin 157 (potatoes), Igor Dutina 60t, Ekkachai 22-23 (a), EM Arts 59b, 157 (onion), EpicStockMedia 156 (k), eurobanks 155 (aspirin bottle), f9photos 155 (backpack), Dima Fadeev 156 (j), FineShine 159t (b), Fotonium 155 (suitcase), David Fowler 155 (k), g215 155 (umbrella), gamble19 152 (e), Gavran333 157 (lettuce), gkrphoto 60b, Volodymyr Goinyk 159t (p), Goodluz 152 (m), Andrii Gorulko 63tr, Peter Gudella 159t (l), Todd S. Holder 17cl, HomeStudio 155 (street map), Ronnie Howard 159t (s), hxdbzxy 82-83 (c), ifong 157 (barley corn), IM_photo 155 (f), IM photo 27l, Infocus 63b (background), irin-k 159t (m), Brian A Jackson 158 (d), javarman 7cl, Jessmine 157 (cabbage), JonMilnes 10tr, Junial Enterprises 152 (o), Mariusz S. Jurgielewicz 158 (coastline), Kamira 159t (n), Evgeny Karandaev 157 (grapes), 157 (orange juice), Sebastian Kaulitzki 158 (b), Robert Kneschke 152 (k), Fatih Kocyildir 155 (notepad), Igor Kolos 153 (g), Viachaslau Kraskouski 59t (background), Veniamin Kraskov 158 (river), Raj Krish 159t (z), kurhan 152 (d), Laboko 157 (cream), Alexandra Lande 155 (c), Philip Lange 155 (a), Nata-Lia 37t, Liviu Ionut Pantelimon 154 (2), Lucky Business 38cl, 153 (d), Luis CÃ © sar Tejo 159t (o), Anatoliy Lukich 87cl, Masalski Maksim 155 (digital camera), Viktar Malyshchyts 157 (lemon), 157 (melon), Xavier Marchant 159t (c), Maridav 57l, 156 (l), Sergio Martinez 157 (roast chicken), michaeljung 10tl, 156 (h), Mny-Jhee 157 (biscuits), Monkey Business Images 38t, 38br, 81 (b), 82 (b), 123, 152 (b), 154 (11), Andrea Muscatello 155 (i), My Good Images 8, 159t (h), Maks Narodenko 157 (bananas), Nattika 157 (plum), Naypong 159t (i), Niderlander 154 (4), Ninell 157 (broccoli), nito 157 (jelly), Nomad_Soul 63t (background), O.Bellini 157 (fizzy drink), Oleg Zabielin 152 (c), Tyler Olson 77cl, 81 (e), Robert Palmer 159t (q), paytai 159t (j), Pelfophoto 154 (3), Perspectives - Jeff Smith 158 (ocean), William Perugini 12br, Vadim Petrakov 158 (waterfall), PhotoBarmaley 51tl, pogonici 157 (yoghurt), Olga Popova 157 (oats), Brian Prawl 155 (n), Mike Price 159t (u), Procy 158 (glacier), Pudi Studio 117cr, Celso Pupo 158 (lake), puwanai 158 (rain forest), Valentina Razumova 157 (orange), Ian Rentoul 159t (d), Yevgen Romanenko 157 (cheese), Federico Rostagno 155 (j), RTimages 100 (d), Jorge Salcedo 72, Atiketta Sangasaeng 94-95, Sasimoto 155 (money belt), Mariia Sats 154 (6), Dan Scandal 155 (alarm clock), Irina Schmidt 98t, sgm 27cr, smereka 159t (x), Ljupco Smokovski 156 (g), Florin Stana 109b, Alex Staroseltsev 157 (kiwi), 157 (pineapple), Swellphotography 157 (coffee), Syda Productions 152 (h), Aleksandar Todorovic 158 (e), 159t (y), Triff 154 (8), Mogens Trolle 159t (e), Thor Jorgen Udvang 155 (l), urfin 157 (milk), Repina Valeriya 157 (wheat), Anke van Wyk 159t (w), Vibrant Image Studio 155 (m), Valentyn Volkov 157 (mango), 157 (watermelon), VR Photos 152 (g), wavebreakmedia 20 (e), 23 (d), Edward Westmacott 157 (Lobster), XiXinXing 152 (a), Alaettin Yildirim 59c, Gary Yim 158 (mountain range), Jacinto Yoder 159t (v), Olena Zaskochenko 155 (waterproof jacket), zcw 157 (mussels); SuperStock: Axiom Photographic / Design Pics 99, Corbis 107cr, 112, imagebroker.net 29c, Juice Images 154 (9), LatitudeStock / Capture Ltd 54-55, Robert Harding Picture Library 74-75 (background), Westend61 107l; The Kobal Collection: Marvel / Paramount 118tr, Mediapro Studios 118bl, Miramax / Dimension Films / Tweedie, Penny 49tl, Recorded Picture Company 47l, 48tl, Riama-Pathe 117t, River Road / Paramount 48tr, Video Vision Entertainment / Distant Horizon / Pathe 118tl, Warner Bros 118br; www. imagesource.com: 154 (1), Photolibrary 20 (a)

All other images © Pearson Education

La impresión y encuadernación se realizó en el mes de julio del 2017, en los talleres de DRUKO INTERNATIONAL S.A. de C.V. Calzada de chabacano #65-E, Col. Asturias, C.P. 06850 Del. Cuauhtémoc, CD de MX.

speakout 2ND EDITION

Pre-intermediate
Students' Book

with DVD-ROM

Antonia Clare • JJ Wilson

CONTENTS

DVD-ROM: DVD CLIPS AND SCRIPTS   BBC INTERVIEWS AND SCRIPTS   CLASS AUDIO AND SCRIPTS

CONTENTS

LISTENING/DVD	SPEAKING	WRITING
	ask and answer questions about holidays and weekends	
listen to stories about offers of marriage	ask and answer personal questions	write about an important year in your life; improve your use of linking words
understand routine exchanges	making conversation	
BBC **Miranda**: watch an extract from a sitcom about a woman called Miranda	talk about important people in your life	write about your best friend
listen to interviews about jobs	talk about what motivates you at work	write an email about work experience
	talk about dangerous jobs	
listen to a man talking about his job	talk about your perfect job	
BBC **The Money Programme: Dream Commuters**: watch an extract from a BBC documentary about commuting	describe your work/life balance	write a web comment about work/life balance
listen to a radio programme about going out in New York	talk about your future plans	write an email invitation
	discuss how you spend your free time	
understand some problem phone calls	make and receive phone calls	
BBC **Going Local: Rio**: watch an extract from a BBC travel programme about visiting Rio de Janeiro	plan a perfect day out	write an invitation for a day out
listen to someone describing how he used his hidden talent	talk about hidden talents	check your work and correct mistakes
	talk about rules in schools	
	give advice and make suggestions for language learners	
BBC **Supersized Earth: The Way We Move**: watch an extract from a BBC documentary about developments that have changed the world	talk about inventions	write a forum post about inventions
	tell a anecdote	
understand travel advice	discuss travel	write an email describing a trip or weekend away
	ask for and give directions	
BBC **Full Circle**: watch an extract from a BBC travel programme	present ideas for an award	write an application for an award
	talk about your lifestyle	
listen to a radio interview with a food expert	discuss food preferences	write about food
listen to conversations between a doctor and her patients	explain health problems	
BBC **Horizon: Monitor Me**: watch an extract from a BBC documentary about health	talk about healthy habits	write a blog post about health advice

COMMUNICATION BANK page 86   AUDIO SCRIPTS page 90

)) LEAD IN

CLASSROOM LANGUAGE

1 A Complete the questions with the words in the box.

> say   to   does   you   are   do

1 What _____ this mean?
2 How _____ you spell it?
3 What page _____ we on?
4 What's the answer _____ number 6?
5 Can _____ repeat that, please?
6 How do you _____ this word?

B Match questions 1–6 above with answers a)–f).

a) OK. Which part? The whole sentence?
b) It's a type of food.
c) Page 63.
d) You don't say the 'k'. Listen: 'knee'.
e) The answer is b.
f) B-a-n-a-n-a.

SPELLING

2 A ▶ L.1   Listen and write down the words you hear.

B Listen again to check.

C Write down ten words in English.

D Work in pairs and take turns. Student A: say your word and then spell it out. Student B: write it down.

PARTS OF SPEECH

3 Match the parts of speech in the box with the words in bold.

> ~~verb~~   adjective   auxiliary   adverb   noun
> article   preposition of place

1 I **studied** here last year.   *verb*
2 We have **a** new teacher.
3 This is a great **school**.
4 The class is **in** Room 14.
5 **Do** you like speaking English?
6 The teachers are **helpful**.
7 I work **quickly**.

TENSES AND STRUCTURES

4 Find one example of each of these things in the text below.

1 present simple
2 present continuous
3 present perfect
4 past simple
5 *going to* for future plans

> My name is Yoko. I was born in Japan, but at the moment I'm living in the United States. I've been here for six months. I'm going to visit my uncle in Canada next year.

QUESTION WORDS

5 Complete the questions with the words in the box.

> who   where   what   when   why   how

1 _____ is your name?
2 _____ do you know in this class (which students)?
3 _____ do you come from?
4 _____ is your birthday?
5 _____ do you come to school: by car or by public transport?
6 _____ are you studying English? Do you need it for your job?

AUXILIARY VERBS

6 Underline the correct alternative.

1 What *do/does/are* you do?
2 Where *do/does/is* she live?
3 What *do/does/did* they do yesterday evening?
4 I *am not/don't/doesn't* know the answers to these questions.
5 The library *don't/not/doesn't* open on Sundays.
6 We *don't/didn't/weren't* go on holiday last year.
7 *Is/Are/Do* you studying at the moment?
8 John *doesn't/isn't/aren't* using the computer, so you can use it.

VOCABULARY

7 Complete the word webs with the words in the box.

> car   shop assistant   bookshop   lawyer   bakery
> uncle   tomato   grandmother   bike   doctor
> supermarket   sugar   train   cousin   pasta

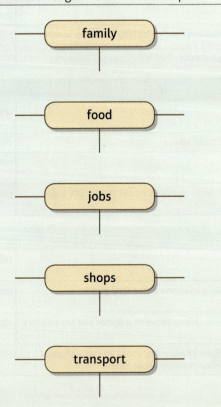

family

food

jobs

shops

transport

1 life

FEELING GOOD? p8

TRUE LOVE p10

NICE DAY, ISN'T IT? p12

SOMEONE SPECIAL p14

BBC
INTERVIEWS

What do you look for in a friend?

1.1))) FEELING GOOD?

G question forms
P stressed words
V free time

VOCABULARY

FREE TIME

1 A Think about three things that make you happy (e.g. *my family*, *walking on the beach*, *eating good food*). Work in pairs and compare your ideas.

B Complete phrases 1–5 with the verbs in the box.

go eat have play spend

1 _go_ shopping/on holiday/for a walk
2 _____ time with family/money/time alone
3 _____ out/with friends/good food
4 _____ time off/a barbecue/a party
5 _____ (a) sport/a musical instrument/games

C Work in pairs. Do any of the activities in Exercise 1B make you happy? Add some more activities to the list.

READING

2 A Read the magazine article. Which of these things do you do already? Which could you do more of?

B Work in pairs. Which of the seven ideas do you think are the most/least important for you? Do you have any other ideas to include?

the seven Secrets of Happiness

Everyone has a different idea of what happiness is, but most of us want to be happier. So, what can we learn from looking at the habits of happy people? Here are seven things to make you happy.

1 Sleep More Most people don't sleep enough. If you want to feel good about life, then try to sleep for at least seven hours a night.

2 Do Some Exercise You don't need to run for 20km or go to the gym every night, but a small amount of exercise will help you feel happy. Go for a short (10–15 minute) walk somewhere beautiful. It wakes up your brain.

3 Give to Others Research shows that giving money or time to help others makes you feel happier. Buying someone an unexpected present or spending some time doing voluntary work will give you a feeling of joy.

4 Be Interested Love what you do and try to learn something new. People who are curious and learn new things experience feelings of satisfaction and happiness.

5 Spend Time with Family and Friends This is probably the most important thing you can do. People who have a strong network of social relationships are not just happier; they live longer, too!

6 Focus on the Moment Try to find opportunities each day to enjoy the small things in life. Spend a little time on your own, and just enjoy the moment.

7 Smile! Smile more (even when you're feeling sad). Smiling can actually make you feel better. People who post big smiley photos of themselves on Facebook actually feel happier because they see the photo every day and it reminds them of happy times.

GRAMMAR

QUESTION FORMS

3 A Read the questions. Think about your answers.

1 How many hours do you usually sleep?
2 Are you good at sport?
3 How much time do you spend doing exercise? Where do you go?
4 What do you do that really interests you?
5 When did you last learn something new? Where were you?
6 What small things in life do you enjoy?

B Work in groups. Ask and answer the questions.

4 A Complete the questions in the tables.

Questions with auxiliaries			
question word	auxiliary	subject	infinitive
Where 2 _____	1 _____ did	you	go? last learn something new?

Questions with *be*			
question word	*be*	subject	adjective/noun/verb + *-ing*, etc.
4 _____	3 _____ were	you you?	good at sport?

B Circle the correct word in bold to complete the rules.

> **RULES**
> 1 In questions with auxiliaries, put *do/does/did* **before/after** the subject.
> 2 In questions with *be*, put *am/are/is/was/were* **before/after** the subject.

▷ page 68 **LANGUAGEBANK**

5 A Put the words in the correct order and add an auxiliary or *be* to make questions.

1 many / your / how / in / people / family?
2 see / often / you / parents / how / your?
3 family / with / you / spending / your / time / enjoy?
4 last / your / when / celebration / family?
5 you / with / live / who?
6 you / often / eat / friends / how / out / with?
7 friend / your / live / where / best?

B ▶ **1.1** Listen and check.

C STRESSED WORDS Look at audio script 1.1 on page 90. Underline the stressed words. Listen again and repeat.

How many <u>people</u> are in your <u>family</u>?

D Work in pairs. Ask and answer the questions.

SPEAKING

6 A Work in pairs. You are going to interview other students. Look at the prompts and make questions about each topic. Choose a third topic to talk about.

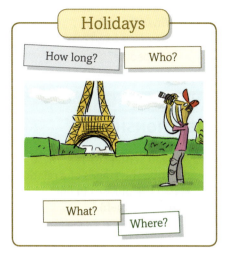

Holidays

How long? | Who? | What? | Where?

Weekend

What? | Where? | Work / Study? | Get up?

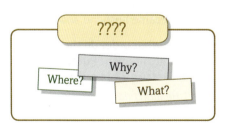

????

Why? | Where? | What?

B Work in groups. Ask and answer the questions.

C Tell the class. Who do you think:

1 has the best holidays?
2 has very busy weekends?
3 enjoys staying at home?
4 does the most exercise?
5 sleeps the most?
6 really knows how to enjoy themselves?

1.2)) TRUE LOVE

G past simple
P past simple verbs: -ed endings
V relationships

SPEAKING

1 Work in pairs. Discuss the questions.

1 Do you believe in love at first sight? Why/Why not?
2 Where are good places to meet new people?

VOCABULARY

RELATIONSHIPS

2 A Read sentences 1–8. These describe the stages of a relationship. Match the phrases in bold with definitions a)–h).

1 He **proposed (to her)**.
2 They **got on well**.
3 They **got married**.
4 They **got engaged**.
5 They **met**.
6 She **accepted**.
7 He didn't **have a girlfriend**.
8 They **fell in love**.

a) agreed to marry
b) asked her to marry him
c) began to love each other
d) have a romantic relationship with a girl
e) said yes
f) had a good relationship
g) first knew each other
h) became husband and wife

B In what order do these things usually happen? Put the phrases 1–8 in Exercise 2A in order.

1 He didn't have a girlfriend.

C Write three true sentences about yourself or a friend. Use the phrases in bold in Exercise 2A.

I met my best friend, Piri, at a conference. We got on well immediately.

speakout TIP

Words like *get* and *have* are used in lots of different phrases in English. Keep lists of these phrases and add new phrases when you learn them. Write down all the phrases you know with *get*. Compare your list with your partner's.

LISTENING

3 A ▶ 1.2 Look at the pictures. They show how three people proposed to their partner. What do you think happened? Listen and check.

B Listen again and answer the questions.

1 In Story 1, where did the boyfriend propose?
2 Why did she say 'it was almost a disaster'?
3 In Story 2, which country were they in?
4 What happened on the boat?
5 In Story 3, how did the boyfriend propose?
6 How did she accept?

C Which stories do the sentences 1–6 come from? Work in pairs and use the sentences to help you re-tell the stories.

1 We were at a restaurant.
2 I didn't say anything. I just gave her the ring.
3 We met at art school.
4 Luckily, she smiled.
5 I accepted, but I didn't tell him.
6 He tried to stop me.

D Discuss. Which do you think is the best story? Why?

GRAMMAR

PAST SIMPLE

4 A Underline examples of verbs in the past simple in Exercise 3C.

B Complete the tables below with the correct form of the verbs in the past simple.

Past simple			
regular		irregular	
appear	_appeared_	go	_____
like	_____	fall	_____
decide	_____	get	_____
try	_____	say	_____

negative	I _____ tell him.
question	_____ they get married?
short answer	No, they _____ ./Yes, they did.

5 A ▶ 1.3 **PAST SIMPLE VERBS: -ed endings** Listen to three different ways to pronounce regular past simple verbs.

1 /d/ **lived** They lived in Africa.

2 /t/ **asked** He asked her to marry him.

3 /ɪd/ **started** They started a family.

B ▶ 1.4 Listen and put the words in the box in the correct column in the table below.

worked   wanted   stopped   smiled   walked
needed   talked   studied   helped   decided

/d/	/t/	/ɪd/
lived	_asked_	_started_

▷ page 68 **LANGUAGEBANK**

6 A Complete the sentences with the correct form of the past simple.

go (x2)   stay   see   cook   spend

1 I _____ my best friend three months ago.

2 I _____ to a wedding last summer.

3 I _____ up all night.

4 I _____ on holiday last month.

5 I _____ a meal for some friends last night.

6 I _____ the day with my sister on Monday.

B Make *When did you last …?* questions for each sentence in Exercise 6A.

When did you last see your best friend?

C Work in pairs and take turns. Ask and answer the questions.

A: When did you last go on holiday?
B: It was a few months ago. I went to Malta with some friends.

SPEAKING

7 A Write down five important dates in your life. Prepare to talk about them.

B Work in pairs and take turns. Ask and answer questions about the dates. Try to guess what happened.

A: 19th July 2006.
B: Did you get married?
A: No, I didn't.
B: Did you start work?
A: Yes, I did.

WRITING

LINKING WORDS

8 A Match 1–4 with a)–d) to make sentences. Link the phrases with a word from the box below.

and   so   but   because

1 In 1998 I finished my degree …

2 I moved house in 2002 …

3 I wanted to learn Italian …

4 They wanted to buy a house, …

a) they didn't have enough money.

b) I could travel around the country.

c) started my first job.

d) I didn't like my flat-mate.

B Complete the web comment with linking words (*and, but, so, because*).

2011 was an important year [1]_____ I met my wife, Ania. We met in an internet chatroom [2]_____ we got on immediately. We started to chat and send emails, [3]_____ we lived in different countries [4]_____ it was difficult for us to be together. Now we live in the UK with our two children.

C Write about an important year in your life. Use linking words (*and, but, so, because*).

F making conversation
P linking
V conversation topics

VOCABULARY

CONVERSATION TOPICS

1 Work in pairs. Discuss the questions.

1 Do you enjoy **having conversations** with people you don't know?
2 What topics do you usually **talk about**?
3 What do you **say** when somebody **interrupts** you?
4 Do you ever **gossip** about celebrities?
5 Are you good at **telling jokes**?
6 Can you think of any bad conversation habits?

2 A Complete the article with the words in the box.

> joke gossip saying conversation
> talk interrupt tells

B Work in pairs. What problem does the article describe? Which tips do you think are good advice?

C Cover the article. How many tips can you remember?

Top Conversation Killers

Do you ever find that you're having an interesting ¹_____ and then suddenly everything goes really quiet and you're not sure why? Next time watch out for these conversation killers.

'You look tired'
There's nothing worse than when a friend who hasn't seen you for a while ²_____ you that you're looking tired or stressed.

Me, Me, Me
This is one of the biggest conversation killers. Don't ³_____ people to talk about yourself. It's a great idea to talk about things you have in common, but just remember to take turns.

'Sorry, what were you ⁴_____?'
It's always easier to talk than to listen, but learning to listen and being interested in the response is an important conversation skill.

'Have you heard what people are saying about … ?'
Don't ⁵_____ or say rude things about people you know, even if it's only a ⁶_____.

Don't be too negative
Try not to ⁷_____ about too many negative topics. As they say, 'Laugh and the world laughs with you, cry and you cry alone.'

FUNCTION

MAKING CONVERSATION

3 A ▶ 1.5 Listen to two conversations. Which conversation (Conversation 1 or Conversation 2) do you think is better? Why?

B Listen again and complete the responses.

Conversation 1

A: Hi, Davide. This is my friend, Rachel.

B: Hi, Rachel. ¹_____ to meet you.

B: Would you like a drink, Rachel?

C: I'd ²_____ a coffee, thank you.

B: Where exactly do you come from?

C: I'm ³_____ Beckley, near Oxford.

Conversation 2

A: Hi, Felicia. Nice day, isn't it?

B: Yes, it's ⁴_____.

A: Did you have a good weekend?

B: Yes, it was ⁵_____. I didn't do much.

A: Did you watch the match last night?

B: Yes, it was ⁶_____.

A: I'll see you later.

B: Yes, see you ⁷_____.

4 Work in pairs and take turns. Student A: look at page 86. Student B: look at page 88.

▷ page 68 **LANGUAGEBANK**

LEARN TO

SOUND NATURAL

5 A ▶ 1.6 **LINKING** Listen to these phrases again. Notice how words are linked.

1 Would‿you like‿a drink?
2 Did‿you have‿a good weekend?
3 This‿is my friend, Rachel.
4 I'd love‿a coffee, thank‿you.
5 Yes,‿it was‿OK.
6 Pleased‿to meet‿you.

B Listen again and repeat.

speakout TIP

Use *so* to help a conversation when you ask another question. *Poland? So, where exactly in Poland do you come from?* You can also use it when you want to change the topic. *So, did you watch the match last night?* Can you add *so* to any questions in Exercise 3B? Practise saying the questions.

SPEAKING

6 A Look at the topics in the box below. Think of five questions you can ask people related to the topics.

| films home next holiday food/drink free time |
| family weather work/studies weekend |

B Talk to as many different people as possible in the class. Start conversations with them. Try to ask at least three of your questions, and then end the conversation. Be careful not to kill the conversation too quickly.

So, what kind of films do you enjoy?
Where exactly do you live?
So, what do you do in your free time?

DVD PREVIEW

1 A Work in pairs and discuss the questions.

1 What kinds of programmes do you enjoy watching on television?
2 Which television programmes are popular in your country at the moment?
3 Do you enjoy watching situation comedies (sitcoms)? Why/Why not?

B Read the programme information and answer the questions.

1 What is Miranda's problem?
2 Why do you think she finds it difficult to answer Mike?

◉›) Miranda   **BBC**

Whatever Miranda tries to do in life, something always goes wrong. Now, she has a boyfriend called Mike, but every time he says the words 'I love you', Miranda panics and doesn't know how to respond. What's the real problem? Is it something to do with her old university friend Gary? And can her best friend, Stevie, help her to work it out?

DVD VIEW

2 A Watch the DVD. Why can't Miranda say 'I love you' to Mike? What's the problem?

B Watch again. Number the sentences in the order you hear them.

a) 'What was your first love?' 'Doughnuts.'
b) 'You love him, but you're not *in love* with him.'
c) 'When he tells me he loves me, I freak out. Can't say it back.' 1
d) 'I wouldn't laugh. It's one of the reasons I love you.'
e) 'You're not in love with your boyfriend. It's only fair you split up with him.'
f) 'What truly makes your heart skip?' 'Gary'.

3 A Who says sentences 1–6: Miranda, Mike, the man, Stevie or Gary? Who are they talking to?

1 'I'm gonna to have to dash. I will see you later.'
2 'What springs to mind when I say, "What do you love?"'
3 'Now we need to work out how you'll end it.'
4 'I'm going to have to write Mike a letter. It's the only way.'
5 'Listen, I really really need your help. Do you think you could spare a few hours this afternoon?'
6 'I'm in love with Gary!'

B Watch again to check your answers.

4 Work in pairs and answer the questions.

1 What do you think Miranda should do now?
2 What do you think will happen next?

speakout a special person

4 A Think about people you know. Who is the best person to:

- go on holiday with?
- talk to about your problems?
- borrow money from?
- go out for an evening with?
- invite to your house for dinner?
- work/live with?
- go to a concert/art gallery with?

B Work in pairs and discuss your answers.

5 You are going to talk about an important person in your life. Think about questions 1–6.

1 Who is this person?
2 What is their relationship to you?
3 How did you meet?
4 How often do you see them?
5 What kind of things do you do together?
6 Why is this person important to you?

6 A ▶ 1.7 Listen to someone describing a friend and answer the questions.

1 When did they meet?
2 Why are they good friends?
3 Does she say anything negative about her friend?

B Listen again and tick the key phrases you hear.

> ### KEY PHRASES
>
> I've known [name] for …
> We met …
> We get on really well [because …] …
> We've got lots of things in common …
> We both enjoy …
> One thing I like about [name] is …
> The only problem with [name] is …
> He/She is one of those people that …
> He/She's a great person.

C Work in pairs and take turns. Student A: tell your partner about your special person. Use the key phrases to help. Student B: ask questions to find out more information about him/her.

writeback a competition entry

7 A Read the competition entry below. Underline three reasons why Julie is the writer's best friend.

Is your friend the 'best friend in the world'? Tell us why.

Julie is the best friend in the world because she is always there for me. Julie is the person I call when I have a problem, or if I need to borrow money. She has helped me through some difficult times. We have known each other for nearly twenty years, so we know everything there is to know about each other. We argue sometimes, but we have the same sense of humour, so our arguments don't last very long. I can talk to Julie about anything and I know she will be a friend forever.

B Write an entry for the competition about your best friend or someone special. Use the questions in Exercise 5 to help you.

V FREE TIME

1 A Complete the questions with the missing word.

1 How often do you _____ a barbecue?
2 What do you usually do when you have time _____ work/ from your studies?
3 How do you usually _____ time with your family?
4 What kind of things do you hate _____ money on?
5 Where is your favourite place to _____ out?
6 Where do you like to _____ shopping?

B Work in pairs. Ask and answer the questions.

G QUESTION FORMS

2 Work in pairs. Complete the application form for your partner. Ask and answer questions using the words in brackets.

A: *What is your name?*
B: *Pedro Gonzales*

APPLICATION FORM

Name: (what)

> *Pedro Gonzales*

Age: (how)

Place of birth: (where)

Marital status: (married)

Address: (what)

Telephone number: (what)

Mobile number: (have got)

Email address: (what)

Occupation: (do)

Hobbies: (have)

3 A Choose some of the topics in the boxes below. Write five questions to ask other students.

 love home family

 work food holidays

B Work in groups. Ask and answer the questions.

V RELATIONSHIPS

4 A Find five mistakes in this paragraph.

> I met Layla at a market. She was selling bread. We started chatting and got well on. At the time I didn't keep a girlfriend, so I asked her on a date. We went to a local bakery! We soon fell to love and I proposed at her after a month. I hid the ring in a piece of cake. Fortunately, she accepted, and she didn't eat the ring! It was a good way to get engaged. A week later we became married.

B Work in pairs and check your answers. Close your books. Student A: re-tell the story. Change two details. Student B: guess the changes.

G PAST SIMPLE

5 A Put the words in the correct order to make questions.

On your last holiday:
1 did / go / where / you?
2 why / there / did / go / you?
3 in / you / a / stay / did / hotel?
4 do / day / during / did / you / the / what?
5 evenings / out / the / you / go / in / did?
6 the / weather / hot / was?
7 you / language / speak / what / did?
8 you / friends / make / new / any / did?

B Work in pairs. Ask and answer the questions in Exercise 5A.

6 A Write a list of ten verbs you learnt in Unit 1. What are the past simple forms?

B Work in pairs and take turns. Student A: say a verb. Student B: say the past simple form.

A: *meet*
B: *met*

C Now use the verbs from Exercise 6A to make questions.

D Ask and answer the questions.

A: *When did you meet your partner?*
B: *We met in 2006.*

F MAKING CONVERSATION

7 A Complete the conversations.

Conversation 1
A: Hi, (name) _____. _____ day, isn't it?
B: Yes, it's _____.

Conversation 2
A: This is my _____ (name) _____.
B: Hi. _____ to meet you.

Conversation 3
A: So, _____ you work here?
B: No, I'm a _____.

Conversation 4
A: Where exactly do you _____ from?
B: I'm _____ (place) _____.

Conversation 5
A: Did you have a _____ weekend?
B: Yes, it was _____. I didn't do _____.

Conversation 6
A: Did you _____ the match last night?
B: Yes, it _____ terrible.

Conversation 7
A: We lost 3–0.
B: Oh _____! I'm _____ to hear that.

Conversation 8
A: I'll _____ you later.
B: Yes, see you _____.

B Work in pairs and practise the conversations.

2)) work

SPEAKING 2.1 Talk about what motivates you at work 2.2 Talk about dangerous jobs
2.3 Discuss likes/dislikes 2.4 Describe your work/life balance

LISTENING 2.1 Listen to interviews about jobs 2.4 Watch an extract from a BBC
documentary about commuting

READING 2.2 Read a newspaper article about dangerous jobs
2.4 Understand a survey about work/life balance

WRITING 2.1 Write an email about work experience
2.4 Write a web comment about work/life balance

BBC INTERVIEWS

◗)) What do you do?

2.1)) THE COMPANY 4 U?

G present simple and continuous
P word stress
V work

VOCABULARY

WORK

1 Discuss the questions.

  1 What are the people doing in the photo?

  2 What sort of company is it?

  3 Would you like to work for a company like this? Why/Why not?

2 A Work in pairs. Match the words in the box with definitions 1–10.

> ~~company~~   employee   salary   office   customer
> employer   staff   task   boss   bonus

  1 a business that makes or sells things or provides services *company*

  2 a person who buys products or uses services

  3 extra money given to a worker (often for especially good work)

  4 a place where many people work at desks

  5 a worker

  6 a job you need to do

  7 a person who manages the workers in the company

  8 everyone who works in the company

  9 a fixed, regular sum of money given to someone for doing a job

  10 a person or business that pays workers to do a job

  B ▶ 2.1   **WORD STRESS**   Listen to the words and repeat.

SPEAKING

3 A Work in pairs. Discuss. What are the most important things for people who work? Number the items below in order of importance. 1 = very important. 8 = not important at all.

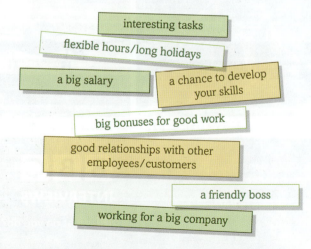

- interesting tasks
- flexible hours/long holidays
- a big salary
- a chance to develop your skills
- big bonuses for good work
- good relationships with other employees/customers
- a friendly boss
- working for a big company

B Compare your ideas with other students.

LISTENING

4 A ▶ 2.2   Listen to someone talking about how companies motivate their staff. How are the pictures (A–D) connected to the ideas?

> **M**   **mo.ti.vate** /ˈməʊtəveɪt $ ˈmoʊtəˌveɪt/ *verb* to make someone want to do something: *Teachers should motivate students to stay in school.*

From Longman WordWise Dictionary.

B Listen and check. Which other ideas do they talk about? Which ideas do you think are the best?

5 A ▶ 2.3   Listen to three employees describing what they are doing. Tick the activities they mention.

> watching a film   choosing a CD   fishing
> studying   waiting for a customer   making coffee
> having a massage   checking emails

B Listen again. Answer the questions.

1 What is the 'agreement' between the two shops?

2 What does the company pay for?

3 Why can the woman start work at 1p.m.?

GRAMMAR

PRESENT SIMPLE AND CONTINUOUS

6 A Read sentences a) and b). Answer the questions.

a) This is the clothes shop.

b) I'm having a break.

1 Which sentence describes something that is always true?

2 Which sentence describes a temporary situation?

3 Which sentence uses the present simple?

4 Which sentence uses the present continuous?

B Read sentences a)–d). Answer the questions.

a) I'm choosing my free CD for the week.

b) I'm checking my emails.

c) I'm studying history.

d) Six of us are doing online courses.

1 Which two sentences refer to this exact moment?

2 Which two sentences refer to the general present, but not to this moment?

▷ page 70   **LANGUAGE**BANK

7 Make two sentences or questions with the prompts. Use the present simple and present continuous.

1 you / work — on a special task at the moment? on Saturdays?

Are you working on a special task at the moment?
Do you work on Saturdays?

2 I / look — for a job at the moment / at my emails when I get to work

3 I / not / use — English for my job / the photocopier at the moment

4 you / watch — the news on TV every day? / TV right now?

5 I / not / read — any good books at the moment / a newspaper every morning

6 you / have — a good time at this party? / a company car?

7 I / sell — my house / IT products to companies in Asia

8 A Make *you* questions with the prompts. Use the present simple or present continuous.

1 think / your salary / good?

Do you think your salary is good?

2 speak / any other languages?

3 why / learn English?

4 study for / an exam / now?

5 work on / a special project / at the moment?

6 have / your own / office?

7 like / your / boss?

B Work in pairs. Choose four or five questions to ask your partner. Find similarities and differences between you and your partner.

WRITING

STARTING/ENDING AN EMAIL

9 A Look at the phrases below. Which are formal (F) and which are informal (I)?

Starting an email

Dear colleagues   *F*
Dear Sir   Hi   Dear Dr Bryce   Hello
Dear All   Hi everyone

Introducing the main topic

I am writing about …   It's about …   Regarding …

Ending an email

See you soon   Best wishes   Bye for now
I look forward to hearing from you   Best regards
Speak soon   Take care   Cheers   Love
Yours sincerely

B Read the email. What work does Vanessa do?

Dear Mr Shaw,

I am writing to apply for the position at your company advertised in JSI. I believe my personal qualities and my experience make me a good candidate for this job.

I worked for Seng Tech for three years, producing designs for apps. Our customers included Sherring Inc. and BTZ Co. I am currently developing mobile apps for two other companies.

I am very motivated by interesting tasks and I am looking for a chance to develop my skills in a bigger company.

I look forward to hearing from you.

Yours sincerely,

Vanessa Chiarollo

C Read the advert and write to BES. Use the prompts below and phrases from Exercise 9A.

1 Say why you're writing and introduce yourself.

2 Say what you're doing now (studying English, etc.).

3 Ask for information about BES's work experience programme.

4 End the email.

BES is an international furniture design company. Based in Ankara, we design and produce household furniture in 15 countries. We are looking for people who want work experience in design, sales and other areas. **Write to Hakan Balik at hbalik@BES.nett.**

2.2)) A RISKY BUSINESS

G adverbs of frequency
P stressed syllables
V jobs

VOCABULARY

JOBS

1 A Work in pairs. Discuss. Which are the best/worst jobs? Think about:

- meeting people
- opportunities to travel
- problems to deal with
- tasks
- hours of work
- salary

B Match the jobs with photos A–G.

> sales rep   fashion designer   IT consultant
> foreign correspondent   personal trainer
> rescue worker   motorcycle courier

C ▶ 2.4   **STRESSED SYLLABLES** Listen and repeat. Underline the stressed syllables.

sales rep

speakout TIP

The stressed part of a word or phrase sounds l o n g e r, **LOUDER** and ^higher than the other parts. Practise saying new vocabulary, focusing on the stressed parts.

▷ page 80 **PHOTOBANK**

2 A Complete the phrases with the words in the box.

> work   deal with   risk   get

1 _____ a good salary/long holidays
2 _____ in a team/under pressure
3 _____ their lives/your health
4 _____ problems/customers

B Use the phrases to talk about the jobs in Exercise 1.
IT consultants get a good salary.

3 A Complete sentences 1–6 with the words in the box.

> get   team   under   deal   holidays   risk

1 People are more motivated when they _____ a good salary.
2 People work better _____ a lot of pressure.
3 It's important that employees get long _____.
4 People who _____ their lives at work should get more money.
5 It's more enjoyable to work in a _____ than alone.
6 These days, people usually _____ with their own IT problems.

B Work in pairs. Discuss. Which of the sentences above do you agree/disagree with? Why?

READING

4 A Work in pairs. Discuss. Which of the jobs in Exercise 1 do you think is the best paid, most interesting or most dangerous? Why?

B Work in groups. Student A: read the text below. Student B: read the text on page 86. Student C: read the text on page 88. Make notes on:

- job
- country
- people interviewed
- why the job is dangerous
- special memories/stories

C Tell your group about your text using the notes.

Danger Rating 6/10

Mountain rescue worker, Austria

Up in the mountains, the view is beautiful. But not for emergency doctor Martin Schmidt, paramedic Marius Adler and helicopter pilot Klaus Hartmann. Their job is to find and rescue people in trouble: climbers caught in an avalanche, injured skiers, even lost walkers. Reporter Lucy Rose met the team and asked them about their work.

Adler says they love their jobs, but they sometimes get angry with the people they rescue. 'Climbers always risk their lives, but when they get into trouble they also risk ours.'

What exactly are the dangers? Hartmann says that, although the sun is shining today, they usually fly in much worse weather conditions, which can be very dangerous. Another problem is that, often, the people they rescue are frightened. They panic, and this makes it difficult for the team.

And what are the best things about the job? Hartmann says, 'Saving lives is its own reward.' And occasionally they get a surprise. 'One time we rescued a woman after a skiing accident. She was badly hurt. Later her husband brought us a huge box of chocolates.' The people they rescue, Schmidt explains, hardly ever say thank you!

GRAMMAR

ADVERBS OF FREQUENCY

5 A Look at sentences 1–9. Put the words in bold in the correct place on the line.

1 He **never** worries.
2 **Often** the people they rescue are frightened.
3 The mountain rescuers **sometimes** get angry.
4 It **usually** involves a few broken bones.
5 Life as a jockey is **rarely** safe.
6 These people **always** risk their lives.
7 The people they rescue **hardly ever** say thank you.
8 **Once in a while** jockeys even die during a race.
9 **Occasionally** they get a surprise.

occasionally/once in a while — always

0% (none of the time) — 100% (all the time)

B Read your text again. Underline all the adverbs or expressions of frequency. Look at the other texts to find more examples.

▷ page 70 **LANGUAGEBANK**

6 A Find and correct the mistakes in sentences 1–6. There is one mistake in each sentence.

1 I work always at night.
2 Once on a while I study at weekends.
3 I ever hardly study alone.
4 I work at home occasional.
5 It is sometime difficult to study and work at the same time.
6 I don't usual miss classes because of work.

B Write four sentences about your job or studies.

I deal with customers once in a while.

C Compare with a partner.

SPEAKING

7 A Work in groups. You are making a TV programme about dangerous jobs. Discuss the questions and choose three jobs for your programme.

1 Which jobs are dangerous? Why? How often are the people in dangerous situations?
2 Which jobs are the most interesting for your TV audience?
3 Who will you interview for the programme? What questions will you ask them?

B Work with another group and compare your ideas.

F expressing likes/dislikes
P intonation: sound interested
V types of work

A

VOCABULARY
TYPES OF WORK

1 A Work in pairs. Look at the types of work below. Answer the questions.

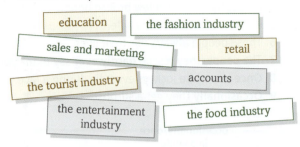

education
the fashion industry
sales and marketing
retail
the tourist industry
accounts
the entertainment industry
the food industry

1 Which industry does a chef, cook and waiter work in?
2 Which industry does a model and fashion designer work in?
3 What types of jobs are there in the entertainment industry?
4 What types of jobs are there in retail?

B Look at photos A–D. Which industries are the people working in?

FUNCTION
EXPRESSING LIKES/DISLIKES

2 A ▶ 2.5 Listen to an interview with someone about his job. What job is it? What does he like about it?

B Listen again and complete the sentences.
1 I **like** _____ outside.
2 I **can't stand** _____ at a desk all day.
3 I **absolutely love** _____ .
4 I **don't like** _____ in a team. I prefer working alone.
5 I **don't mind** _____ my hands dirty.
6 I'm **keen on** _____ new things.
7 I **hate** _____ under pressure.
8 I'm **not very keen on** _____ for a company. I want to be my own boss.

C Read the sentences. Which phrases in bold are very positive (+ +), positive (+), negative (–), or very negative (– –)? Which are not positive or negative (*)?

3 A Which of the statements in Exercise 2B is true for you?

B Work in pairs. Find out three things that your partner loves/likes/hates and write sentences about them. Use the phrases in Exercise 2B to help.

Maria can't stand smoking.

▷ page 70 **LANGUAGEBANK**

LEARN TO
RESPOND AND ASK MORE QUESTIONS

4 A ▶ 2.6 Read and listen to the extracts from the audio script. Notice how the listener responds and complete the phrases. The first has been done for you.

M: One good thing about my job is that I like working outside.

W: I [1] _see_ .

M: I travel a lot and I absolutely love travelling, particularly in South America and Australia.

W: Right. And what [2] _____ your colleagues, people you work with?

M: I don't like working in a team. I prefer working alone.

W: [3] _____ **? And what about** the type of work?

M: You're always discovering new things.

W: That's great. It [4] _____ **wonderful.**

B ▶ 2.7 **INTONATION: sound interested** Listen and repeat the phrases in bold. Notice the intonation. Copy the intonation to sound interested.

C Look at audio script 2.6 in Exercise 4A. Underline other examples of comments and questions. Write them in the table.

comments	*I see.*
questions	*And what about …?*

5 A Work in pairs. Student A: complete sentences 1–4. Student B: complete sentences 5–8.

1 I got a new job as a _____.
2 Yesterday I bought a new _____.
3 I'm going on holiday to _____.
4 Last night I saw _____.
5 I've always wanted to _____.
6 Yesterday I learnt how to _____.
7 I watched a great film about _____.
8 This morning I met _____.

B Work in pairs and take turns. Student A: read a sentence. Student B: respond and ask a follow-up question.

A: I just got a new job as a ski instructor!
B: Really? When do you start?

SPEAKING

6 A Work in pairs. What is the perfect job for you? Think about your job now or a job you'd like in the future. Make notes on the:

• industry (entertainment, tourism, medical …)
• type of work (creative, manual, information-based …)
• skills (networking, writing, planning …)
• hours (9-5, flexible …)
• location (outside, in an office, travelling …)
• people (work alone, in a team, in a large corporation …)

B Work with other students. Talk about your perfect job. As you listen, respond and ask questions.

My perfect job is in the tourist industry. I like meeting new people and I absolutely love showing people around my city.

DVD PREVIEW

1 Work in pairs. Discuss the questions.

1 How do you get to college/work?
2 How long would you be prepared to travel to school/work (one hour/three hours)?

2 A Read the programme information and answer the questions.

1 What was Justin unhappy about before?
2 What did he decide to do?

◉)) The Money Programme: Dream Commuters

BBC

The Money Programme is a BBC documentary series. Dream Commuters tells the story of a man who was **fed up with** his journey to work and his lifestyle. Every day there was a lot of **traffic** on the roads and the **commute** to work took a long time. He wasn't happy with his work/life balance. So he bought a **property** in France and took his family to live there. He now takes cheap **flights** to work. He is one of a growing number of **commuters** who live in another country. He says it has **transformed** his life.

B Match the words in bold in Exercise 2A with meanings 1–7.

1 completely changed
2 journeys in a plane
3 people who travel to work
4 cars, motorbikes, etc. on the road
5 journey to work
6 a building or land that you own
7 unhappy with something, so you want to change it

DVD VIEW

3 A Watch the DVD. Do you think Justin's life is better now? Why/Why not?

B Are the sentences below True (T) or False (F)?

1 More and more people are choosing to live abroad and commute to their jobs in the UK.
2 Justin is manager of an online business based in the UK.
3 Justin's commute costs him hundreds of pounds every week.
4 Justin's journey home is about 70 miles.
5 Justin's wife and children stay in France while he travels to the UK every week.

4 Watch the DVD again. What exactly do they say? Underline the correct alternative.

1 'We were fed up with *waiting in the airport/the commuting and the traffic.*'
2 'He's one of a group of *travellers/commuters* who take the same flight to Toulouse every week.'
3 'We looked on the internet and we saw properties available *much cheaper/more expensive* than in Britain.'
4 'That's the house down there. With the *swimming pool/terrace.*'
5 'We've just transformed our *house/lifestyle.*'

5 Work in pairs. Discuss the questions.

1 Could you be a 'dream commuter' with your present job/studies?
2 Where would you choose to live and how would you get to work?

speakout work/life balance

6 Read the text and discuss the questions.

> In the UK, people work 43.5 hours per week on average. Men work 46.9 hours. In France, the average working week is 35 hours. Research also shows that 16 percent of UK workers work over 60 hours per week. At home in the UK, working parents play with their children for only 25 minutes per day. 1 out of 8 (12.5 percent) fathers see their children only at the weekend.

1 Is the work/life balance the same in your country?
2 Do you think people work too much? What problems can this cause?
3 Are you happy with your work/life or study/life balance? Why/Why not?

7 ▶ 2.8 Listen to an interview with a student. Does she have a good work/life balance? Tick the key phrases you hear.

> **KEY PHRASES**
>
> How much time do you spend … (sleeping/relaxing/commuting)?
> I spend a lot of time … (working/doing exercise)
> Do you ever … (have a holiday)?
> What about your … (social life/weekends)?
> How do you spend your weekends?

8 A Write some questions about work/life balance. Use the things in the box to help you.

> exercise/sport   social life   family
> weekends   enjoyable hobbies   holidays
> work/study habits

How much time do you spend with your family?

B Work in groups and take turns. Ask and answer your questions. Find someone who has a similar work/life balance to you.

writeback a web comment

9 A Read the entry to www.worklife247.nett. Answer the questions.

1 Is this a stressful job? Why/Why not?
2 Would you like a job like this?

 22-10-16 Posting 1

I'm a personal trainer. I eat well and I do a lot of exercise. I spend about five hours a day working with clients. In general, I think my work/life balance is good. I take time off every few months just to relax, and I rarely get stressed. Once in a while I go out partying. For me, a balanced lifestyle is really important. When I was younger, I worried if I missed a day of exercise. These days I don't worry about it.

My only problem is the one-hour commute. I hate taking the train every day and it's expensive. I'm planning to move house so I can live near the gym where I work and walk to work every morning.

| Comment |

B Think about your work/life balance and write a comment for www.worklife247.nett.

PRESENT SIMPLE AND CONTINUOUS

1 Work in pairs. Which verb can you use for a) and b)? Put each verb into the present simple or present continuous.

1 **a)** Don't switch off the TV! I *'m watching* it.
   b) I love that programme! I _watch_ it every week.

2 **a)** Can you call me back later? I _____ my homework.
   b) I try to keep fit. I _____ yoga and aerobics every day.

3 **a)** I love tennis, but I _____ badly.
   b) Sorry, I can't hear you because Matthew _____ the piano.

4 **a)** I _____ about twenty text messages a day, usually to friends.
   b) She _____ a book. It will be published next year.

5 **a)** Daddy can't come home now. He _____ late at the office.
   b) Usually he _____ from 9a.m. to 5p.m. from Monday to Friday.

6 **a)** I like to spend time with friends. That's what _____ me happy.
   b) I _____ some coffee. Do you want some?

7 **a)** She loves the school. She _____ a lot of friends there.
   b) Jill _____ some problems with her phone. Can you check it?

8 **a)** He only met his real father last month. They _____ to know each other now.
   b) In the UK, about 50 percent of married couples _____ divorced.

9 **a)** She always _____ a book to her son before he goes to sleep.
   b) I _____ his new book at the moment. It's really good.

10 **a)** Hi Tim! I'm in town for a week. I _____ an old friend.
   b) When we go to London, we usually _____ the National Gallery.

2 A Make six true sentences about your life/job. Use a word/phrase from each box.

| at home   my friends   in bed   at the weekend in the bath   on Friday evening   my family during my holidays   at my desk |

| work   drink   play   do   sing   eat   write   talk call   visit |

| often   sometimes   rarely   never   always   usually once in a while   occasionally   hardly ever |

B Work in pairs and compare your sentences.

A: I rarely work at my desk.
B: Do you often work at home?

ADVERBS OF FREQUENCY

3 A Match questions 1–7 with answers a)–g).

1 How often do you play sport?
2 Do you usually get up before 7a.m.?
3 How often do you phone your mother?
4 Do you eat a lot of meat?
5 How many texts do you send in a week?
6 Do you ever go camping?
7 How often do you read a newspaper?

a) Yes, my children wake me up at 5.30a.m.
b) I don't know. Maybe twenty.
c) Very rarely. I watch the news on television.
d) I play football once in a while.
e) No, hardly ever. I prefer fish.
f) Once a week. We always speak on Sundays.
g) Yes, occasionally. But it usually rains.

B Work in pairs and take turns. Ask and answer questions 1–7.

WORK AND JOBS

4 Work in pairs and take turns. Student A: choose a word/phrase from the box. Student B: choose another word/phrase and explain the connection between them.

| IT consultant   office   staff   work in a team foreign correspondent   sales rep   risk their lives fashion designer   boss   deal with customers   task motorcycle courier   company   get a good salary opportunity   rescue worker   personal trainer deal with problems |

A: IT consultant
B: An IT consultant deals with problems related to technology.

EXPRESSING LIKES/DISLIKES

5 A Work in pairs. How well do you know your partner? Think of questions for answers 1–6.

1 I absolutely love it.
2 I can't stand it.
3 I don't like it very much.
4 I don't mind it.
5 I'm not very keen on it.
6 I like it.

B Ask your partner the questions. Ask follow-up questions to find out more.

A: Do you like Italian food?
B: I absolutely love it.
A: What's your favourite dish?
B: Spaghetti Bolognese.
A: Really? How often do you eat it?

3 time out

FREE IN NYC p28

RELAX! p30

CAN I TAKE A MESSAGE? p32

RIO DE JANEIRO p34

SPEAKING **3.1** Talk about your future plans **3.2** Discuss how you spend your free time **3.3** Make and receive phone calls **3.4** Plan a perfect day out

LISTENING **3.1** Listen to a radio programme about going out in New York **3.3** Understand some problem phone calls **3.4** Watch an extract from a BBC travel programme about visiting Rio de Janeiro

READING **3.2** Read about how people spend their free time around the world

WRITING **3.1** Write an email invitation **3.4** Write a plan of a perfect day

BBC INTERVIEWS

What do you like doing in your free time?

3.1)) FREE IN NYC

G present continuous/*be going to* for future
P fast speech: *going to*
V time out

VOCABULARY

TIME OUT

1 A Complete the word webs with the verbs in the box.

| have   go   get   see   go to |

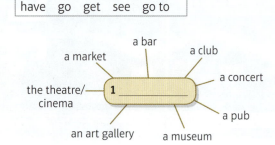

a bar

a market   a club

the theatre/   a concert
cinema   1 _____

an art gallery   a pub

a museum

an exhibition   a comedy show

2 _____

some live music   a band

sightseeing   dancing

4 _____

shopping

a snack

3 _____

some tickets   the bus

dinner   a free meal

5 _____

a drink   an evening out

B Work in pairs and take turns. Ask and answer questions using the phrases in Exercise 1A.

A: *How often do you go to a museum?*
B: *Not very often.*

▷ page 81 **PHOTOBANK**

LISTENING

2 A Work in pairs. Discuss the questions.

1 What kind of things do you like to do when you visit a city?

2 Where can you go/what things can you do for free, or very cheaply, where you live?

B ▷ 3.1 Listen to a radio programme. Answer the questions.

1 Is New York an expensive city to live in?

2 Are there lots of free things to do there?

3 How much money do the journalists have to spend?

4 What do they have to do?

3 A Complete the information about Rafael and Carmen's plans.

Rafael

1 He plans to start the day with a delicious bagel and then to spend the morning in _____.

2 He's going to the _____ of American Finance.

3 He's taking the Staten Island Ferry to see _____ of New York.

4 In the evening, he's going to see some _____ music.

Carmen

5 She's going to see a free _____ exhibition.

6 She's going to Times _____ because she likes the atmosphere.

7 She's going to an _____ restaurant near there.

8 In the evening, she's going to a _____ class.

B Listen to the programme again to check your answers. Which places in the photos do the speakers talk about?

C Work in pairs. Discuss. What do you think of the two plans? Which things would you like/not like to do?

GRAMMAR

PRESENT CONTINUOUS/*BE GOING TO* FOR FUTURE

4 A Read sentences a)–d) and answer the questions.

a) I'm going to see a free art exhibition.
b) I'm meeting a friend.
c) I'm going to see some live music.
d) I'm not going running.

1 Do the sentences refer to the present or the future?
2 Is there a definite time and place for the plans?
3 What tenses do the sentences use?

B ▶ 3.2 **FAST SPEECH:** *going to*
Listen to the pronunciation of *going to* in fast speech /ˈɡʌnə/. Listen and repeat the sentences.

▷ page 72 **LANGUAGE**BANK

5 A Make sentences or questions with the prompts. Use the present continuous or *be going to*.

1 we / go / cinema / Friday
2 you / go / stay / at / home / this evening?
3 she / not / work / this weekend
4 what time / we / meet / tomorrow?
5 I / go / watch / football match / later
6 they / go out / for a pizza / Saturday

B Change two sentences so they are true for you.

C Work in pairs and compare ideas.

SPEAKING

6 A Think about your future plans. Make notes about:
- places/people you plan to visit
- a film you want to see
- something delicious you want to eat

	you	your partner
tonight	*visit friend*	
this weekend		
next week/month		
later this year/next year		

B Work in pairs and take turns. Ask and answer questions about your plans (What? Where? Who with? Why?). Add notes to the table.

A: *What are you going to do tonight?*
B: *I'm going to visit an old friend.*

WRITING

INVITATIONS

7 A Put the emails in the correct order.

> To
> Hi Sonia – I'm going to be in New York next week. Sue and I are meeting for a drink on Tuesday evening at 6.30p.m. Would you like to come?
> Annabel

> To
> I'd love to. Sounds great! See you there.
> S

> To
> We're going out for a meal. Do you want to meet us for dinner? We're having a pizza at Mario's at 8p.m.
> A

> To
> Great to hear from you. I'm sorry, but I'm busy. I'm doing an exercise class from 6p.m. to 7.30p.m. What are you doing afterwards?
> Sonia

B Look at the emails in Exercise 7A. Underline two phrases for inviting and two responses.

C Write emails with the prompts.

> To
> Hi Matt
> What / you / do / tonight? A few people / come / watch / football / my house. Want / come?
> Ali

> To
> Tilly
> What / do / weekend? Would / like / dancing / Saturday night?
> Frank

> To
> Ali
> Great / hear. Love / to. Time / everyone / come?
> Matt

> To
> Sorry / busy / Saturday evening. Want / go cinema / Sunday?
> T

> To
> That / great / idea. Love / to. What / want / see?
> Frank

D Work in pairs. Choose an activity from Exercise 6 and write an email inviting another pair to the event.

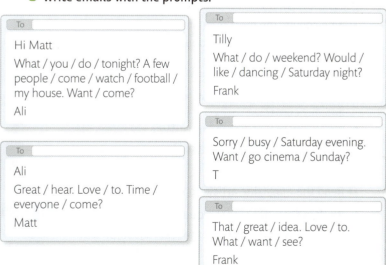

G questions without auxiliaries
P stress in compound nouns
V places to visit

VOCABULARY
PLACES TO VISIT

1 A Look at the words in the box and answer the questions.

1 Are they usually indoors or outdoors?
2 What free time activities do we usually do in these places?

> concert hall   countryside   sports field
> nightclub   street market   shopping mall
> nature trail   waterfront

B Write the words in the correct place and add as many other places as you can in one minute. Compare with other students.

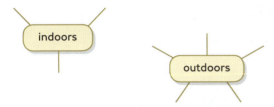

indoors

outdoors

2 A ▶ 3.3 **STRESS IN COMPOUND NOUNS** Listen to the words in the box in Exercise 1A. Underline the stressed syllables. Which word is usually stressed in compound nouns (nouns made of two words)?

concert hall

B Listen again and repeat.

READING

3 A Work in pairs. Read the questions about how different nationalities spend their free time, and guess the answers.

1 Who spends the most time on the internet?
2 What is the world's most popular sport?
3 Who spends the most time outdoors?
4 Which country has the most bars per person?
5 Which country has the most popular galleries and museums?
6 Which nation watches the most TV?
7 Which country parties the most?
8 Who exercises the most?

B Read the magazine article to find the answers.

C Work in pairs. Discuss the questions.

1 Is there any information in the text that surprises you? Why?
2 How do people spend their free time in your country? Are the activities in 1–8 popular?

How the World Spends its free time

1 Internet
People from Canada spend, on average, 43.5 hours per week online, 8 hours longer than the next highest, the USA. One reason: Canada has long, cold winters so people spend lots of time indoors.

2 Sport
Football is king. In second place, surprisingly, is cricket. Only a few nations play the game seriously, but it's very popular in India, which has 1.2 billion people.

3 Outdoors
New Zealanders spend the most time outdoors. The countryside is perfect for hiking, mountain climbing, and water sports. If you live in New Zealand, you're never more than two hours' drive from the sea. And then there is the rugby, too …

4 Bars
Spain has six bars per 1,000 inhabitants, easily the highest number. In Spain, a bar is for families, not just drinkers. It's a meeting place and often an eating place (try the tapas!).

5 Galleries and Museums
The UK has six of the top 20 most visited art galleries/museums in the world, including the National Gallery, the British Museum and Tate Modern.

6 TV

The biggest TV-watchers are in Thailand. They spend 22.4 hours a week watching TV. In second place comes the Philippines (21 hours) and in third place, Egypt (20.9 hours), famous for its never-ending soap operas!

7 Party!

It's impossible to say who parties the most, but Brazil's annual carnival makes it a good choice. Some of the best cities for partying include Bangkok (friendly people, great nightclubs), Berlin (live music scene), and the island of Ibiza (dance music).

8 Exercising

The biggest exercisers are people from Greece and Estonia. Over 80 percent of people in those countries exercise regularly. In both countries, football and the Olympic sports are the most popular, but Estonia has one very special game: ice cricket!

GRAMMAR

QUESTIONS WITHOUT AUXILIARIES

4 Read the examples and answer questions 1–3.

a) Subject questions

Question: **Who** *exercises the most?*
Answer: **Greeks** *exercise the most.*

b) Object questions

Question: *What did* **you** *do last night?*
Answer: **I** *went to a party.*

1 Which question asks us to name the subject (the people who do the action): a) or b)?

2 Which question asks for other information about the subject: a) or b)?

3 Which type of question uses the auxiliary?

▷ page 72 **LANGUAGEBANK**

5 Complete the questions for the answers in italics with the words in the box.

| makes   did   Who (x 2)   won   Which   do   is |

1 _____ invented basketball?
A Canadian called James Naismith invented basketball.

2 _____ country makes the most films?
India makes the most films.

3 What _____ people do when it's too cold to go out?
They watch TV or read!

4 _____ exercises more: the Japanese or the Germans?
The Germans exercise more.

5 Which sport _____ Brazil famous for?
Brazil is famous for football.

6 Who _____ the first football World Cup?
Uruguay won the first World Cup.

7 Which country _____ the most cars?
China makes the most cars.

8 What _____ you do last night?
I stayed at home.

SPEAKING

6 A Ask other students questions to find out:

1 who listens to music the most frequently
How often do you listen to music?

2 who exercises the most
Do you do a lot of exercise?

3 who spends the most time on the internet

4 who regularly goes to art galleries and/or museums

5 who has been to the theatre or cinema in the last four months

6 who goes to the most parties

7 who watches the most TV

8 who is the biggest sports fan

B As a whole class, answer the questions in Exercise 6A.

Juan listens to music most frequently. He listens to music on the way to and from work and for two hours every evening!

3.3)) CAN I TAKE A MESSAGE?

F making a phone call
P linking: can
V collocations

SPEAKING

1 Work in pairs. Discuss the questions.

1 Do you prefer speaking on the phone or in person?
2 Have you ever made a call or taken a message in English? What happened?

VOCABULARY

COLLOCATIONS

2 A Look at phrases 1–7 below. Have you done any of these on the phone recently? Have you done any in English?

1 book a table
2 arrange to meet friends
3 have a chat
4 cancel a booking/reservation
5 check train times
6 change a ticket
7 talk business

B Work in pairs and compare your answers.

A: Have you booked a table on the phone recently?
B: Yes, I booked a table at a restaurant last week.

FUNCTION

MAKING A PHONE CALL

3 A ▶ 3.4 Listen to four people making phone calls. Why are they phoning?

B Listen again and complete the notes.

Conversation 1

Sun. May 16: Jack Hopper, table for _____ people.
Time: _____.

Como's
RESTAURANT

Conversation 2

RSA THEATRE

2 tickets for James _____.
New date: _____.

Conversation 3

Dinner with Mary and the gang, Pauly's at _____ on _____ night.

Conversation 4

Date: 22nd August. Time: 2.20.
Witherton's Ltd
To: Ally Sanders. Caller: Kim Brower.
Message: Cancel _____. Please call back.

4 Complete the sentences with the words in the box.

| it's back for leave here take can |

Start the call
Caller: Hello, this is Andy./Hello, ¹_____ Andy. (NOT ~~I am Andy~~)
Receiver: Hello, Paul speaking.

Ask to speak to someone …
Caller: ²_____ I speak to … ?
Receiver: Who's calling?

When the person the caller wants isn't there …
Caller: Can I ³_____ a message?
Receiver: I'm afraid she's not ⁴_____ at the moment. Can I ⁵_____ a message? I'll ask her to call you ⁶_____.

Finish the call
Caller: See you soon. Goodbye.
Receiver: Thanks ⁷_____ calling. See you soon. Goodbye.

LEARN TO

MANAGE PHONE PROBLEMS

6 A Look at the phrases in bold in the extracts below and match them to problems a)–e).

a) we need to hear something again   *2, 6*

b) the speaker is speaking too fast

c) the speaker is speaking too quietly

d) when we are not sure the information is correct

e) the speaker isn't sure the listener heard anything

Extract 1

C: OK, one moment. ¹**Can I just check?** What's the name, please?

D: The tickets are booked in the name of James King.

C: ²**Sorry, I didn't catch that. Did you say** King?

D: James King.

C: OK, yes. Two tickets for July the tenth. What date would you like to change to?

D: What dates do you still have seats for?

C: There's nothing on the twelfth or thirteenth. There are two seats for the eleventh, but they're separate. We have …

D: ³**Sorry, can you slow down, please?**

Extract 2

E: Hello?

F: Hello, it's Mary here. Hello? ⁴**Can you hear me OK?** It's Mary here.

Extract 3

F: Are you doing anything on Saturday? Because a few of us are going out for dinner.

E: Sorry, Mary, ⁵**can you speak up, please?** I'm at the station and I can't hear a thing.

Extract 4

H: It's 01823 2766.

G: ⁶**Can you repeat that, please?**

B ▶ 3.5   **LINKING: *can*** Listen and repeat the phrases. Notice how *can* and *you* are linked in connected speech: /kənju:/

7 A ▶ 3.6   Listen and write an appropriate response.

B ▶ 3.7   Listen to check.

speak**out** TIP

Before you make a phone call, think carefully about the words you will use. How will you start the conversation? What information do you want? Write down some key words that you will use and expect to hear.

SPEAKING

8 Work in pairs. Student A: turn to page 86. Student B: turn to page 88.

---

5 A Underline the correct alternative to complete the phone conversations.

Conversation 1

Sasha:	Hello. Sasha ¹*here/speaks*.
Mustafa:	Hi, ²*I'm/it's* Mustafa.
Sasha:	Hi, Mustafa. How are you?
Mustafa:	I'm fine, thanks. How about you?
Sasha:	Very well, thanks.
Mustafa:	Are you busy? Do you want to have lunch in that Turkish place on Broad Street?
Sasha:	That sounds good. What time?
Mustafa:	One o'clock?
Sasha:	Great.
Mustafa:	OK. ³*Speak/See* you soon.
Sasha:	OK. Bye.

Conversation 2

Receptionist:	Anderson Products.
Sasha:	Hello. Can I ⁴*connect/speak* to the HR Manager?
Receptionist:	One moment. Who's ⁵*called/calling*?
Sasha:	It's Sasha Barnes here.
Receptionist:	I'm afraid he ⁶*isn't/not* here at the moment. Can I take a ⁷*message/call*?
Sasha:	Please tell him to call me ⁸*return/back*. I'm waiting in the Turkish restaurant!

B Work in pairs and practise the conversations. Take turns to change roles.

▷ page 72 **LANGUAGE**BANK

DVD PREVIEW

1 Work in pairs and discuss.

  1 When you visit a new city, what kind of things do you like to do?

  2 Do you like to see and do the things a tourist would do, or do you prefer to spend time with the local people? Why?

2 A Work in pairs and discuss.

  1 What do you know about Rio de Janeiro in Brazil?

  2 Would you like to go there? Why/Why not?

B Read the programme information. What kind of things do you think the locals will do in Rio?

▶) Going Local: Rio   BBC

Going Local takes its presenters to fantastic cities around the world and asks them to explore the city by doing a series of challenges. However, to complete the challenges, they need to throw away the guidebook and ask the people who know best – the locals. In this episode Rafael Estophania travels to Rio de Janeiro, the city of sand and samba, to find out how the *cariocas* (locals) spend their time.

DVD VIEW

3 A Which of these activities do you think the presenter tries to do?

  1 find somewhere good to eat

  2 use public transport with good views

  3 eat exotic fruit

  4 play a game with the locals

  5 dance samba

  6 play music

B Watch the DVD to find out.

4 A Correct the information in the sentences.

  1 Rio is the home of sunshine, ~~salsa~~ and the Sugarloaf Mountain. *samba*

  2 You can view all the *favelas* from the train.

  3 The locals tell him to go to the supermarket to find exotic fruit.

  4 The cashew nut tastes like a mixture of strawberries and lemons.

  5 The men like to play frescoball in the park.

  6 They play music with a local band on the street.

B Watch the DVD again to check your answers.

5 Work in pairs. Discuss the questions.

  1 Would you enjoy any of the things the presenter does? Which ones?

  2 When did you last do any of these things? Where were you?

speakout a day in your city

6 A  **3.8** Listen to Alessandro talking about his plans for a day out in Pisa. Number the activities in the order he talks about them.

a) have a pizza _____

b) go to a market _____

c) have a coffee ___1___

d) walk through the old city _____

e) have lunch in a restaurant _____

f) go to a park _____

B Listen again and use the key phrases to complete sentences 1–6.

> **KEYPHRASES**
>
> We're starting the day …
>
> We're going to …
>
> Afterwards, for lunch we're …
>
> In the afternoon, we're planning to …
>
> In the evening, we're …
>
> It's going to be …

1 … spend the morning walking through the market.

2 … a day to remember.

3 … with a coffee and a fresh pastry.

4 … go a little outside Pisa.

5 … going back towards the Leaning Tower.

6 … going to one of the best restaurants I know.

7 A Work in groups. You are going to plan 24 hours in a city of your choice. Plan your day in detail. Try to include areas that only locals would know about. Use questions 1–6 to help you.

1 Which city are you planning to visit?

2 What are you going to do there?

3 How are you going to get around?

4 What are you going to eat/drink? Where?

5 What are you planning for the evening?

6 What is going to make the day special?

B Work with other students and tell them about your plans. Which plans do you think are the best?

writeback an invitation

8 Write an invitation. Describe the day you have planned and give it to someone in another group. Use the emails on page 29 to help you.

V TIME OUT

1 Cross out one phrase which is not possible in each sentence.

1 I went to *a bar/sightseeing/the market*.
2 Do you want to get *the bus/ a snack/an art gallery*?
3 They went to *the art gallery/ the museum/a snack*.
4 She has gone *a pub/ sightseeing/dancing*.
5 Can we have *a club/dinner/ a drink*?

G PRESENT CONTINUOUS/*BE GOING TO* FOR FUTURE

2 A Put the words in the correct order to make questions.

1 are / what / doing / tonight / you?
2 you / weekend / are / this / doing / special / anything?
3 dinner / evening / is / this / your / who / cooking?
4 you / holiday / are / on / going / when?
5 are / going / city / you / to / visit / which / next?
6 after / to / are / lesson / going / the / what / do / you?

B Work in pairs and take turns. Ask and answer the questions.

V PLACES TO VISIT

3 Work in pairs and take turns. Student A: choose a word from the box and describe it. Student B: guess the word.

concert hall	countryside
sports field	nightclub
street market	shopping mall
nature trail	waterfront

It's a place where …
A: It's a place where people play outdoor sports.
B: A sports field.

G QUESTIONS WITHOUT AUXILIARIES

4 A Make questions with the prompts. Add a question word and put the verb into the correct form.

1 famous works / include / *Romeo and Juliet* and *Hamlet*?
   Whose famous works include Romeo and Juliet and Hamlet?
2 be / an actor / before / he became US President?
3 1975 Queen album / include / the song *Bohemian Rhapsody*?
4 be / a fourth great Renaissance painter, besides Leonardo, Michelangelo and Titian?
5 'John' / win / an Oscar for his song *Can you Feel the Love Tonight* from *The Lion King*?
6 Bob Marley song / include / the words *Let's get together and feel alright*?
7 watery Italian city / have / an international art exhibition every two years?
8 member of the Dion family sell / 200 million records before 2007?
9 hit songs / include / *I'm like a bird*, *Promiscuous* and *Maneater*?

B Do the quiz above. Each answer begins with the last two letters of the previous answer.

1 Shakespea<u>re</u>
2 Re _ _ _ _
3 _ _ight at the Ope_ _
4 _ _pha_ _
5 _ _t_ _
6 _ _e Lo_ _
7 _ _ni_ _
8 _ _ li _ _
9 _ _ lly Furtado

C Check your answers on page 86.

F MAKING A PHONE CALL

5 A Complete the phone call with the words in the box.

here	it's	back	like	can

A: Hello there, [1]_____ Billy Blue.
B: Hello, Billy. How are you?
A: I'm absolutely fine, thank you.
B: So, Bill, what [2]_____ I do for you?
A: I'd [3]_____ to speak to Mrs Chow.
B: Sorry, she's not [4]_____ right now.
A: Any idea when she'll be [5]_____?
B: Never. Today she got the sack.*

*If you *get the sack*, it means you lose your job.

B Complete the message with the words in the box.

call	leave	this	message
busy			

Hello, [1]_____ is Pete and Paul.
Sorry, there's no one here at all.
We're probably [2]_____, in a meeting,
Or maybe in a restaurant, eating,
Or maybe in a bar watching a game,
But [3]_____ a [4]_____ and your name.
We'll [5]_____ you back some time soon,
And pigs might fly* around the Moon.

Pigs might fly is an idiom that means 'it will never happen'.

C Work in pairs and take turns. Read the conversation in Exercise 5A and the message in Exercise 5B. Concentrate on the rhythm.

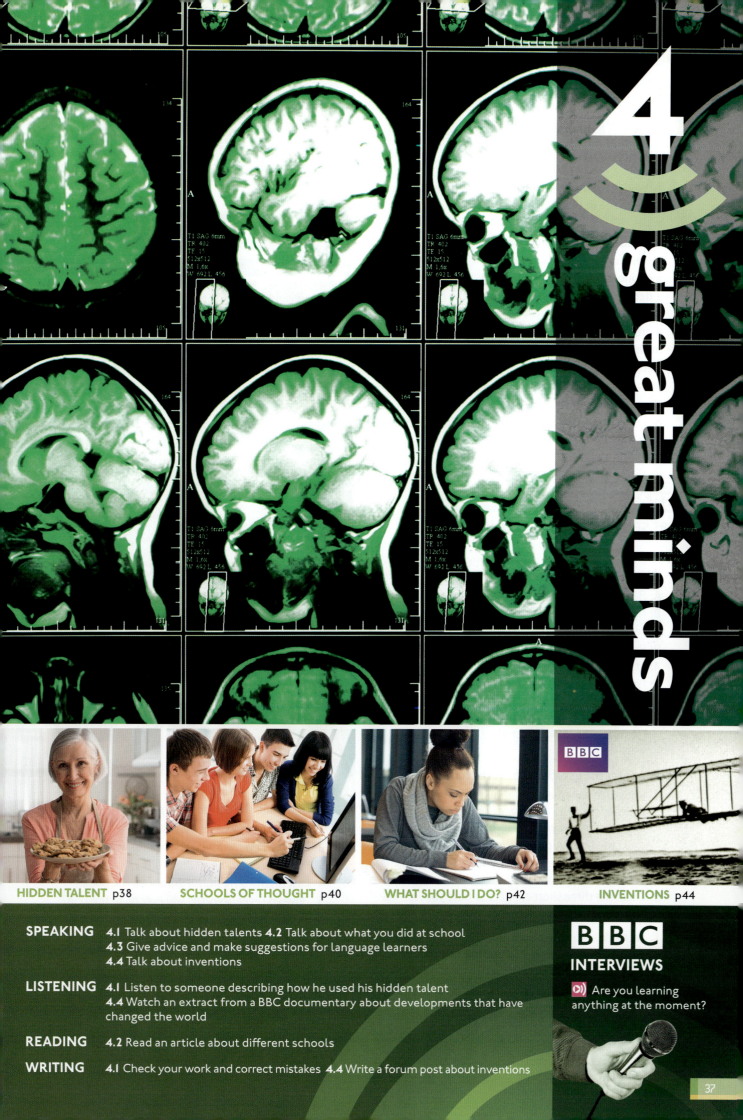

4)) great minds

SPEAKING   4.1 Talk about hidden talents 4.2 Talk about what you did at school
4.3 Give advice and make suggestions for language learners
4.4 Talk about inventions

LISTENING   4.1 Listen to someone describing how he used his hidden talent
4.4 Watch an extract from a BBC documentary about developments that have
changed the world

READING   4.2 Read an article about different schools

WRITING   4.1 Check your work and correct mistakes 4.4 Write a forum post about inventions

BBC INTERVIEWS

O)) Are you learning anything at the moment?

G present perfect + *ever/never*
P weak forms: *have*
V *make* and *do*

VOCABULARY

MAKE AND *DO*

1 A Work in pairs. Which of the phrases in bold below can you see in the pictures?

Make …

a speech in front of more than fifty people

a meal for more than eight people

a phone call in a foreign language

a decision that changed your life for the better

Do …

a project with a big team

business in another language

well/badly in an exam

your homework on the way to school

B Which of the activities in Exercise 1A have you done: a) in the last 24 hours? b) in the last week? c) in the last month? Which have you never done? Compare your answers with other students.

GRAMMAR

PRESENT PERFECT + *EVER/NEVER*

2 A ▶ 4.1 **Listen and read the conversation below. Which tenses do the speakers use?**

A: Have you ever made a speech in public?

B: No, never. Have you?

A: Yes, I have. I made a speech at work.

B: Really? When did you do that?

A: At a conference last year. I was really nervous.

B: I'm not surprised. OK, have you ever made friends with someone from another country?

A: No, I haven't, but my brother has. He met a woman from Chile in 2014. In fact, they got married a week ago!

B Answer the questions about the conversation.

1 Underline two questions about general experiences (where the exact time is not important). How are they formed?

_____ you (*ever*) + past participle … ?

2 Find two sentences which say <u>when</u> the actions happened in the past. Which verb tense is used?

3 Circle the three short answers to *Have you … ?* questions.

C **WEAK FORMS:** *have* Listen again. Notice how *have* is pronounced in the questions. How is it different in the short answers?

▷ page 74 **LANGUAGE**BANK

3 A Underline the correct alternative.

1 She *has been/was* on TV yesterday.

2 *Have you ever written/Did you ever write* a speech?

3 I*'ve never eaten/never ate* snails.

4 Last night I *have finished/finished* the book.

5 *Have you ever been/Did you ever go* to the USA?

6 He *has finished/finished* the project this morning.

B Complete the sentences.

1 I've …

2 Yesterday I …

3 I've never …

4 I've always …

5 When I was a child, I …

C Work in pairs and compare your answers.

4 A Write the past participles in the table below. Check your answers on page 67.

catch	_caught_	give	_____
keep	_____	swim	_____
make	_____	sleep	_____
drive	_____	lose	_____
do	_____	win	_____
fly	_____	buy	_bought_
come	_____	pay	_____
cross	_____	grow	_____

B ▶ 4.2 Match the verbs which have rhyming past participles. Then listen and check.

caught /kɔːt/ – bought /bɔːt/

C Work in pairs. Use the verbs above to make six *Have you ever …?* questions. Use the ideas in the box to help you.

> fish   anything expensive   a bus   a prize   all day   a plane
> plants   in a river

D Work in pairs and take turns. Ask and answer the questions.

A: Have you ever caught a fish?
B: Yes, I have. I caught three last weekend!

LISTENING

5 A ▶ 4.3 Look at the pictures and listen to an interview with Mario, the boy in the story. As you listen, answer questions 1–3.

1 What was Mario's hidden talent?
2 When did he start to use his talent?
3 How did he use his talent to change his job?

Mario's Café

B Listen again and complete the extracts.

1 I've always _____ cooking.
2 Then in my twenties I started to _____ meals for my friends.
3 I had the idea to _____ my food at work.
4 I wanted to _____ something more interesting.
5 _____ you ever thought, 'Oh, I prefer my old office job'?
6 It's the best decision I've ever _____.

SPEAKING

6 A Think about your hidden talent or something you love doing. Write notes about the following questions.

1 What is the talent?
2 Have you ever done it in public?
3 Do you practise? When/Where?
4 Is it/Will it be useful in your job/future job?

B Work in groups and take turns. Describe your hidden talent.

I am good with numbers. I can do difficult sums in my head without using a calculator.

WRITING

CORRECTING MISTAKES

7 A Read the paragraph below. Find nine mistakes and correct them. Use these symbols:

gr = grammar   p = punctuation
sp = spelling

My Hidden Talent

My talent is that I can sing really well. I've always like music I sing all kinds of songs, including rock, pop and classical music I first discovered this abillity when I was young. I often listened to music and sang at the same time. I've doing it many times at parties, in front of my freinds, and in karaoke bars. There is no magic secret I just listen carefuly and am practising on my own.

speakout TIP

Don't make the same mistake twice! Look through your corrected written work. Do you repeat your mistakes? Write down the correct form <u>in a different colour</u>.

B Write a paragraph about your hidden talent or about someone you think is very talented (a sportsperson, actor, singer, writer, etc.).

C Work in groups. Read the paragraphs and correct any mistakes.

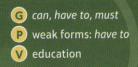

G *can, have to, must*
P weak forms: *have to*
V education

VOCABULARY

EDUCATION

1 Work in pairs. Discuss the subjects in the box. Which subjects did you like at school? Were there any subjects you didn't like? Why/Why not?

> maths   science   history   literature   art
> languages   IT (information technology)

▷ page 82 **PHOTOBANK**

2 A Complete the phrases with the verbs in the box.

> make   wear   do/take   give   play   study

1 _____   art/music
               a foreign language
               online
2 _____   sport
               games
               a musical instrument
3 _____   mistakes
               friends
4 _____   a test
               exams
5 _____   a performance
6 _____   a school uniform

B Which of the things above did you do at school? Did you enjoy them? Write (+), (−) or (?) (no experience), next to each one.

C Work in pairs and compare your answers. Who enjoyed their school experience more?

READING

3 A Work in pairs. Discuss. Who was your favourite/ least favourite teacher at school? Why? Were your teachers traditional in their approach to teaching? Do you think this was good or bad?

B Read the text. Match paragraphs 1–3 with topics a)–c) below.

a) making mistakes is OK
b) a school where students make the decisions
c) children watch videos outside class

C Read the text again. Discuss. Which of the ideas in the text do you think is the best? Which is the worst? Would these methods work in your country?

ARE TRADITIONAL WAYS OF LEARNING

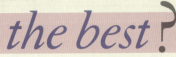

the best?

Read about some alternative schools of thought . . .

1 THE ALTERNATIVE SCHOOL

The Alternative School, in Lancashire, UK, offers a different type of schooling for young people who are having problems in mainstream education. The school offers an innovative and interesting educational programme, which is designed specifically for the individual. Students can decide when they come to school, and which subjects they want to study. They don't have to come to school every day. They can choose to start with just a few hours a week. The school uses an 'open door' policy where students are allowed to leave lessons if they are bored or unhappy.

2 THE FLIPPED CLASSROOM

Many classrooms around the world are adopting a flipped classroom approach. This learning model switches classroom learning and homework. In a traditional classroom, the teacher explains the lesson to the students in the classroom, and the students study homework outside class, where they have to work on their own, and can't ask anyone for help. So, in a flipped classroom, children can watch a video of their teacher giving a lecture on the subject at home. They don't have to do any written work. When they come back to the classroom, they have to do the more traditional exercises, but they can ask the teacher or their classmates for help if they don't understand.

3 STARTING YOUNG

A child learning music with the Suzuki method has to start as young as possible. Even two-year-old children can learn to play difficult pieces of classical music, often on the violin. They do this by watching and listening. They learn by copying, just like they learn their mother tongue. The child has to join in, but doesn't have to get it right. 'They soon learn that they mustn't stop every time they make a mistake. They just carry on,' said one Suzuki trainer. The children have to practise for hours every day and they give performances once a week, so they learn quickly. 'The parents must be involved too,' said the trainer, 'or it just doesn't work.'

GRAMMAR

CAN, HAVE TO, MUST

4 Read sentences 1–6 and put the verbs in bold in the correct place in the table.

1 Students **can** decide when they come to school.
2 (The students) **can't** ask anyone for help.
3 They **have to** do the more traditional exercises.
4 At *The Alternative School*, you **don't have to** come to school every day.
5 They **mustn't** stop every time they make a mistake.
6 The parents **must** be involved, too.

possible/allowed	not possible/not allowed
can	
necessary	**not necessary**

▷ page 74 **LANGUAGEBANK**

5 A Complete the text with *have to/don't have to, must/mustn't, can/can't*. There may be more than one possible answer.

Do I have to go to school today?

They ¹_____ (not necessary) wear a uniform, and they ²_____ (not necessary) wait for the school bus. These are two of the advantages of being home-schooled. But there are more. 'You ³_____ (possible) choose which subjects you want to study,' says Jasmin, aged fourteen. 'You ⁴_____ (necessary) work hard, but you ⁵_____ (possible) choose to work when you feel like it.' Jasmin is one of 55,000 children in the UK who doesn't go to school. She stays at home for her education, and she's much happier. 'School is all about rules: you ⁶_____ (necessary) be at school at 8.30a.m., you ⁷_____ (not allowed) wear trainers, you ⁸_____ (not allowed) use your mobile phone in class, etc. I prefer being at home.' Jasmin's mother, Terry, educates her four children at home. 'Some people think that children who study at home ⁹_____ (not allowed) go to the exams and get the same qualifications, but they ¹⁰_____ (allowed), and they do!'

B ▶ 4.4 **WEAK FORMS:** *have to* Listen and check.

C Listen and notice the pronunciation of *have to* /hæftə/.

D Listen again and repeat.

6 Work in pairs. Discuss two or three similarities and differences between home-schooling and going to a normal school. Do you think home-schooling is a good idea? Why/Why not?

SPEAKING

7 Work in pairs. Read the statements. Are the rules the same or different in your country? Do you think this is a good or a bad idea? Discuss.

1 In the UK, children have to learn a foreign language at school.
2 In the UK, you can take exams in art, cooking and sport at school.
3 Children in Thailand have to sing the national anthem in the morning.
4 In Singapore, children must learn most subjects (maths and science) in English.
5 In France, children don't have to wear uniforms to school.
6 In Japan, children mustn't be late for school, or they can't get in.
7 In Spain, children don't have to eat at school. They can go home for lunch.
8 In the UK, children can eat a vegetarian meal at lunch.
9 Children in Poland must repeat the year if they fail their exams.

F giving advice
P silent letters
V language learning

SPEAKING

1 A Read the quotes about learning. Do you agree with any of them? Why/Why not?

> **We learn by doing.**
>
> *A little knowledge is a dangerous thing.*
>
> *Anyone who stops learning is old, whether at twenty or eighty.*
>
> **The best way to learn is to teach.**

B Compare your ideas with other students.

VOCABULARY

LANGUAGE LEARNING

2 A Read sentences 1–7. Then match the words in bold with definitions a)–g).

1 I **re-read** articles we use in class.
2 I **look up** new words in a dictionary.
3 I watch films with **subtitles.**
4 I **go online** to read the news in English.
5 I **chat** to other learners.
6 I **note down** new phrases in my notebook.
7 I listen to English songs and I try to **memorise** them.

a) find information in a book/on a computer
b) read again
c) talk (possibly on the internet)
d) study until you remember
e) words on a film which translate what a character says
f) write
g) use the internet

B Work in pairs. Discuss the questions.

1 Which of the activities above do you do? How often?
2 Which do you think are the most important/useful for learning English?
3 Do you have any other ideas on how to improve your English?

FUNCTION

GIVING ADVICE

3 A Read the website message below and think of three things Zeynep can do to improve her English.

> Hello, everyone. In two months I'll start work at an international company. The only problem is I need to improve my English quickly. I did well in my recent English exam, but I need to do business in English, and I know it'll be more difficult. Do you have any good ideas?
> **Zeynep**

B Work in pairs and compare your answers.

4 Read the replies and discuss. Which ideas have you tried? Which do you think are the most useful ideas?

 Hi Zeynep. I think you should use message boards to make new friends. Then you can chat with them online in English and it doesn't matter if you make mistakes.
Ahmed L

 Zeynep, go online and find a business website you like. When you don't understand some words, you should look them up and write them in a notebook.
Ruby 335

 You shouldn't worry. They gave you the job, so you're good enough. Relax and just watch some movies in English.
Marie 98

 Why don't you use graded readers? They're enjoyable and they'll help you learn new words.
Ana Kosicka

 Zeynep, I think it's a good idea to use language learning apps, as these help you measure your progress.
Jung-sun Huang

5

A Look at the replies in Exercise 4 again. Complete phrases 1–6 below.

1 I _____ you should …
2 Find/Write _____
3 You should _____
4 You shouldn't _____
5 Why _____ you _____ …?
6 I (don't) think it's a good _____ to …

B Discuss. Which phrases have the same meaning?

C ▶ 4.5 **SILENT LETTERS** How is *should* pronounced? Which letter is silent? Listen and repeat.

6

A ▶ 4.6 Listen to two teachers discussing language learning. What problems do they mention?

B Work in pairs. Complete the notes in the table.

problem	advice
Students too shy to speak. Worry about 1 _____ _____.	Give students time to 2 _____. Let them practise in 3 _____.
Students have problems 4 _____.	Watch film clips on YouTube. Watch the mouth, 5 _____, body language. Use 6 _____ the second time.

C Listen again to check.

D Work in pairs. Discuss the questions.

1 Do you have the problems mentioned in the recording?
2 What do you think of the advice?
3 Can you add any other advice?

LEARN TO

RESPOND TO ADVICE

7

A Read the extracts below. How did the listener respond? Listen again and write the response.

1 They can take notes first.
2 Let them practise in groups before they speak in front of everyone. This'll give them confidence.
3 And using subtitles? Some teachers say we shouldn't use them. Ever!
4 They can see which words are swallowed.

B Read the responses. Mark them (✓) I agree, (✗) I disagree or (?) I agree but not completely.

1 That's a good idea.
2 I suppose so.
3 You're right.
4 I'm not sure that's a good idea.

▷ page 74 **LANGUAGEBANK**

8

A Look at pictures A–D below. What do you think the problems are?

1
A: I think _____ in the food industry. (you / work)
B: That's _____ idea. (good)

2
A: You _____ so much time watching TV. (not / spend)
B: _____ right.

3
A: _____ we find you a personal trainer? (why)
B: I _____ a good idea. (not sure)

4
A: I think _____ idea to start going shopping together. (good)
B: I _____. (suppose)

B Complete the conversations in pictures A–D using the words in brackets.

9

Work with two other students. Take turns to ask for and respond to advice. Student A: turn to page 86. Student B: turn to page 88. Student C: turn to page 89. Read your situation and explain it to the others.

I've got this problem …

DVD PREVIEW

1 Work in groups. Discuss the questions.

1 Do you ever travel by aeroplane? How frequently?
2 Have you ever flown long distances? If so, did you enjoy the experience?
3 What do you know about the invention of the aeroplane? (Who? Where? When?)

2 Read the programme information. Why does Dallas Campbell go to the USA?

◀)) Supersized Earth: The Way We Move **BBC**

Supersized Earth looks at amazing developments that have changed the modern world. This programme shows the start of aeroplane travel. Dallas Campbell goes to the USA, where the Wright brothers first flew a glider, an early type of aeroplane without an engine, in 1902. Campbell tries out a replica (a perfect copy) of the glider to see if he can fly it.

3 A Read the sentences. What do you think the words and phrases in bold mean?

1 The brothers' first journey **triggered a whole century of innovation**.
2 The **invention** the Wright brothers are known for is the aeroplane.
3 They began to **conquer** the skies.
4 The brothers **achieved** this in a simple way.
5 The first plane **launched a revolution** in the way we travel.

B Match the words/phrases in bold in Exercise 3A with meanings a)–e) below.

a) were successful at something
b) caused one hundred years of new ideas
c) started something that changed society
d) a new creation
e) become the master of (something)

DVD VIEW

4 A Watch the DVD and answer the questions.

1 What does Dallas Campbell tell us about the Wright brothers' first flight?
2 Does Dallas Campbell fly the glider successfully?

B Which words complete the notes? Choose the correct alternative. Watch the DVD again to check.

1 On 17 December *1903/1913* the Wright brothers made a journey.
2 They travelled *120 miles/120 feet*.
3 A year before flying a plane, the brothers built *a glider/a plane engine*.
4 Dallas Campbell says the plane 'helped transform our *travel/planet*.'

5 Work in pairs. Discuss. What new information did you learn from the programme?

speakout inventions

6 A Look at the list of inventors and their inventions. What do you know about these people? What other famous inventors do you know?

Johannes Gutenberg (1395–1468): the printing press
Alexander Graham Bell (1847–1922): the telephone
Thomas Edison (1847–1931): the light bulb
Tim Berners-Lee (b. 1955): the internet

B ▶ 4.7 Listen to two people talking about important inventions. Which do they mention?

1 Which idea do they think is very good?
2 Which idea do they disagree about?
3 What is the third idea they talk about?

C Listen again and tick the key phrases you hear.

> **KEYPHRASES**
>
> I think the most important …
> For me, …
> That's true, but …
> In my opinion, …
> Another invention that I see as really important is …
> Definitely.
> That's right.
> I agree.

7 A Work in pairs. Which three inventions do you think are the most important? Use the ideas in Exercise 6A or choose your own ideas.

B Tell the rest of the class about your choices. Do you all agree?

writeback a forum post

8 A Read about an online survey and then read a post by a commenter. What is the survey about and what does the person think of it?

World Changers

We asked 15,000 people from 15 countries to name the most important inventions in history. Here are the top ten:

1 wheel   6 electricity
2 telephone   7 refrigerator
3 antibiotics   8 internet
4 language   9 engine
5 aeroplane   10 iPhone

I think the list includes some very important inventions, but in my opinion there are also some strange choices. Some of them, e.g. language and electricity, aren't inventions at all. These are discoveries of natural things and shouldn't be on this list. I'm also surprised that the toilet and the printing press aren't in the top ten. For me, these are essential. Without the toilet, there would be a lot more disease, and without the printing press, modern communications would be very different: we would have fewer books, magazines and newspapers. Also, I'm amazed that the iPhone is at number ten! How many people in the world actually have an iPhone? It seems strange to include it in a list of basic needs like the wheel and antibiotics.

Nick G

B Write a post saying what you think of the top ten inventions. Explain your reasons. You can also add other suggestions for inventions you think should be included.

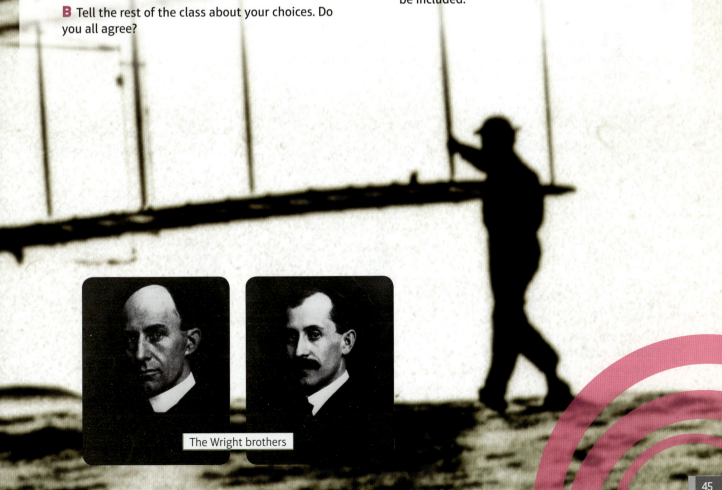

The Wright brothers

ⓥ MAKE AND DO

1 A Complete the questions with *makes* or *does*.

Who in your family …

1 _makes_ decisions about where you go on holiday?

2 _____ most of the meals?

3 _____ a lot of homework?

4 _____ the most phone calls?

5 _____ projects at work?

6 _____ speeches?

B Work in pairs and take turns. Ask and answer the questions.

ⓖ PAST SIMPLE OR PRESENT PERFECT + EVER/NEVER

2 A Complete the sentences with the correct form of the verb in brackets.

Questions

1 _____ in the sea? (you / ever swim)

2 _____ on holiday last year? (you / go)

Negatives

3 _____ Africa. (I / never visit)

4 _____ last night. (I / not go out)

Affirmatives

5 _____ in more than one country. (I / live)

6 _____ in a restaurant last weekend. (I / eat)

B Work in pairs and take turns. Guess your partner's answers to questions 1–2.

C Are sentences 3–6 true for your partner? Ask and answer questions to find out.

ⓥ EDUCATION

3 A Match 1–7 with a)–g) to make questions.

1 Do you play

2 When you take

3 How do you feel when you make

4 At school, did you

5 Have you ever given a

6 Do you ever study

7 Did you study

a) online?
b) performance of anything?
c) exams, do you get nervous?
d) study art?
e) any sport particularly well?
f) a foreign language at school?
g) mistakes?

B Work in pairs and take turns. Ask and answer the questions.

ⓖ CAN, HAVE TO, MUST

4 A Underline the correct alternative to complete the sentences.

1 In Australia, you *must/can/don't have to* drive on the left.

2 In the UK, you *have to/can/can't* smoke in pubs and restaurants.

3 You *can't/have to/must* talk on your mobile phone during an examination.

4 Children are lucky. They *don't have to/must/can* worry about paying bills!

5 In the UK, you *have to/can't/mustn't* be 17 years old before you can ride a motorcycle.

B Write down one thing:

- you can/can't do in your country
- you have to do next week
- you mustn't do during an exam
- you don't have to do at the weekend
- you must do when learning a language
- you mustn't do while driving
- you have to do every day
- you don't have to do when you are a child

C Work in pairs and compare your ideas.

ⓥ LANGUAGE LEARNING

5 A Complete the questions.

1 Do you r_____ - r_____ articles to help you understand them?

2 When's the last time you went o_____ to study English?

3 Do you like watching films with sub_____? Why/Why not?

4 Have you ever used a ch_____ room in English?

5 Which words from this unit are you going to mem_____?

B Work in pairs and take turns. Ask and answer the questions.

ⓕ GIVING ADVICE

6 A Complete the tables below with phrases for giving/responding to advice.

giving advice

responding to advice

B Work in pairs. Complete the conversation in different ways.

A: Why don't we _____?
B: That's a _____.
A: I think/don't think _____.
B: OK. Let's _____.

C Practise and act out your conversation.

5)) travel

FANTASTIC FILM TRIPS p48   **TRAVEL TIPS** p50   **YOU CAN'T MISS IT** p52   **FULL CIRCLE** p54

BBC INTERVIEWS

)) Do you enjoy travelling to different countries?

5.1)) FANTASTIC FILM TRIPS

G past simple and past continuous
P weak forms: *was/were*
V transport

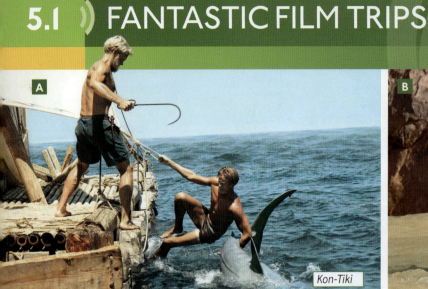

A

Kon-Tiki

B

Into the Wild

VOCABULARY

TRANSPORT

1 Work in pairs and answer the questions.

1 How many types of transport can you think of in two minutes? Make a list.

2 What do you think is the best way to travel? Why?

▷ page 83 **PHOTOBANK**

READING

2 Work in pairs. Look at photos A–C and discuss the questions.

1 What types of transport do you think appear in the films above?

2 Where do you think the people are going?

3 Work in groups. Student A: read the text on this page. Student B: read the text on page 87. Student C: read the text on page 89. As you read, make notes about your text.

1 Who made the journey?

2 Why did they want to go?

3 Where did they go?

4 Take turns to tell your group about your text. Which story do you think sounds the most interesting?

KON-TIKI

In the middle of the twentieth century the Norwegian explorer and writer Thor Heyerdahl developed a theory. He believed that people from South America travelled to Polynesia 1,500 years ago and settled there. At the time, very few others believed his theory. They thought the journey was too difficult without modern technology. While others were discussing the theory, Heyerdahl decided to test it.

Using only materials and technology available to the people of that time, Heyerdahl and his team of five sailors (and a parrot) built a wooden raft*. On 28 April 1947 they left from Peru and crossed the Pacific.

While they were sailing, huge waves crashed into the raft, and whales and sharks came close. 101 days and 4,300 miles later they arrived in Polynesia. At the time, no one knew this type of journey was possible. But perhaps the most amazing thing about the journey was that Thor Heyerdahl didn't know how to swim!

Heyerdahl later wrote a book about the journey, and in 2012 a Norwegian film called *Kon-Tiki* came out, based on the trip.

***raft**: a flat boat usually made of wood

speakout TIP

Make short notes. Don't write full sentences. Choose only important information. Try to use your own words. *The sun was shining when they began their journey that Friday morning.* ➡ *Sunny when they left.* Find a sentence in one of the texts. Make a note of the main idea in three or four words.

5 Discuss the questions.

1 Which (parts of the) journeys sound enjoyable/terrible/frightening?

2 Why do you think the stories were made into films?

3 Can you think of any other journeys that have been made into films?

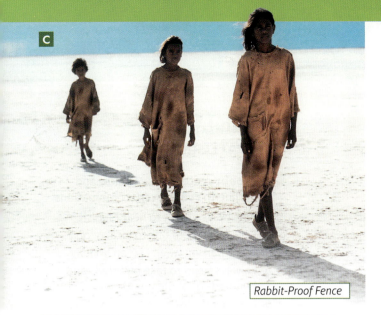

C

Rabbit-Proof Fence

GRAMMAR

PAST SIMPLE AND PAST CONTINUOUS

6 A Look at sentences a)–c) and answer the questions.

a) While they **were sailing**, huge waves **crashed** into the raft.

b) While he **was living** wild, he **wrote** a diary.

c) When it **was raining**, the girls **decided** to escape.

1 What tenses are the verbs in bold?

2 Which action started first in each sentence (*sail* or *crash*, etc.)?

3 Which action took a longer period of time?

4 Which actions are background information and which are main events?

B Underline the correct alternative to complete the rules.

> **RULES**
>
> 1 Use the *past simple/past continuous* for background actions that continue for a long time.
> 2 Use the *past simple/past continuous* for shorter actions that move the story forward.

C Find one more example of the past simple and the past continuous in the same sentence in your text.

▷ page 76 **LANGUAGE**BANK

7 A Make sentences with the prompts.

1 I / run / start to snow. So …

I was running when it started to snow. So I went home!

2 I / wait for a bus / meet my boss. So …

3 I / watch TV / recognise my best friend! So …

4 I / walk home / find $5,000 in a bag. So …

5 We / travel by plane / a man with a gun stand up. So …

6 We / ride our bicycles / a cow walk across the road. So …

7 We / eat in a restaurant / see a mouse. So …

8 I / study in my room / hear loud music next door. So …

B Work in pairs and compare your ideas.

8 A ▶ 5.1 Listen to some ideas for Exercise 7A. Are they similar to yours?

B **WEAK FORMS:** *was/were* Listen again. Notice how *was* /wəz/ and *were* /wə/ are pronounced. Then listen and repeat the first part of the sentences.

9 Work in pairs and take turns. Student A: make sentences with the past simple and the past continuous. Use a prompt from A and a prompt from B. Student B: respond with another sentence beginning with *So …* .

A: I was sleeping in my bed when I heard a strange noise.
B: So I called the police.

A
- sleep
- ride my motorbike
- *deal with a problem*
- go for a drink
- **feel sick**
- go to a concert
- make a call
- *sit in a train*
- have some time off
- watch a film

B
- get hungry
- buy a speedboat
- *crash*
- decide to change job
- start to feel tired
- fall asleep
- **see the love of my life**
- **check my voicemail**
- read your email
- **hear a strange noise**

SPEAKING

10 A Describe something that happened to you on a trip or journey. Think about questions 1–8 and make notes.

1 Where and when did you go?

2 Who were you with?

3 What was the form of transport?

4 How long did the trip take?

5 What places did you see during the journey?

6 Did anything go wrong during the journey?

7 What happened while you were travelling?

8 How did you feel?

Last summer I went on holiday to Turkey. I stayed in Istanbul for two days and then went to the coast. One day, while I was travelling by boat, I dropped my bag into the water. I lost my camera and my passport. It was a disaster!

B Work in groups. Tell your stories. Which were the most interesting and/or funniest stories you heard?

VOCABULARY

TRAVEL ITEMS

1 Work in pairs. Discuss the questions.

1 Do you travel light?
2 What do you usually pack when you go away for a short trip/long holiday?

2 A Work in pairs. Look at the words in the box and choose two things for travellers 1–3 below.

> suitcase notebook digital camera souvenirs
> waterproof clothes dictionary walking boots sun hat
> backpack money belt binoculars map umbrella

1 a grandmother visiting her grandchildren in Australia
2 a student travelling around the world
3 a tourist visiting the sights in New York

B ▶ 5.2 **STRESSED SYLLABLES** Listen and repeat the words. Underline the stressed syllables.

C Work in pairs. Discuss. Which of the things in Exercise 2A do you take on holiday with you?

▷ page 83 **PHOTOBANK**

LISTENING

3 A ▶ 5.3 Listen to people describing what they take on holiday. Which of the items in Exercise 2A do the travellers mention?

B Work in pairs and complete the notes.

1 I try to learn _____.
2 I love _____.
3 I take a lot of _____.
4 I usually spend my holidays in _____.
5 I sometimes travel in _____ places.
6 I don't carry too much _____.
7 I write things down because I like to _____ them.

C Listen again to check.

GRAMMAR

VERB PATTERNS

4 A Look at sentences 1–9 below and underline the verb + verb combinations.

1 We always <u>expect to hear</u> English.
2 I always <u>want to talk</u> to local people.
3 I <u>love walking</u> when I go on holiday.
4 I always seem to take hundreds and hundreds of photos.
5 I usually choose to go to a warm place.
6 I enjoy travelling in wild places.
7 If you decide to go walking, a backpack is easier to carry.
8 It's best to avoid carrying too much money.
9 I need to write things down.

B Complete the table below with the verbs in the box.

> ~~expect~~ want seem choose enjoy
> decide avoid need

verb + -ing	verb + infinitive with to
	expect

C Work in pairs. Add the verbs in the box below to the table above. Which two verbs can go in both columns?

> hope finish imagine hate
> would like love

▷ page 76 **LANGUAGEBANK**

5 Cross out the verb combination that is not possible in each sentence.

1 I *hope/~~enjoy~~/expect* to get a free plane ticket.
2 I *want/would like/imagine* to visit Australia.
3 She *loves/avoids/needs* travelling.
4 Where did you *like/decide/choose* to go on your next holiday?
5 They *hate/want/love* working with tourists.
6 He doesn't *seem/need/enjoy* to know this area well.
7 Do you *like/expect/love* going to different countries?
8 Why did you *avoid/decide/hope* to become a travel writer?

6 A Complete the sentences and make them true for you. The next word must be either the infinitive with *to* or the *-ing* form of a verb.

1 When I travel:
  I always avoid …
  I hate …
  I love …
2 On my last holiday:
  I chose …
  I decided …
  I enjoyed …
3 For my next holiday:
  I want …
  I hope …
  I would like …

B Work in pairs and compare your ideas.

SPEAKING

7 Work in pairs. Discuss the questions.

1 What type of holidays can you see in the photos? Which do you prefer? Why?
2 Is there anything that you really love doing when you are on holiday?
3 When you travel, do you try to learn about the place, its customs and its language? Why/Why not?
4 Do you enjoy visiting tourist areas, old cities, new cities, or none of these?

A: *I really like sightseeing holidays. I love spending time looking at beautiful old buildings.*
B: *I love taking photos. I put them on my Facebook page when I get back.*
A: *Me, too.*

WRITING
USING SEQUENCERS

8 A Work in pairs. Read an email describing a trip and discuss. What were the good/bad things about the trip?

To paolo.moncello@flu.edi   inbox 12
From igonzalez@ab.esp

Hi Paolo,

I hope you're well. I've just got back from my trip to Poland. It was wonderful. First we flew to Warsaw. We were only there for two days, but we managed to see lots of interesting sights like the Royal Castle and the National Museum. Then we had a day in Kraków, which was beautiful, especially the huge square in the Old Town. Unfortunately, after a while, it started raining so we spent the afternoon chatting with locals in a bar. After that, we took a train to Łódź. I loved it. We visited various museums and walked along the famous Piotrkowska Street. Finally, we caught the plane back home. It was a great trip and we met lots of really friendly Poles, who promised to visit us in Spain!

Love,

Irina

B Underline five words/phrases that help us to understand the order of events. The first one has been done for you.

C Write an email to a friend about a trip or a weekend away. Use the words you underlined.

5.3))) YOU CAN'T MISS IT

F asking for/giving directions
P intonation: questions
V tourism

VOCABULARY

TOURISM

1 Work in pairs. Look at the words in the box. Which things can you see in the photos?

> tour guide   boat trip   coach tour   tourists
> sightseeing   natural wonder   tax-free shopping

2 A Look at the title of the text below. Discuss. What do you think the man does? Why do you think he works in three countries every day?

B Read the text to find out.

C Discuss. Would you like Juan's job? Why/Why not?

THE MAN WHO WORKS IN THREE COUNTRIES EVERY DAY

JUAN OLIVEIRA was born in Argentina, grew up in Paraguay and now lives in Brazil. He says he loves the three countries equally, and he works in all three of them every day.

Juan is a tour guide in Foz do Iguaçu, a Brazilian town which is close to the borders of both Argentina and Paraguay. He takes tourists around the Iguaçu Falls, one of the great natural wonders of the world.

First, he shows tourists the waterfall from the Brazilian side. Then they cross the border to see the water from the Argentinian side. After that, they go on a boat trip which takes them under the waterfall. Finally, he takes them on the short journey to Ciudad del Este in Paraguay to do some tax-free shopping.

He says the Falls are amazing, especially in the rainy season. He sees them every day and he never gets tired of them.

FUNCTION

ASKING FOR/GIVING DIRECTIONS

3 A ▶ 5.4 Look at the map. Where is the tourist? Now listen and follow the routes on the map. For each route, write the destination (the country) on the map.

B Listen again and read audio script 5.4 on page 93. Underline useful phrases for giving directions.

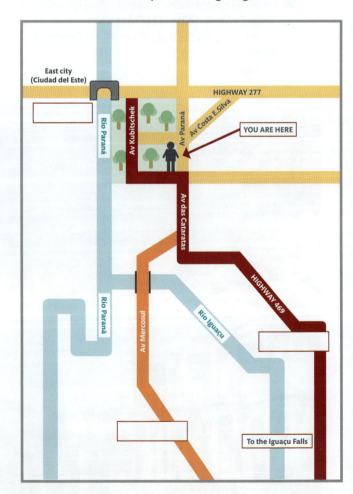

4 Label pictures A–J with the phrases in the box.

> go along the main road   go straight on
> in front of you   go past the turning   go left
> take the first right   at the corner   cross a bridge
> keep going until you reach (the border)
> go through the (centre of the town)

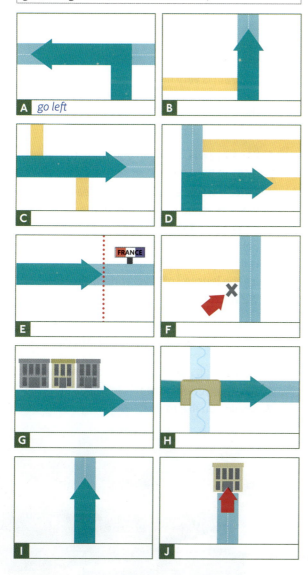

A *go left*

B

C

D

E FRANCE

F

G

H

I

J

5 A ▶ 5.5 Listen to three conversations. Are the statements true (T) or false (F)?

1 Speaker 1 takes the bus.
2 Speaker 2 has a map.
3 Speaker 3 will see a restaurant before arriving at The Grand Motel.

B Complete the notes. Listen again to check.

Conversation 1 Carnival

It takes _____ minutes. Go straight on. You'll hear the _____!

Conversation 2 Plaza Hotel

Go past the cinema. Take the first _____. Keep going for _____ minutes. You'll see the _____.

Conversation 3 The Grand Motel

Go to the end of this street. Go _____ and go past the _____. It's on the _____.

▷ page 76 **LANGUAGEBANK**

LEARN TO

SHOW/CHECK UNDERSTANDING

6 A ▶ 5.6 Read and listen to the extracts from the audio script. Are the phrases in bold asking for information (A), explaining directions (E) or showing understanding (U)?

Extract 1

A: **Can we walk?** *A*

B: Yes, **it takes about ten minutes** from here. *E*

Extract 2

C: **Excuse me, can you help me?** I'm looking for the Plaza Hotel. **Is this the right way?**

D: Um … Plaza Hotel, Plaza Hotel. Yes, **keep going**, past the cinema and take the first left.

C: **OK.**

D: Then keep going for about fifteen minutes until you reach the end of the road. And **you'll see** the sign for the hotel. **You can't miss it.**

C: OK. **Can you show me on the map?**

D: Sure.

Extract 3

E: Excuse me, we want to get to The Grand Motel. **Is it far?**

F: Umm … sorry, I've no idea. Jim, do you know?

G: What?

F: The Grand Motel?

G: The Grand Motel? Yeah, it's just over there. Just go to the end of this street. Go left and go past the … um … there's a restaurant. Go past the restaurant and it's on the left.

E: On the left. **So I need to** go to the end of the street, turn left, go past the restaurant and it's on the left.

B Which phrases mean:

1 Am I going in the right direction?
2 Continue.
3 It's easy to see it.

C ▶ 5.7 **INTONATION: questions** Listen to five questions. Which words are said louder and with a higher voice: words at the beginning (*is, can*) or near the end of the question? Listen again to check.

7 Work in pairs. Look at audio script 5.5 on page 93 and practise the first two conversations.

SPEAKING

8 Work in pairs. Student A: look at the map on page 87. Student B: look at the map on page 89. Ask for and give directions.

A: *How do I get to the station?*
B: *Go straight on until you reach the Greek restaurant, then turn right.*

DVD PREVIEW

1 A Have you ever been on a long and/or difficult journey? What can you remember about it? Tell other students.

B Read the programme information and answer the questions.

1 What does Michael Palin do?
2 Where does he travel to in *Full Circle*?
3 How does he travel in this episode?

◉) Full Circle   BBC

Michael Palin is an actor and travel writer. In *Full Circle*, he went on a journey through the seventeen countries along the Pacific coast. While travelling 50,000 miles in ten months, he saw and discovered things beyond his dreams. He learnt how to cook eggs in a volcano and how to make music with horses' bones in Chile! In this episode, Michael travels across the Andes from Arica in Chile to La Paz in Bolivia in a small train.

DVD VIEW

2 Watch the DVD. Was it an enjoyable journey? Which of the problems below do the people mention?

- the food is terrible
- the train gets very hot
- the air is thin and it's difficult to breathe
- the train is very noisy
- the train stops a lot because of animals/cars on the track
- the train is very slow

3 A Work in pairs. What do you think the words/phrases in bold mean?

a) **Twice a week**, a railway service leaves Arica. *1*
b) We've **reached** the Bolivian border. __
c) It's going to **take two hours**. __
d) Some passengers are **local**. __
e) Is it the **journey of a lifetime**? __
f) It's the **journey of (everyone's) dreams**. __
g) We've **crossed** the Andes at 16.4 miles an hour. __

B Watch the DVD again. Number the sentences in Exercise 3A in the order you hear them.

4 Work in groups. Discuss the questions.

1 What do you think of this journey?
2 Would you like to do it? Why/Why not?

speakout an award

5 A Read the text and answer the questions.

1 What is the award?

2 What will the winner do?

> **Journey of my Dreams** is an award of €5,000 for the best idea for an original and inspiring journey anywhere in the world. The winner will receive training in film-making and will record their experiences for a future programme.

B ▶ 5.8 Listen to someone describing her journey.

1 Where does she want to go?

2 What does she want to do there?

C Listen again and tick the key phrases you hear.

> **KEY PHRASES**
>
> We would like to go to …
> The trip is going to take …
> Some of the problems we're going to face include …
> We want to experience the local culture …
> Our plan is to speak to the local people …
> We hope to find out about their traditions …
> It should be an inspiring trip.
> This is the journey of my/our dreams.

6 A You are going to apply for the award. Work in pairs. Decide:

• where/how you are going to travel
• what you would like to experience/see/do
• which people you are going to stay/work with
• why you deserve the award

B Present your ideas to the class. Use the key phrases to help you. Who should win the award?

writeback an application

7 A Read the application. Match paragraphs 1–3 with headings a)–c).

a) Goals and objectives

b) Details of the plan

c) Introduction

> ## APPLICATION FORM
>
> **1** _____
>
> We would like to go to Easter Island to live with the local people for three months. Easter Island is one of the great mysteries of the world. It has many famous stone statues of heads, but no one knows who made them or why.
>
> **2** _____
>
> Our plan is to talk to the islanders about their history and about their present and future. We will ask them about their lives and what they think of the statues. We want to learn how the world's most isolated people live: what they eat, what they do for entertainment and what they think of the modern world of computers and other technology.
>
> **3** _____
>
> We will record all of the interviews on film. We will also keep a diary of our own experiences on the island. Eventually, we hope to make a TV documentary and write a book about our time on the island.

B Write your application for the award. Use the model in Exercise 7A to help you.

V TRANSPORT

1 A Choose four types of transport from the box below. Write a sentence about each type. Don't mention the name.

> train tram minibus taxi
> motorbike ferry speedboat
> coach lorry helicopter

It travels through water and is very fast.

B Work in pairs and take turns. Student A: read your sentences. Student B: guess which type of transport it is.

A: *It's a fast type of transport. It goes on the road. It has two wheels.*

B: *A motorbike.*

G PAST SIMPLE AND PAST CONTINUOUS

2 A Put the verbs in brackets into the past simple or past continuous.

1 While they (walk), they (see) a fence.
   While they were walking, they saw a fence.
2 While they (cross) the sea, a terrible storm nearly (destroy) the raft.
3 They (run) away one night while it (rain).
4 While he (wander) in the wilderness, he (meet) some people who helped him.
5 When the men (sail) on the ocean, they (see) many sea creatures.
6 While he (live) in an abandoned bus, he (realise) he might die.

B Work in pairs. Discuss. Which films from Lesson 5.1 do the sentences go with?

3 Work in pairs and take turns. Ask and answer the question.

Where were you and what were you doing at these times yesterday?

6:00	10:00	13:00
16:00	19:00	22:00

V TRAVEL ITEMS

4 A Add the vowels.

1 stcs *suitcase*
2 bckpck
3 wtrprf clths
4 wlkng bts
5 sn ht
6 svnrs
7 bnclrs
8 ntbk
9 dgtl cmr
10 mny blt

B Work in pairs. Decide which of the items above are important for the holidays below.

beach walking sightseeing adventure

A sun hat is important for a beach holiday.

G VERB PATTERNS

5 A Complete the sentences with the correct form of the verbs in brackets.

1 I sometimes choose _____ (go) somewhere on holiday because a friend recommends it.
2 I hope _____ (visit) more cities in my own country this year.
3 I seem _____ (have) good luck with the weather when I go on holiday. It never rains!
4 I want _____ (travel) to places where tourists never go.
5 I always avoid _____ (travel) by boat because I get sick.
6 I don't enjoy _____ (fly) very much.
7 I can't imagine _____ (go) on a camping holiday – I prefer hotels!
8 I wouldn't like _____ (have) a holiday with a big group of people.

B Work in pairs. Discuss. Are sentences 1–8 true for you? Why/Why not?

F ASKING FOR/GIVING DIRECTIONS

6 A Find and correct the mistakes. There are two mistakes in each conversation.

Conversation 1
A: Excuse me. I'm looking for the Natural History Museum. Is this right way?
B: Keep going until you reach the crossroads. It's in the right.

Conversation 2
A: Hello. We want to go to the Italian Embassy. Is far?
B: No. Just turn left and you'll see the sign for it. You can't miss.

Conversation 3
A: Excuse me, do you know where the university is?
B: Keep going long the main road. Then you'll see a sign and it's in front to you.

B Work in pairs and practise the conversations.

C Work in pairs and take turns.

Student A: ask for directions:
• from a well-known place in the town to Student B's house
• from Student B's house to the school

Student B: ask for directions:
• from the school to a nearby restaurant
• from a nearby restaurant to a well-known place in the town

A: *OK. How do I get from the station to your house?*
B: *Well, you take the first right …*

6 fitness

BBC INTERVIEWS

What do you do
to keep fit?

57

6.1)) KEEPING FIT

G present perfect + *for/since*
P sentence stress
V health

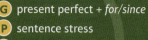

Get moving!

A lot of us spend most of our working day sitting at the computer. If you add this to the seven hours we spend sleeping, we could easily find that we spend nearly two thirds of our day without moving at all. We all know that exercise is good for both the body and the brain. Even a short amount of exercise every day can help us to feel happier and more relaxed. So, how does the world keep fit? We've looked at some of the latest exercise trends from around the world.

TOWERRUNNING China

Have you ever worked in an office block and wondered how you can get fit? Perhaps you should try Towerrunning. It's a sport you can do in the skyscrapers of almost any big city, but Asian cities can be particularly good. All you need to do is start at the bottom of an office tower, and run up all the stairs until you get to the top. Towerrunning has become popular all around the world with important races taking place in some of the world's tallest towers, like Taipei 101, the Empire State Building in New York, and the China World Trade Centre, Beijing.

PILOXING® USA

If you enjoy dance classes like Zumba, but you also want to get rid of your anger, then PILOXING® might be for you. PILOXING® started in the USA, but has travelled quickly to countries like the UK. The sport is a mixture between boxing, pilates and dance. PILOXING® uses the power and speed of boxing, whilst building your muscles and strength with pilates. All of this happens to non-stop loud music, and you learn some great dance moves too.

PADDLE BOARDING Brazil

When it comes to the end of a long day, what could be better than a paddle board on the ocean? It might look easy, but paddle boarding is a tough sport. You need to be strong to keep your balance. However, if you bring your board down to the water at 'golden hour' just before sunset, the water is calm and the ocean will make you forget all your problems.

VOCABULARY

HEALTH

1 A Look at the words/phrases in the box. Are these things good (+) or bad (–) for your health?

> junk food   exercise classes   fizzy drinks   fresh fruit/vegetables
> stress/worrying   alcohol   vitamins   running   caffeine   relaxing

B Work in pairs and compare your ideas. Group the vocabulary under the following headings: *food/drink, exercise, general habits.* Can you add any more words/phrases to each group?

C Work in pairs and take turns. Ask and answer the questions.

1 What do you do to keep fit and healthy?
2 Do you do anything which is not healthy?

A: What do you do to keep fit and healthy?
B: I eat lots of fruit. How about you?
A: I cycle to work every day.

▷ page 84 **PHOTOBANK**

READING

2 A Discuss. What sports can you see in the pictures? Do you know anything about these sports?

B Read the text to find out more information about each sport. Which of the sports would you like to try? Why?/Why not?

C Work in pairs. Answer the questions.

1 According to the article, why is exercise good for you?
2 Why is Towerrunning popular in Asian cities?
3 How is PILOXING® similar to other sports?
4 When is a good time to go paddle boarding? Why?

GRAMMAR

PRESENT PERFECT + *FOR/SINCE*

3 A Read sentences a) and b) and answer questions 1–4 below.

a) I've done paddle boarding *since* 2014.

b) He's lived in Asia *for* five years.

1 When did the speaker in a) start paddle boarding?
2 Is she still paddle boarding now?
3 When did the person in b) move to Asia?
4 Does he still live in Asia?

B Underline the correct alternative to complete the rules.

> **RULES**
>
> 1 Use the present perfect to look back at something that started in the past and *finished/continues now*.
> 2 Use *for/since* to talk about a period of time (how long) and use *for/since* to talk about a point in time (when something started).

C Complete the table with the phrases in the box.

> ~~2005~~ ~~ages~~ July a long time Saturday
> I left university two weeks/months/years 2p.m.
> last night an hour or two
> I was a child/teenager

for	since
ages	*2005*

▷ page 78 **LANGUAGEBANK**

4 A Complete the sentences using the verbs in brackets and adding *for/since* as appropriate.

1 I _____ (do) karate _____ I was a child.
2 I _____ (have) this phone _____ two months.
3 I _____ (know) Marcia _____ I was at school.
4 We _____ (live) in this town/city _____ ten years.
5 I _____ (want) to buy a new car _____ a long time.

B Change two or three of the sentences so they are true for you. Compare your sentences with a partner.

5 A ▶ 6.1 Listen to the questions and write short answers with *for* and *since*. Don't write the questions.

1 *by the sea*
2 *for five years/since 2005*

B Work in pairs and compare your answers. Try to remember the questions.

6 ▶ 6.2 **SENTENCE STRESS** Listen and write the questions. Listen again and underline the stressed words.

1 *How long have you lived there?*

SPEAKING

7 A Write questions for each topic beginning *Do you …?* and *How long have you …?*

home

Do you …?
live in the city centre?

How long have you …?
lived there?

hobbies/sport

Do you …?
_____

How long have you …?
_____

things you have (possessions)

Do you …?
_____

How long have you …?
_____

work/study/school

Do you …?
_____

How long have you …?
_____

B Work in groups. Ask and answer the questions. Try to find out more information.

A: Do you have a car?
B: Yes, I do.
A: How long have you had it?
B: It's very old. I've had it for about ten years.
A: What kind of car is it?
B: It's a VW Golf.

C Tell the class about the students in your group.

6.2)) THE FUTURE OF FOOD

G *may, might, will*
P intonation: certainty/uncertainty
V food

VOCABULARY

FOOD

1 A Work in pairs. How many types of food can you think of for each of the categories below? Make a list.

vegetables   *desserts*   *meat*   **fruit**

B Compare your lists with other students.

▷ page 85 **PHOTOBANK**

C Work in pairs. Discuss the questions.

1 What is your favourite food?
2 Do you ever eat food from other countries/cultures? If so, what?
3 Which of the dishes in the photos do you often/sometimes/never eat? Would you like to try any of them?

falafel

sushi

paella

burrito

LISTENING

2 A Work in pairs. Look at the pictures and read the sentences about food of the future. Do you think they are true (T) or false (F)?

1 In the future, more people may eat insects.

2 In the future, we will be able to make food from mud, wood and seaweed.

3 In the future, kitchen tools (e.g. knives) might give us information about the food in the kitchen.

B ▷ 6.3 Listen to an interview with a food expert and check your answers.

C Complete sentences 1–6. Then listen again to check.

1 We may see some changes, things that you might not understand as food g_____.
2 Insects are rich in protein, low in fat, and easy to f_____.
3 Scientists have already found ways to create meat in the l_____.
4 We're also looking at ways to make proteins out of things like mud and wood and also s_____.
5 Other developments on your kitchen table include an intelligent k_____.
6 Really giving people more i_____ about their food.

speakout TIP

When we aren't sure of a word we hear, we can often guess: What letter does the word begin with? How many syllables does it have? Do we recognise the ending of the word (e.g. *-tion, -y, -ed*)? Does the context tell us the type of word (e.g. noun, verb, adjective)? After guessing, check with a friend, your teacher or the audio script.

GRAMMAR

MAY, MIGHT, WILL

3 A Read sentences a)–d) and answer the questions about the phrases in bold.

a) We **might see** them (insects) on menus.

b) We **may see** some changes.

c) An intelligent knife **will tell** you all about the food it's cutting.

d) It tastes awful now, but … it **won't** in the future.

1 Which one is negative?

2 Which ones mean 'probably, but we don't know'?

3 Which one is a strong prediction about the future?

▷ page 78 **LANGUAGE**BANK

B ▶ **6.4** INTONATION: certainty/uncertainty
Listen to four sentences. In which sentences are the speakers uncertain?

C Listen again. Notice how the speakers say *will*, *might*, *may* and *won't*. When the speaker is not sure, do *will*, *might*, *may* and *won't* sound longer or shorter?

4 A Write responses to sentences 1–7. Use the prompts in brackets with *might/might not*, *may/may not* or *will/won't*.

1 We're having a picnic. (rain)   *It might rain.*

2 I'm becoming a vegetarian. (lose / weight)

3 Let's go to the best restaurant in town. (be / expensive)

4 I want to stop eating junk food. (feel / healthier)

5 Let's go to the café for breakfast. (not / be / open)

6 I want to try eating octopus. (not / like / it)

7 I'm going to do a cooking course. (enjoy / it)

B Work in pairs and take turns. Student A: say something is going to happen. Student B: respond using *may*, *might*, *will* or *won't*. Continue the conversation.

A: We're having a picnic.
B: It might rain.
A: Don't be so negative! The sun's shining.
B: That's true, but you should take an umbrella.

SPEAKING

5 A Work in pairs. Do you agree with sentences 1–6 below? Tick the four most interesting sentences.

1 In the future, nobody will be hungry for long.

2 People won't eat animals in the future.

3 More people might grow food to save money.

4 Families won't have time to eat together.

5 The next generation may not know how to cook; they will order food on the internet.

6 I might learn how to cook in the future.

B Compare your ideas with other students.

A: Number 1 might happen, but it won't happen soon.
B: I agree. There is enough food in the world, but it is not reaching the people who need it.

WRITING

SENTENCE STRUCTURE

6 A Work in pairs. Read the extract from a blog below and discuss the questions.

1 When and why did Fernanda move from her home city?

2 What does she say about Colombian food and Colombian cooking?

3 What food did she try in the US and who made it?

how **important** *is* food *in* your life

Fernanda Huerta-Gonzalez, from Colombia, talks about food.

In my late twenties I moved from my home in Medellin, Colombia, to the United States to continue my studies. It was a good move, but I missed my family and friends. I also missed Colombian food. In my country we have a lot of special dishes like *mondongo* and *peto*, and we take our time preparing food. People say we cook with love!

While in the US, I met other international students, and twice a month we got together and cooked for one another. It was wonderful, and I tasted food from many countries: Libya, Poland, Tunisia, Peru and Japan. I also made many good friends. My time in the US taught me the importance of food as a part of culture and a way to bring people together.

B Compare the two examples below. What do you notice about the length of the sentences?

I was in my late twenties. I went to the United States. I went to continue my studies.

I was in my late twenties when I went to the United States to continue my studies.

speak**out** TIP

Short sentences may sound unconnected. Long sentences can be difficult to understand. Try to use *and* only once in a sentence. In the next sentence, use *also*. Look at your last piece of writing. Can you use this tip to improve sentence structure?

C Find two examples of the *and/also* pattern in the blog.

D Choose one of the topics in the box below and write a paragraph. Use different sentence lengths.

cooking   restaurants   favourite food   family meals

I love cooking.
One of my favourite restaurants is …

6.3)) HOW ARE YOU FEELING?

F seeing the doctor
P difficult words: spelling v. pronunciation
V illness

SPEAKING

1 A Work in pairs. Answer the questions.

1 Do you think men or women go to the doctor more often?
2 Why do you think this is?
3 What reasons do you think people give for not going to see a doctor?

B Read the text to check your answers.

C Work in pairs. Discuss. Do you think any of the excuses in the text are good reasons to avoid seeing the doctor?

VOCABULARY

ILLNESS

2 A Match problems 1–4 below with advice a)–d).

1 You have **got a headache/ backache.**
2 You have **caught a cold/flu.**
3 You have **broken your arm/leg.**
4 You have a **sore throat** and a **bad cough.** You also have a **high temperature.**

a) Take some **medicine/antibiotics.**
b) Go to the hospital for an **X-ray.**
c) **Get some rest,** and **drink lots of hot drinks.**
d) Take some **painkillers/pills.**

B ▶ 6.5 **DIFFICULT WORDS: spelling versus pronunciation** Check your pronunciation. Listen and repeat.

C Work in pairs. Discuss. What do you do when you have a cold/headache/ flu to make yourself feel better?

A: I usually go to bed with a hot drink. How about you?
B: I don't do anything. I just carry on working.

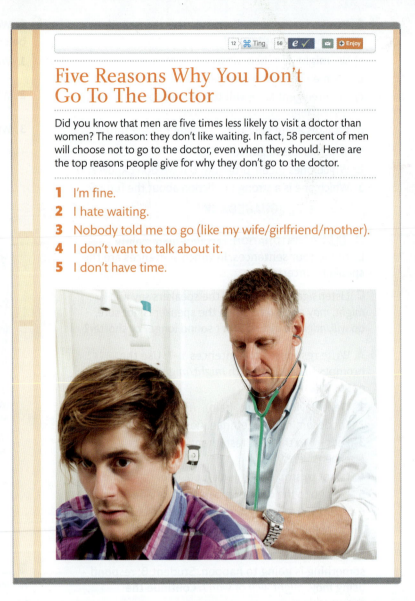

12 ⌘ Ting 56 e ✓ ✉ ⊕ Enjoy

Five Reasons Why You Don't Go To The Doctor

Did you know that men are five times less likely to visit a doctor than women? The reason: they don't like waiting. In fact, 58 percent of men will choose not to go to the doctor, even when they should. Here are the top reasons people give for why they don't go to the doctor.

1 I'm fine.
2 I hate waiting.
3 Nobody told me to go (like my wife/girlfriend/mother).
4 I don't want to talk about it.
5 I don't have time.

FUNCTION

SEEING THE DOCTOR

3 A ▶ 6.6 Listen to two conversations between a doctor and her patients. Answer the questions.

1 What problem(s) does the patient have?
2 What does the doctor suggest?

B Complete sentences 1–6 below with the words in the box.

~~matter~~ problem hurt look worry pills

1 What's the *matter* ?
2 How long have you had this _____ ?
3 I'll give you some _____ .
4 Can I have a _____ ?
5 Where does it _____ ?
6 It's nothing to _____ about.

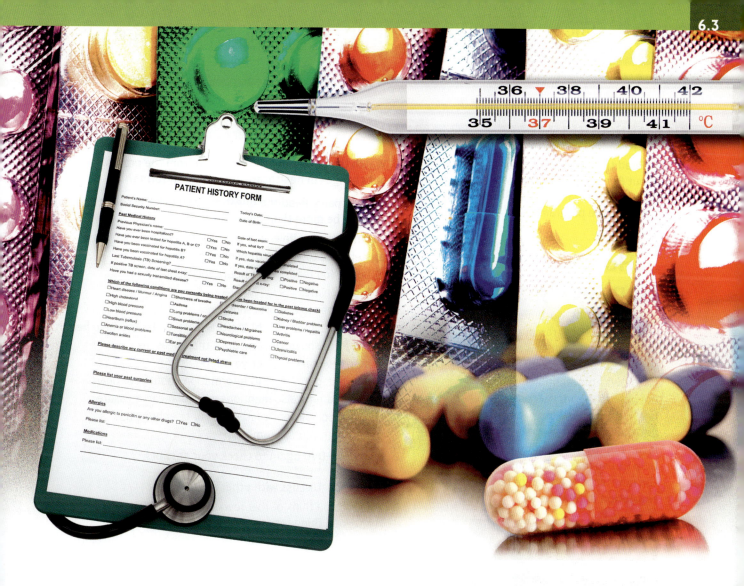

C Complete sentences 1–5 below with the words in the box.

painful   sleep   sick   hurts   worried

1 I feel _____/terrible.
2 I can't _____.
3 I'm _____ about …
4 It _____ when I walk.
5 It's very _____.

D Listen to the conversations again to check your answers.

▷ page 78 **LANGUAGEBANK**

4 Underline the correct alternative.
1 My head *hurts/pain/sore*.
2 I've got a really bad *flu/cold/sick*.
3 She feels *cough/sick/a temperature*.
4 I think I've *broken/sore/hurting* my arm.
5 Where does it *hurt/pain/sore*?
6 It's nothing to *problem/matter/worry* about.
7 I'll *give/take/look* you some pills.
8 How long have you had this *ill/matter/problem*?

LEARN TO

PREDICT INFORMATION

5 A Work in pairs. Look at the conversation. What do you think the missing words are?

Doctor: What's the ^{1}_____?
Patient: I've got a really bad ^{2}_____. I feel ^{3}_____.
Doctor: How long have you had the ^{4}_____?
Patient: About a ^{5}_____.
Doctor: Can I have a ^{6}_____?
Patient: It's very ^{7}_____.
Doctor: I'll give you some ^{8}_____.

B ▷ 6.7 Listen to check your answers.

C Listen again and practise saying the phrases.

speakout TIP

When you are going into a situation that you can plan for (a visit to the doctor, a trip to a restaurant, etc.), first try to predict the conversation. This will help you to understand words/phrases when you hear them.

6 Work in pairs. Student A: turn to page 87. Student B: turn to page 89. Role-play the conversations. Before you start, try to predict what the other person will say.

DVD PREVIEW

1 A Read the programme information about *Horizon: Monitor Me*. What type of things will you learn from watching the programme?

Horizon: Monitor Me

BBC

Horizon is a BBC documentary series. In this programme, Dr Kevin Fong looks at new **apps** that are changing people's lives. He shows how technology can now **measure** our exercise, sleep, food, drink, etc. When we use this information to **monitor** ourselves, it can improve our health and help us live longer. Dr Fong thinks the new technology might be a revolution in **healthcare**.

B Match the words in bold with meanings 1–4.

1 find out the size or quantity of something
2 carefully watch something to see how it changes over time
3 a small, special programme that you download onto a mobile phone
4 the service that looks after people when they are sick

DVD VIEW

2 A Watch the DVD. What did you learn from the programme about changes in healthcare and self-monitoring?

B Work in pairs. Read the questions and tick the correct options. There may be more than one answer.

1 You might be healthier if you knew how much/many:
   a) steps you took.　　**d)** people you met.
   b) books you read.　　**e)** hours you slept.
   c) food you ate.

2 Dr Fong goes to a sports shop to:
   a) see some apps.　　**b)** look at how bicycles can help health.

3 Blaine Price shows Dr Fong apps that measure:
   a) steps you take.　　**c)** your food.
   b) your sleep.　　　**d)** information about your heart.

4 The programme also mentions apps that can measure:
   a) your blood-alcohol level.　　**c)** your telephone use.
   b) how high you can jump.

C Watch the DVD again to check your answers.

3 Work in pairs. Discuss with other students.

1 What do you think of this 'revolution in healthcare'? Is it a good thing for society?
2 Have you ever used an app? Do you think they help/could help you in your daily life?

speakout create a health regime

4 A Read the notes on the health of three people and answer the questions.

1 What health problems do they have now?
2 What problems might they have in the future?

> **Marcin**, 44, machine operator, 1.83 m, 108 kg
> Diet: eats mainly junk food, no vegetables, 6 cups of coffee daily
> Fitness/Sleep: no exercise, sleeps 7 hours a night
> Social life: goes out with friends 3 nights a week
> Goal: lose 14 kg and get fit for football

> **Paulina**, 22, student, 1.73 m, 50 kg
> Diet: eats fresh fruit/vegetables, no meat, vitamins
> Fitness/Sleep: does yoga, sleeps 6 hours a night
> Social life: has few friends, stresses about studies
> Goal: gain 6.5 kg, have more energy

> **Alvaro**, 68, retired bank manager, 1.75 m, 95 kg
> Diet: eats meat twice a day
> Fitness/Sleep: has backache (takes painkillers), no exercise, sleeps 8 hours
> Social life: many friends, watches TV 6 hours a day
> Goal: be fit enough to play with grandchildren

B ▶ 6.8 Listen to a health expert saying how one of the three people can improve their health. Which person is the expert talking about?

C Listen again. Tick the key phrases you hear.

> **KEY PHRASES**
>
> To get healthy, you need …
> There are some changes he can make.
> For example, he needs to [do some exercise/stop eating junk food] …
> He could try [going for walks/cycling/doing exercise classes] …
> He should spend time [exercising/seeing friends] …
> He must lose weight.
> Maybe he could [eat less meat/stop drinking fizzy drinks] …
> It's a good idea to …

5 A Work with other students. Plan a health regime for the other two people in Exercise 4. Think about how they can become healthier if they change their diet, exercise, and lifestyle.

B Work with another group and compare your ideas.

writeback health advice

6 A Read the problem below and answer the questions.

1 What health problems does Ahmed have?
2 Why is he writing?

I'm worried about my health. Every winter I get sick. I get a cough or a sore throat and sometimes I have a high temperature. I also get really bad headaches. Generally, I try to live healthily. I don't eat much junk food, and I exercise at least once a week. The problem is, I have a stressful job and I never sleep for more than six hours. Winter is coming and I don't want to spend it lying in bed and taking antibiotics. I've heard it's a good idea to monitor my food and exercise, but I'm not sure about this. What can I do?

Ahmed al Muntari

Hi Ahmed, Sorry to hear you have health problems during the winter. That sounds tough! I have a few ideas that might help you. Firstly, …

B Complete the blog post replying to Ahmed. Try to include advice about some of the following: diet, sleep, exercise, using apps to monitor your health.

(V) HEALTH

1 A Make questions with the prompts below for a class survey.

1 go / exercise classes
2 eat / junk food / drink / fizzy drinks
3 time / relaxing
4 take / vitamins
5 go / running
6 stress / worrying
7 drink / caffeine
8 eat / fresh fruit / vegetables

B Work in groups and take turns. Ask and answer the questions.

C Tell the class what you found out.

(G) PRESENT PERFECT + FOR/SINCE

2 A Write the name of:

1 a place you haven't been to since you were a child
2 something you have only had for a few months
3 someone you have known since you were a teenager
4 something you haven't done since you left school
5 something you have wanted to do for a long time
6 a sport/hobby you have done for more than five years

B Work in pairs and compare your ideas. Ask and answer questions about each thing.

A: I haven't played tennis since I left school. Have you?
B: Yes, I love tennis.

(V) FOOD

3 Find twelve types of food in the word snake.

onioncreampineapplelemoncarrotwheatchickencakeoatsjellycheesemussels

4 A Work in pairs. Divide the food in Exercise 3 into these categories. There are two words for each category.

desserts	dairy
fruit	vegetables
grains	meat/seafood

B Add words to each category.

(G) MAY, MIGHT, WILL

5 A Match statements 1–6 to responses a)–f).

1 I've drunk eight cups of coffee.
2 I've started buying fresh vegetables.
3 I've stopped smoking.
4 I've stopped taking vitamins.
5 I've started doing yoga classes.
6 I've decided to run a marathon.

a) You won't cough all the time.
b) You might feel less stressed.
c) You may get more colds.
d) You may not be fit enough.
e) You will taste the difference.
f) You might not sleep well tonight.

B Work in pairs and take turns. Student A: use the prompts in the box to make statements with *I've decided to ... .* Student B: respond using *may/may not, might/might not, will/won't.*

buy a house in Monaco
give up eating meat
write a book join a boxing club
get a pet tiger live in Jamaica
become a dancer
do a degree in physics
marry an astronaut
go into politics

A: I've decided to buy a house in Monaco.
B: It might be expensive!

6 Work in groups and take turns. Ask and answer the questions.

1 What do you think may happen to your country in a few years' time?
2 Who do you think will win the next World Cup?
3 Where might you be in five years' time?
4 What job will you do in the future?
5 What will you do on your next birthday?
6 Where will you go on your next holiday?

(F) SEEING THE DOCTOR

7 A Complete the questions with the correct form of the verbs in the box.

catch feel give break can have

1 Have you (or anyone in your family) ever _____ your arm/ leg? Where? How?
2 Do you often _____ colds or flu? What do you do to get better?
3 Is there any food that makes you _____ sick?
4 Do you ever find you _____ not sleep? What do you do?
5 When was the last time the doctor _____ you some pills?
6 What do you do when you _____ got a headache?

B Work in pairs and take turns. Ask and answer the questions.

IRREGULAR VERBS

Verb	Past simple	Past participle
be	was	been
beat	beat	beaten
become	became	become
begin	began	begun
bite	bit	bitten
blow	blew	blown
break	broke	broken
bring	brought	brought
build	built	built
burn	burned/burnt	burned/burnt
buy	bought	bought
catch	caught	caught
choose	chose	chosen
come	came	come
cost	cost	cost
cut	cut	cut
deal	dealt	dealt
do	did	done
draw	drew	drawn
dream	dreamed/dreamt	dreamed/dreamt
drink	drank	drunk
drive	drove	driven
eat	ate	eaten
fall	fell	fallen
feel	felt	felt
fight	fought	fought
find	found	found
fly	flew	flown
forget	forgot	forgotten
forgive	forgave	forgiven
freeze	froze	frozen
get	got	got
give	gave	given
go	went	gone
grow	grew	grown
hang	hung	hung
have	had	had
hear	heard	heard
hide	hid	hidden
hit	hit	hit
hold	held	held
hurt	hurt	hurt
keep	kept	kept
know	knew	known
learn	learned/learnt	learned/learnt

Verb	Past simple	Past participle
leave	left	left
lend	lent	lent
let	let	let
lie	lay	lain
lose	lost	lost
make	made	made
mean	meant	meant
meet	met	met
pay	paid	paid
put	put	put
read	read	read
ride	rode	ridden
ring	rang	rung
run	ran	run
say	said	said
see	saw	seen
sell	sold	sold
send	sent	sent
set	set	set
shake	shook	shaken
shine	shone	shone
show	showed	shown
shut	shut	shut
sing	sang	sung
sit	sat	sat
sleep	slept	slept
smell	smelled/smelt	smelled/smelt
speak	spoke	spoken
spend	spent	spent
spell	spelt	spelt
spill	spilled/spilt	spilled/spilt
stand	stood	stood
steal	stole	stolen
swim	swam	swum
take	took	taken
teach	taught	taught
tear	tore	torn
tell	told	told
think	thought	thought
throw	threw	thrown
understand	understood	understood
wake	woke	woken
wear	wore	worn
win	won	won
write	wrote	written

GRAMMAR

1.1 question forms

Yes/No questions are questions that only require a *Yes* or *No* answer.

For questions in the present and past simple, put the auxiliary *do/does/did* before the subject.

A: *Does he live here?*   **B:** *Yes, he does.*

For questions with *be*, put *be* before the subject.

A: *Is he married?*   **B:** *No, he isn't.*

Wh- questions are questions which ask for more than a *Yes/No* answer. Use the same word order as *Yes/No* questions.

question word	auxiliary *do/does/did*	subject	infinitive
Where	does	he	live?
When	do	you	see your parents?
Why	did	they	phone me?

question word	*be*	subject	adj/noun/verb + *-ing*, etc.
Why	are	you	sad?
What	is	he	doing?

Use *who* for people.   **Who** is your boss?

Use *where* for places.   **Where** is the bathroom?

Use *what* or *which* for things.

What music do you like?

Which do you prefer, football or rugby?

Use *when* for time.   **When** do you want to meet?

Use *how often* for frequency.

How often do you go to English lessons?

Use *how long* for length of time/distance.

How long does the lesson last?

Use *how much/many* for quantity.

How much does this cost?

How many brothers do you have?

Use *why* for reasons.   **Why** are you studying English?

Use *what time* for a time.   **What time** do you start work?

Note:

Which has a limited number of possible answers.

Which do you want, the red or the blue jumper?

What has a large number of possible answers.

What music do you like?

1.2 past simple

past simple regular verbs			
+	I/you/ he/she/it/ we/they	worked	in a restaurant.
–		didn't work	
? Did		work	in a restaurant?

past simple irregular verbs			
+	I/you/ he/she/it/ we/they	went	out.
–		didn't go	
? Did		go	out?

Use the past simple to talk about finished actions in the past. In negatives and questions, use the auxiliary *did* + infinitive. Do not use *did* in negatives and questions with the verb *be*.

I wasn't very happy. NOT *I ~~didn't be~~ happy.*

spellings: regular past simple verbs		
verbs ending in:	rule	example
	+ *-ed*	start – started
-e	+ *-d*	live – lived
-y	*-y* + *-i* + *-ed*	marry – married
consonant-vowel-consonant	double the consonant + *-ed*	stop – stopped

Form the past simple with regular verbs by adding *-ed*. Many common verbs have an irregular past simple form. Look at the list on page 67.

Use the past simple to talk about finished actions in the past.

1.3 making conversation

making conversation	response
This is my friend (name).	Hi (name). Pleased to meet you.
Would you like a drink?	I'd love a coffee, thank you.
Nice day, isn't it?	Yes, it's lovely.
Where exactly do you come from?	I come from …, near …
So, do you work here?	No, I'm a student.
Did you have a good weekend?	Yes, it was OK. I didn't do much.
Did you watch the match last night?	Yes, it was terrible.
We lost 3-0.	Oh no! I'm sorry to hear that.
I'll see you later.	See you soon.

PRACTICE

1.1

A Complete the questions. How many can you answer?

1 _____ states are there in the USA?
2 _____ was the first person to walk on the Moon?
3 _____ is the largest island in the Mediterranean Sea?
4 _____ is H_2O?
5 _____ did the Berlin Wall come down?
6 _____ is Lake Wanaka?
7 _____ country is famous for samba?
8 _____ long is the River Nile?

B Match questions 1–8 in Exercise 1.1A with answers a)–h).

a) Brazil
b) Neil Armstrong
c) 9 November 1989
d) in New Zealand
e) 50
f) water
g) 6,695 km
h) Sicily

C Find and correct the mistakes. There is a mistake in each sentence.

1 How much this cost?
2 You have any brothers or sisters?
3 What time starts the film?
4 How often do you playing football?
5 Who your new teacher is?
6 Do want you to come and have a pizza?
7 Why don't you liking grammar?
8 Where you go on holiday last year?

1.2

A Complete the story with the correct form of the verbs in the box. Use the past simple.

ask (x2)   email   say   get (x2)   arrive   see
know   fall   decide

A single father-of-two [1] _asked_ his American girlfriend to marry him only four minutes after he [2] _____ her for the first time

Carl Dockings, 36, from Wales, met Danielle on the internet.

'We [3] _____ on so well. We always [4] _____ what the other was thinking.' He said they [5] _____ and talked in chat rooms. They [6] _____ in love even before exchanging pictures.

After ten months, Carl [7] _____ to fly 4,000 miles to meet Danielle in person. He [8] _____ the important question at Chicago's O'Hare Airport soon after he [9] _____.

The 26-year-old [10] _____ 'yes' and the couple [11] _____ married four months later.

They now live in his home city with their daughter Isabel.

B Put the verbs in brackets into the correct form of the past simple.

1 My grandfather _____ (teach) me how to paint.
2 Where _____ you _____ (grow up)?
3 We _____ (meet) in Ireland last year.
4 At first we _____ (not get on) very well.
5 I _____ (leave) college and _____ (get) a job in an office.
6 I _____ (live) in the USA, so we _____ (not see) each other for six months.
7 _____ you _____ (enjoy) the concert last night?
8 They _____ (not have) children.
9 My sister _____ (finish) her degree last year.
10 She _____ (study) Russian.

1.3

A Find and correct the mistakes. There is a mistake or missing word in each sentence.

1 This is ~~the~~ ^my^ friend, Sara.
2 Hi. Pleased to know you.
3 Do you like a drink?
4 Where exact do you come from?
5 Did you have good weekend?
6 I see you later.

B Put the words in the correct order to make sentences.

1 meet / to / you / pleased
2 coffee / would / I / a / love
3 do / what / so / you / do?
4 I / you / see / 'll / later
5 come / where / do / from / exactly / you?
6 soon / see / you

GRAMMAR

2.1 present simple and continuous

	present simple	present continuous
+	I work at home. He watches TV.	I'm working at home. He's watching TV.
–	She doesn't study now. We don't text in class.	She isn't studying now. We're not texting in class.
?	Does he live with you? Where do the workers have lunch?	Is he living with you? Where are the workers having lunch?

Use the present simple to describe something that is always or generally true.

It is common to use these words with the present simple: *sometimes, usually, every day, often.*

I usually get up at 7a.m.

Use the present continuous to talk about:
* an activity happening right now, at the time of speaking.
* a temporary activity happening around now (maybe at the moment, but maybe not).

spelling with *-ing* forms

verbs ending in:	rule	example
-e	-e + *-ing*	take – taking
vowel + consonant	double the consonant + *-ing*	run – running
-ie	-ie + *-y*	die – dying
-y	+ *-ing*	study – studying

Form the present continuous with the verb *be* + the *-ing* form of the verb.

It is common to use these words with the present continuous: *now, at the moment, currently, this month.*

I'm living with my parents at the moment.

Some verbs are not usually used with continuous tenses: *be, know, like, love, understand, want,* etc. These are called 'state verbs'.

I want to go to bed now. NOT
I ~~am wanting~~ to go to bed now.

2.2 adverbs of frequency

Use adverbs of frequency to say how frequently you do something. Some of the most common are: *never, rarely, occasionally, sometimes, often, usually, always.*

There are several adverbial phrases of frequency, e.g. *hardly ever, once in a while, every day/month/year.*

With *be*, put the adverb **after** the verb.

I am always here.
They were usually early.

We usually put the adverb **before** other verbs.

I sometimes spoke to him.
We hardly ever ate there.

With auxiliary or modal verbs, we usually put the adverb **after** the auxiliary or modal.

She doesn't stay here. → *She doesn't usually stay here.*
We haven't visited them. → *We have never visited them.*
I can help. → *I can always help.*

Adverbs of frequency can also go at the beginning, middle or end of a sentence.

Occasionally I go dancing.
I occasionally go dancing.
I go dancing occasionally.

Always and *never* do not normally go at the beginning or end of sentences.

Once in a while and *every day/month/year* usually go at the beginning or end of sentences.

There are other phrases to show how frequently something happens:

every day = one time per day   *I have a shower every day.*

once a week = one time per week
She writes to me once a week.

twice a week = two times per week
They go shopping twice a week.

2.3 expressing likes/dislikes

There are a number of verbs and other phrases to show likes and dislikes. After these verbs and phrases, we usually use the *-ing* form.

positive
I **like** sing**ing**/meat. I **absolutely love** swimm**ing**/tennis. I'**m keen on** runn**ing**/beach holidays.

Note: We can also use *like* + infinitive.
Like + infinitive means 'do as a habit' or 'choose to do'.
I like to go to bed early.

negative
I **can't stand** smok**ing**/computers. I **don't like** work**ing**/rock music. I **hate** watch**ing** TV/films. I'**m not very keen on** work**ing**/fruit.

Note: *I don't mind* means 'It's OK for me. I don't like it or dislike it'.

I don't mind sleeping on the floor.

PRACTICE

2.1

A Complete the conversations with the correct form of the verbs in the box. Use the present simple or present continuous.

> eat   be   wait   know   work   wear   play

1 **A:** It takes him ten minutes to get to work.
  B: I know. His house _____ far from the office.

2 **A:** Isn't your son an actor?
  B: Yes, but at the moment he _____ in a restaurant.

3 **A:** What is all that noise? I'm trying to work!
  B: I _____ with the children.

4 **A:** What _____ you _____ about the new software program?
  B: The new software program? Absolutely nothing.

5 **A:** Why _____ you _____ that jacket in the office? It's really warm!
  B: Because I'm cold!

6 **A:** Would you like some beef?
  B: No, thanks. I _____ meat. I'm a vegetarian.

7 **A:** Why are you standing there?
  B: I _____ for a taxi.

B Find and correct the mistakes. There is a mistake in five of the sentences.

1 John works in sales and he is going to the office every day at 8a.m.
2 The new employee says she's eighteen, but I'm not believing it.
3 At the moment, I'm doing a task for my boss.
4 Don't buy a bottle of wine for her. She isn't drinking alcohol.
5 I can't speak Chinese, but my friend teaches me.
6 Excuse me, is anybody sitting here?
7 I'm taking art classes this term.
8 Hey! What do you do with that knife?

2.2

A Put the words in the correct order to make sentences.

1 I / dinner / at / weekend / cook / sometimes / the
  I sometimes cook dinner at the weekend.
2 once / I / while / go / in / swimming / a
3 I / money / waste / never / my
4 Najim / often / tennis / play / doesn't
5 Akiko and Toshi / evening / stay / usually / the / home / at / in
6 why / late / are / always / you?
7 I / work / Fridays / rarely / late / on
8 Mary / ever / hardly / deals / with / customers
9 occasionally / a / team / work / I / in

B Underline the correct alternative.

1 *Always/Usually/Hardly ever* our IT consultant deals with these problems; it's his job.
2 I get up early *never/rarely/every day* and go to work at 6a.m.
3 You *sometimes/every week/once in a while* need to risk your life in this job.
4 We *often/never/rarely* see each other – maybe once a year.
5 We *occasionally/always/rarely* work under pressure; we never have a chance to relax.
6 *Often/Hardly ever/Once in a while* I speak to my boss – maybe once a month.
7 We have a summer party *every year/always/never*.
8 I deal with customers *rarely/often/occasionally*, but only if my boss is out.

2.3

A Complete the sentences with one word.

1 I like _____ to music while I study. It helps me concentrate.
2 I _____ mind getting up early for my job. It's no problem for me.
3 Stefania is keen _____ travelling so she's studying tourism.
4 Mick _____ like talking to customers. He says it's boring.
5 Lorenzo absolutely_____ dancing. He's really good at samba.
6 I can't _____ working at the weekend.

GRAMMAR

3.1 present continuous/*be going to* for future

present continuous				
+	I	'm	spending	the day with my grandmother on Saturday.
–	We	're not	playing	football this evening.
?	What	are	you	doing	at the weekend?

It is common to use the present continuous to talk about things happening now or temporary situations. It is also possible to use the present continuous to talk about definite future plans and arrangements.

It is common to use an expression of future time with the present continuous, e.g. *this weekend*, *tomorrow morning*, *later*.

be going to				
+	I	'm going to	take	some time off work.
–	They	're not going to	win.	
?	Is	it	going to	rain?	

Use *be going to* + infinitive to talk about future plans and predictions.

Usually, we can use both the present continuous and *be going to* to talk about plans.

I'm meeting my girlfriend later.
I'm going to meet my girlfriend later.

But there is a small difference:

For plans which involve other people and have a fixed time and place, the present continuous is more common.

We're having a barbecue on Saturday. (We have invited people, bought food and drink, etc.)

For plans which do not involve other people, *be going to* is more common.

I'm going to stay in and read a book.

When *be going to* is followed by the verb *go*, it is possible to omit *go to*.

I'm going to (go to) the cinema.

3.2 questions without auxiliaries

subject	verb		answer
Who	sent	the present?	David.
What	causes	this problem?	The water pipes.
Whose guitar	cost	$300?	Mine.
Which footballers	played	for that team?	Beckham and Cole.

When *who*, *what*, *which* or *whose* is the **subject** of the sentence, do not use an auxiliary verb (*do*, *did*, etc.). The verb is in the third person.

Who ate all the pies? Joe ate all the pies.
Which students forgot their homework? Ben and Meg forgot their homework.

When *who*, *what*, *which* or *whose* is the object of the sentence, use an auxiliary verb as usual.

What do you do? I work in a bank.
Whose book did you use? I used Tom's book.

3.3 making a phone call

caller	
start the call	Hello, this is Andy. Hello, it's Wendy. (NOT I am Wendy.)
ask to speak to someone	Can I speak to …?
when the person you want isn't there	Can I leave a message?
finish the call	See you soon. Goodbye.

receiver	
start the call	Hello. Paul speaking.*
find out who is speaking	Who's calling (please)?
when the person the caller wants isn't there	I'm afraid she's not here at the moment. Can I take a message? I'll ask her to call you back.
finish the call	Thanks for calling.

*We say this when we answer the phone at work.

PRACTICE

3.1 **A** Match prompts 1–4 with pictures A–D.

1 play / football
2 stay home / watch TV
3 go / cinema
4 have / meeting

B Look at the pictures and make sentences with the prompts. Use the present continuous.

Next week

This evening

Saturday

Next weekend

C Put the verbs in brackets into the correct form of the present continuous or *be going to*.

A: What ¹_____ you _____ (do) tonight?
B: I ²_____ (go) John's house party.
A: Really? We ³_____ (be) there, too.
B: Great! ⁴_____ you _____ (take) any food or drink?
A: Yes, we ⁵_____ (bring) some food, but we
     ⁶_____ (not bring) drink.
B: What type of music ⁷_____ he _____ (have)?
A: He's got a DJ and he ⁸_____ (play)
     dance music.
B: It sounds great. How ⁹_____ you _____ (get) there?
A: We ¹⁰_____ (drive). Do you want a lift?

3.2 **A** Find and correct the mistakes. There is a mistake in five of the questions.

1 Do you like reading?
2 Who does read the most in your family?
3 Who be your favourite writer?
4 Which books have become famous recently?
5 What did be your favourite book when you were
  a child?
6 Who did write it?
7 How often you read on the internet?
8 Where and when do you like to read?

B Make questions with the prompts. Use the past simple. One question needs an auxiliary verb.

1 What colour / be / The Beatles' / submarine?
2 Who / write / *Stairway to Heaven*?
3 Whose / home / be / Graceland?
4 Which country / Diego Rivera / come from?
5 Who / paint / the *Mona Lisa*?
6 Which painter / invent / Cubism?

3.3 **A** Put the words in the correct order to make a phone conversation.

A: speaking / David
B: it's / Johnson / hello / Mark
A: can / Mr / help / how / I / you / Johnson?
B: to / like / Sara / please / I'd / to / speak / Torres
A: the / afraid / here / I'm / she's / moment / not / at
B: a / leave / I / can / message?
A: course / of / yes
B: you / me / her / can / ask / call / to / back?
A: problem / no
B: number / 0276 765356 / is / my
A: repeat / you / that / can / please?
B: 0276 765356
A: calling / thanks / OK / for
B: Bye

GRAMMAR

4.1 present perfect + *ever/never*

present perfect: positive and negative				
+	I/You/We/They	have ('ve)	finished	the project.
	He/She/It	has ('s)		
−	I/You/We/They	haven't/(have never)	visited	Mexico.
	He/She/It	hasn't/(has never)		

present perfect: questions				short answers		
Have	I/you/we/they	(ever) played	chess?	Yes,	I/you/we/they	have.
				No,		haven't.
Has	he/she/it			Yes,	he/she/it	has.
				No,		hasn't.

Form the present perfect with *have/has* + past participle.

The past participle is verb + *-ed* for regular verbs. For a list of irregular verbs, see page 67.

Use the present perfect to talk about past experiences without saying an exact time.
I've been to Warsaw.

When we want to say an exact time, we use the past simple.
I went to Warsaw in 2007.

Use *ever* with the present perfect to mean 'during your life until now'. *Never* is the negative of *ever*.

*Have you **ever** visited Madrid?*
*She's **never** been to a nightclub.*

Spoken grammar 1: When we are asked a *Have you ever …?* question, we often reply: *No, never* instead of *No, I haven't.*

A: *Have you ever been to the Maldives?*
B: *No, never.*

Spoken grammar 2: When we want to repeat the same *Have you ever …?* question, we usually say *Have you?*

A: *Have you ever been to Zurich?*
B: *No, have you?*

4.2 *can, have to, must*

Use modal verbs *can/can't, have to/don't have to, must/mustn't* to talk about present obligation.

Use *can* to talk about something which is possible/allowed.
*You **can** use dictionaries during the exam.*

Use *can't* to talk about something which is not possible/allowed.
*You **can't** park here.*

Use *must/mustn't/have to* to talk about rules or things that are necessary.
*We **have to** study for our exam.*
*You **must** return the books to the library before Friday.*
*You **mustn't** chew gum in the classroom.*

Use *don't have to* to talk about something that is not necessary (but it is possible/allowed).
We don't have to be there until eight o'clock. (But we can get there earlier if we want to.)

Use *he/she has to* in the positive, and *he/she doesn't have to* in the negative.
*She **has to** pay for the exam.*
*He **doesn't have to** do any extra work.*

4.3 giving/responding to advice

phrases for giving advice	example
I think you should …	I think you should study more.
You should …	You should hear her play the trumpet.
You shouldn't …	You shouldn't be late all the time.
Why don't you …?	Why don't you finish your homework later?
I (don't) think it's a good idea to …	I think it's a good idea to take some lessons.
Find/Write …	Find a cheap hotel on the internet.

phrases for responding to advice
That's a good idea.
I suppose so.
You're right.
I'm not sure that's a good idea.

PRACTICE

4.1

A Find and correct the mistakes. There is one mistake in each sentence.

1 Have you ever saw the film *Titanic*?
2 Two days ago she's been to a museum.
3 Unfortunately, we have ever won the lottery.
4 Has ever she visited you?
5 I haven't meet your brother.
6 In 2011, they've travelled to Geneva.
7 Have you seen that TV programme last Wednesday?
8 He never has played a musical instrument.

B Complete the conversations with the correct form of the verbs in the box. Use the past simple or present perfect.

make   eat   visit   hear   do   work

Conversation 1
A: _____ (ever) business in China?
B: Yes, I have. I did business there in 2014.

Conversation 2
A: Peter Duvall is a diplomat, isn't he?
B: Yes, he _____ all over the world.

Conversation 3
A: She loves travelling, doesn't she?
B: Yes, she _____ fifteen countries last year.

Conversation 4
A: _____ many speeches?
B: No, he hasn't. That's why I'm worried.

Conversation 5
A: Is Coldplay's new CD good?
B: I don't know. I _____ it.

Conversation 6
A: Have you ever tried sushi?
B: Yes, we _____ some yesterday!

4.2

A Underline the correct alternative.

1 We *have to/has to* get up early to catch the train.
2 Children *can't/can* stay with their parents if they are very quiet.
3 I'm afraid I *can't/must* leave work early. It's not allowed.
4 They *have to/don't have to* put a notice on the door so you know which room to go to.
5 You *can/don't have to* park your car here. It's free on Saturdays.
6 You *mustn't/have to* smoke in the office. It's against the law.
7 You *can't/have to* leave your coat on the floor. Hang it up!
8 We *must/don't have to* worry about transport. A taxi will take us to the airport.

B Complete the sentences with *can/can't, have to/don't have to* or *must/mustn't*.

1 You _____ leave the room when you have finished the exam. (it's allowed)
2 We _____ book a table. That restaurant is never busy on Mondays. (it's not necessary)
3 You _____ log in using your PIN number. (it's necessary)
4 You _____ eat as much as you like. (It's allowed)
5 Sadie _____ bring extra clothes. I have got lots here. (it's not necessary)
6 You _____ wear jeans in the nightclub. (it's not allowed)
7 Harry _____ work on his pronunciation. (it's necessary)
8 You _____ do that. It's illegal! (it's not allowed)

4.3

A Put the words in the correct order to make sentences.

a) a / idea / that's / good
b) think / I / out / after / lesson / go / should / the / we
c) not / I'm / sure / I / much money / haven't got / because
d) for / we / a / out / meal / why / go / don't ?
e) OK / to / Butler's Café / let's / coffee / a / for / go

B Put sentences a)–e) in the correct order to make a conversation.

GRAMMAR

5.1 past simple and past continuous

	past simple	past continuous
+	I watched a film yesterday.	I was watching a film yesterday.
–	He didn't play here.	He wasn't playing here.
?	Did you talk to John?	Were you talking to John?

Use the past simple to talk about completed actions.
*I **ate** a salad last night.*
Use the past continuous to talk about actions in progress at a particular time.
*At 8a.m. yesterday I **was travelling** to work.*

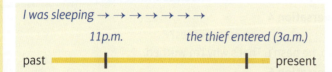

I was sleeping → → → → → → →
11p.m.   the thief entered (3a.m.)
past ————————————————— present

It is common to use the past simple and the past continuous together to tell stories. The past continuous describes an action that starts first, but is interrupted by a second action. Use the past simple for the second (usually short) action.
*What **were** you **doing** when the bus **crashed**?*
*I **was sleeping** when the thief **entered** the house.*
It is common to use *when* or *while* to link the two actions. Use *while* before the continuous action.
While I was sleeping, it started to rain.
Use *when* before the continuous action or the short action.
*When we **were talking**, the bus appeared.*
*We **were talking** when the bus **appeared**.*
Do NOT use *while* before the short action.
I was sleeping ~~while~~ it started to rain.

5.2 verb patterns

Sometimes we use two verbs together.
*I **love playing** football.*
After some verbs, put the second verb in the infinitive with *to*.
*She decided **to go** to Mexico.*
*We need **to make** a phone call.*
After some verbs, use the *-ing* form.
*I enjoy runn**ing**.*
*They avoided travell**ing** by bus.*

some common verb patterns	
verb + *-ing*	verb + infinitive with *to*
enjoy	choose
finish	hope
avoid	expect
imagine	would like
stop	decide
like	seem
don't mind	want
spend (time)	need
	help
	promise

Many verbs that show preference (things that we like or don't like) are followed by *-ing*, e.g. *like, enjoy, don't mind*.
After some verbs it is possible to use the *-ing* form OR the infinitive with *to*, e.g. *love, hate*.
*I love **dancing**. I love **to dance**.*
*I hate **getting up** early. I hate **to get up** early.*
There is little change in meaning.

5.3 asking for/giving directions

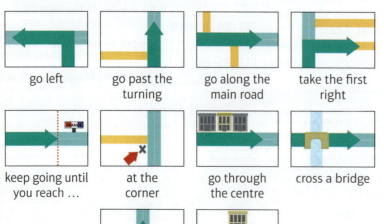

go left

go past the turning

go along the main road

take the first right

keep going until you reach …

at the corner

go through the centre

cross a bridge

go straight on

in front of you

useful questions	directions	saying you understand
Can we walk? Excuse me, can you help me? Is this the right way? Can you show me on the map? Is it far?	It takes about twenty minutes. Keep going … You'll see … You can't miss it.	OK, so I need to … Right.

PRACTICE

5.1

A Complete the story with the correct form of the verbs in brackets. Use the past simple or past continuous.

Alvin Straight, a 73-year-old, [1]_____ (live) quietly on his farm in Iowa, USA, when he heard the news that his brother, Lyle, was seriously ill. After ten years with no contact between the brothers, Alvin [2]_____ (decide) to visit Lyle. Alvin couldn't drive so he [3]_____ (buy) a lawnmower, which moved at five miles per hour, and [4]_____ (begin) the 250-mile-journey.

While he [5]_____ (travel), he met many people, including a priest and a teenage girl who was running away from her family. He helped them all simply by talking about life. Some of them also [6]_____ (help) him. For example, one day when he [7]_____ (drive) the lawnmower, it broke down. While two mechanics [8]_____ (fix) it, he met a friendly couple and [9]_____ (stay) with them.

The journey took him six weeks. And [10]_____ the story _____ (end) happily? See the 1999 film, *The Straight Story*, to find out!

B Make sentences with the prompts and the correct form of the verbs in the box. Use the past simple or past continuous.

pass   know   like   play   dance   swim   travel   have

1 He / tennis when he hurt his leg.
2 Sarah / the job because it was boring.
3 While they / they met lots of other tourists.
4 How / you / my name?
5 Who / you / with in that nightclub when I saw you?
6 I / in the sea when I saw the shark.
7 I / my exam?
8 The thief broke in while Jack / breakfast.

5.2

A Complete the sentences with the correct form of the verbs in the box.

live   read   drink   swim   visit   have   play   finish

1 They want _____ the monuments tomorrow morning.
2 I can't imagine _____ in that flat – it's so small!
3 I don't like _____ water from a bottle.
4 They decided _____ football this morning.
5 Would you like _____ dinner in this restaurant?
6 Do you enjoy _____ in the sea?
7 I hope _____ my degree next year.
8 I love _____ books about adventures.

B Find and correct the mistakes. There are eight mistakes in the advertisement.

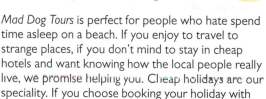

✱ **Are modern holidays too boring for you?**
✱ **Would you like doing something more exciting?**

Mad Dog Tours is perfect for people who hate spend time asleep on a beach. If you enjoy to travel to strange places, if you don't mind to stay in cheap hotels and want knowing how the local people really live, we promise helping you. Cheap holidays are our speciality. If you choose booking your holiday with *Mad Dog Tours*, you can expect living your dreams!

5.3

A Match 1–10 with a)–j) to make sentences or questions.

1 Excuse me, can   a) about an hour.
2 Is this the   b) need to go left here.
3 Is   c) restaurant on your right.
4 Can you show   d) it far?
5 It takes   e) right way?
6 You can't   f) going.
7 Can we   g) me on the map?
8 So I   h) you help me?
9 You'll see the   i) walk?
10 Keep   j) miss it.

B Underline the correct alternative to complete the conversations.

Conversation 1

A: Excuse me, how do I get to the swimming pool?
B: You need to go [1]*along/at/with* the main road. Keep going until you [2]*go/have/reach* the town hall. Then [3]*go/make/be* left and it's [4]*the/in/to* front of you.

Conversation 2

A: Excuse me, is this the right way to the Bach Concert Hall?
B: No, you need to turn around, then [5]*do/cross/go* the bridge. After that, you [6]*have/are/take* the first right and go [7]*at/with/through* the centre of town. The concert hall is at the [8]*first/corner/cross* of Ducane Road and Bright Street.

GRAMMAR

6.1 present perfect + *for/since*

Use the present perfect to talk about things that started in the past and are still true now.

We've been married for fourteen years.

(We got married fourteen years ago and we are still married now.)

Use *since* to talk about the specific time something started, e.g. *1992, last week, Monday, I was a child.*

We've known each other since we were children.

(We are friends now.)

He has played football since 2002.

Use *for* to talk about a period (length) of time, e.g. *ten years, two months, a long time, an hour, a few weeks.*

I haven't seen him for a few weeks.

I've lived in Barcelona for twenty-five years.

To ask about the length of time, use *How long have you …?*

How long have you worked for Dell?

Use the past simple, not the present perfect, for things which happened at a specific time in the past.

I moved to Spain in 2001. NOT

I ~~have~~ moved to Spain in 2001.

6.2 *may, might, will*

Use *may/might* + infinitive to talk about probable situations.

We also use *may/might* + infinitive to talk about future possibilities.

I might go to the party.

They might not arrive today.

We may have some problems.

She may not like the dress.

Do not use contractions with *might not* and *may not.*

The question form with *might* is rare.

The question form with *may* is used for asking permission. It is a very polite form.

May I sit here?

May I open the window?

Use *will* + infinitive to talk about a future prediction. The negative of *will* is *won't* (or *will not*).

I will be home at 9p.m. tonight.

She won't come here tomorrow.

Will they win the match?

In spoken English, use the contracted form of *will* (*'ll*) in positive sentences. Do not use it in questions.

I'll be home at 9p.m. tonight.

It is common to use *think/don't think* + *will.*

I think she'll get the job.

I don't think I'll go to university next year.

6.3 seeing the doctor

doctor
What's the matter/problem?
How long have you had this problem?
Where does it hurt?
Can I have a look (at …)?
It's nothing to worry about.
I'll give you some pills/antibiotics/medicine.

patient
I feel sick/terrible.
I can't sleep.
I'm worried about …
It hurts when I walk/talk.
It's very painful.

WHERE DOES IT HURT?

PRACTICE

6.1 **A** Underline the correct alternative.

1 I *didn't do/haven't done* much work *for/since* my boss left.

2 I *didn't go/haven't been* to China *for/since* 2010.

3 She *has been/was* a doctor *for/since* more than forty years. She retired in 2012.

4 Hi, Angela. How are you? I *haven't seen/didn't see* you *for/since* ages.

5 I *left/have left* university in 2000. I've worked in this company *for/since* about fifteen years.

6 I *didn't see/haven't seen* Sam yesterday. In fact I *didn't see/haven't seen* him *for/since* Monday.

7 He's really tired. He hasn't stopped working *for/since* 5.30a.m.

8 She *hasn't driven/didn't drive* a car *for/since* she had the accident.

B Complete the sentences with *for* or *since*. Put the verbs in brackets into the correct form of the present perfect or past simple.

1 I've lived in this city _____ 2011. I _____ (come) here with my family.

2 I _____ (buy) this house in 2005, so I _____ (live) here _____ more than ten years.

3 I _____ (know) Marissa _____ a long time. We _____ (meet) in 1998.

4 They _____ (move) to Australia last December, so they _____ (be) there _____ nearly a year.

5 We _____ (not be) back to Russia _____ 1990.

6 He _____ (not see) his father _____ he left home.

7 I've been learning English _____ I _____ (start) school.

8 She _____ (have) that car _____ ages!

6.2 **A** Match statements 1–6 with responses a)–f).

1 I'm hungry because I missed breakfast.

2 You eat too much junk food.

3 I'm just going out to get a snack.

4 The film was really good.

5 She looks a bit stressed.

6 We want to visit the museum this afternoon.

a) I won't be long.

b) I think she'll need a holiday soon.

c) We may not have time.

d) You might get fat.

e) I may have an early lunch.

f) I think my father might enjoy it.

B Find and correct the mistakes. There is a mistake in each sentence.

1 I don't will know my exam results until August.

2 Will you to go to university next year?

3 Anna is very busy so she may not comes tonight.

4 The traffic is heavy so they may to be late.

5 Edson mights be the best player we have ever seen.

6 I might go not to the exercise class today.

7 We'll to be back at 6p.m.

6.3 **A** Complete the conversation with phrases from the boxes on page 78.

Doctor: Good morning. I'm Dr Gordon. ¹_____ _____ _____?

Patient: ²_____ _____ _____. I've got a sore throat, and a cough.

Doctor: ³_____ _____ _____ _____ _____ _____ _____?

Patient: About a week.

Doctor: Have you got a temperature?

Patient: Yes, I think so.

Doctor: ⁴_____ _____ _____ _____ at your throat?

Patient: Yes. It's ⁵_____ _____. ⁶_____ _____ when I talk.

Doctor: Right. ⁷_____ _____ _____ some medicine. Take this for one week, and if you don't feel better, come back to see me again.

Patient: Thank you.

Lesson 2.2 JOBS

1 Match photos A–P to the jobs.

1 accountant
2 architect
3 businessman/woman
4 chef
5 electrician
6 estate agent
7 housewife
8 lawyer
9 PA (personal assistant)
10 plumber
11 receptionist
12 sales assistant
13 scientist
14 soldier
15 TV presenter
16 vet

2 Work in pairs. Discuss. Which jobs do you think are dangerous/enjoyable/boring? Why?

Lesson 3.1 TIME OUT

1 Match photos A–O to the activities 1–15.

collect:
1 stamps
2 coins

go to:
3 a concert
4 a nightclub
5 the gym

go to/see:
6 an exhibition
7 a show

play:
8 cards
9 chess
10 computer games
11 board games
12 hang out with friends
13 join a club
14 surf the net
15 walk/cycle/skate through a park

2 Work in pairs. Discuss. Which of these have you never done? Which would you like to do?

PHOTO BANK

1 **Answer the questions.**

1 Where did you go to primary school?
2 Which subjects did you enjoy at secondary school?
3 Have you been to university? What did you/would you like to study?
4 Is the education system in your country similar to the one in England?

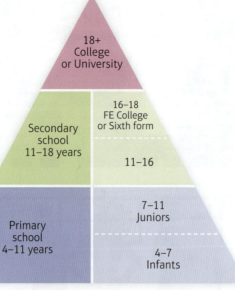

State Education in England

18+ College or University

16–18 FE College or Sixth form

Secondary school 11–18 years

11–16

7–11 Juniors

Primary school 4–11 years

4–7 Infants

maths

physics

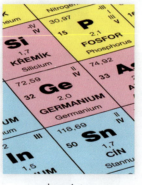

chemistry

biology

geography

history

languages

art

design and technology

PE (Physical Education)

IT (Information Technology)

RE (Religious Education)

drama

Lesson 5.1 TRANSPORT

1 Match photos A–N to the types of transport.

1 aeroplane
2 coach
3 ferry
4 helicopter
5 hot air balloon
6 lorry
7 minibus
8 moped
9 motorbike
10 ship
11 speedboat
12 taxi
13 tram
14 underground

2 Work in pairs. Discuss. Which types of transport do you use regularly? Which do you think are the most enjoyable ways to travel?

Lesson 5.2 TRAVEL ITEMS

1 Match photos A–R to the travel items.

1 alarm clock
2 aspirin
3 binoculars
4 dictionary
5 digital camera
6 first aid kit
7 map
8 money belt
9 notebook
10 backpack
11 soap
12 souvenirs
13 suitcase
14 sun hat
15 travel guide
16 umbrella
17 walking boots
18 waterproof clothes

2 Work in pairs and take turns.
Student A: describe an item.
Student B: guess the item.

A: *You wear these when it is raining.*
B: *Waterproof clothes.*

PHOTO BANK

1 A Check the meaning of sports 1–30 below.

1 badminton
2 basketball
3 boxing
4 cricket
5 cycling
6 football
7 golf
8 hockey
9 horse racing
10 horseriding
11 jogging
12 judo
13 karate
14 ping pong/ table tennis
15 rollerblading
16 rugby
17 running
18 sailing
19 scuba-diving
20 skateboarding
21 skiing
22 squash
23 snorkelling
24 snowboarding
25 surfing
26 swimming
27 tennis
28 volleyball
29 windsurfing
30 yoga

B Which sports can you see in photos A–M?

2 Work in pairs. Discuss. Which sports are popular in your country? Which have you tried?

net

bat

ball

racket

Lesson 6.2 FOOD

1 Which of these foods do you a) never eat b) eat a lot of?

2 Which types of food/drink do you think are a) very good b) very bad for your health?

GRAINS

corn | wheat

oats

MEAT AND FISH/SEAFOOD

chicken | duck | beefsteak | leg of lamb

fish | shrimps | mussels | lobster

DAIRY

milk | cheese

cream | yoghurt

DESSERTS

jelly | cake

biscuits | ice cream

DRINKS

tea | coffee

orange juice | fizzy drink

VEGETABLES

soya beans | potatoes | carrots | spinach | broccoli | cabbage

lettuce | peas | onion | garlic | cucumbers | courgettes

FRUIT

pineapple | apple | orange | grapes | grapefruit | bananas

kiwi fruit | mango | melon | watermelon | plums | lemon

COMMUNICATION BANK

Lesson 1.3

4 A Student A: make questions or comments with the prompts for Student B. Listen to Student B's responses.

1 would / like / drink?
2 watch / match / last night?
3 nice / day?
4 work / here?

B Listen to Student B's questions and comments. Choose the correct response.

1 Hi, Pete. Pleased to meet you./
  Dear Mr Pete. How do you do?
2 Yes, thanks. I didn't do much./
  Yes, thank you. I am enjoying it.
3 I'm coming from Toledo, near Madrid./
  I'm from Toledo, near Madrid.
4 It's nice to meet you./
  Yes, see you soon.

Lesson 3.5

4 C Answers to quiz

2 Reagan
3 *A Night at the Opera*
4 Raphael
5 Elton
6 One Love
7 Venice
8 Céline
9 Nelly Furtado

Lesson 4.3

9 A Student A: explain your problem. Then listen and respond to the advice.

Your son is eighteen years old and lives at home. He needs to study for his exams, but in the evening he goes out with friends until late. He often misses lessons or falls asleep when he is studying. At home you do all the cooking and cleaning and give your son money every week.

B Listen to another student's problem. Give the student some advice.

Lesson 2.2

4 B Student B

Danger Rating 8/10

Motorbike courier, Brazil

In Brazil, they are called motoboys, and on average, one of them dies in traffic every day. Foreign correspondent Peter Lane met the motoboys of São Paulo. He learnt that accidents are not the only problem – there are also robberies. It happened to Roberto Coelho.

'It was terrible, a really bad time for me. I lost everything. We don't have insurance and the company doesn't help us.' The motoboys usually earn just $450 a month.

Lane asks, 'When you know the streets are dangerous, why do you still drive so fast?' Coelho says it's because they often work under time pressure. 'We know it's dangerous, but we have no choice.'

Lane also spoke to some car drivers. One said, 'These motorcycle couriers are so dangerous. They drive too fast and they don't care about the rules of the road.' Another said, 'Most of them are just kids. It's no surprise they have accidents.'

Once in a while, they try to change the traffic laws – they want the motoboys to drive like everyone else. But the changes all failed, so the motoboys continue to risk their lives in one of the most dangerous jobs in the world.

Lesson 3.3

8 Student A: think about what you are going to say when you receive and make phone calls in these situations. Role-play the situations with Student B.

Answer the phone

1 You work for Nova Restaurant. Take a message.
2 You work for Amber Cinema. Answer the phone and tell a customer the times of the film *The Magic Hat*: 2.30p.m., 5.00p.m., 7.30p.m. and 10.00p.m., with a special extra showing at 12.00p.m. at the weekend.
3 Answer the phone normally. Listen and respond to the invitation.

Make a call

4 You are calling Ripping Yarns, a theatre company. You would like six tickets for *Hamlet* for Friday.
5 You are calling Brandon's Restaurant. You want to change your reservation from 7.30p.m. on Tuesday to 8.00p.m. next Wednesday There will now be ten people, not five, so you need a bigger table.
6 Ask your partner if he/she wants to go for a snack after class.

Lesson 5.1

3 Student B: read the text and make notes.

INTO THE WILD

When Chris McCandless graduated from Emory University, USA, he knew he wanted more from life than a normal career. He gave away his savings – $24,000 – to charity, abandoned his car, burned the money in his wallet, and gave himself a new name: Alexander Supertramp. He rejected the modern world and decided to experience life alone and in the wild.

With hardly any equipment or technology, McCandless went into the Alaskan wilderness*. While he was travelling, he met several people who helped him, giving him rides and food. One man even offered to adopt him as a grandson, but McCandless decided to keep going, into the wild.

Eventually he ended up in an abandoned bus, hunting and picking plants for food. While he was living wild, he wrote a diary. It described his day-to-day life and the difficulties and pleasures he had from living in nature. McCandless stayed in the bus for four months and then his diary stopped. Eventually his body was found by a hunter.

Following a book describing his life, a film came out based on his adventures.

*__wilderness:__ a wild area where no one lives

Lesson 6.3

6 A Student A: you are a doctor seeing a patient. Use the prompts to ask questions and make suggestions.

- how long?
- where / hurt?
- when / hurt?
- how / you / hurt?
- take painkillers
- get lots of rest
- don't do sport

Start like this:
Hello. How can I help you?

B Student A: now you are a patient seeing a doctor. Use the prompts to explain your problem.

- bad cough / few months
- tried antibiotics
- no temperature / don't feel ill
- smoke / ten cigarettes a day

Lesson 5.3

8 Student A: look at the map and ask Student B for directions to:

- a nightclub called Risky Business
- a restaurant called The Waterfall
- the Screen by the Pond cinema
- a pub called The Courier's Rest
- the Museum of Fashion and Design

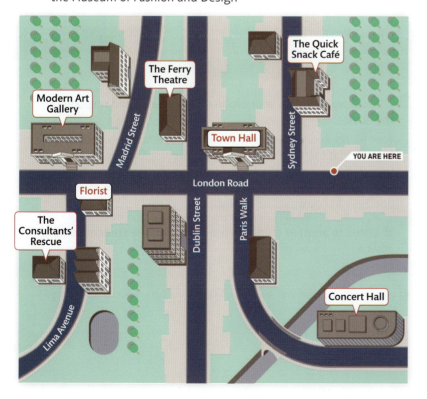

Lesson 1.3

4 A Student B: listen to Student A's questions and comments. Choose the correct response.

1 I'd love an orange juice, please./
  I like orange juice, please.
2 Yes, it was brilliant./Yes, it's lovely.
3 Yes, nice to meet you./Yes, it's lovely.
4 No, I'm a student. / No, I'm working.

B Make questions or comments with the prompts for Student A. Listen to Student A's responses.

1 this / friend / Pete
2 have / good / weekend?
3 where / exactly / from?
4 see / later

Lesson 3.3

8 Student B: think about what you are going to say when you make and receive phone calls in these situations. Role-play the situations with Student A.

Make a call

1 You are calling Nova Restaurant. You booked a table for Saturday, but you have to cancel it.
2 You are calling Amber Cinema. Ask what time the film *The Magic Hat* is showing.
3 Invite your partner to a film this evening. Say the name and time of the film.

Answer the phone

4 You work for Ripping Yarns, a theatre company. Answer the phone and confirm a ticket reservation.
5 You work for Brandon's Restaurant. A customer wants to change his/her reservation. Take the message and confirm if it is possible.
6 Answer the phone normally. Listen and respond to the invitation.

Lesson 2.2

4 B Student C

Danger Rating 6/10

Jockey, France

'Bang!' goes the gun. The gates open and the horses come running out. All eyes are on them. Money, fame and glory are the prizes.

Horse riding looks so beautiful that it is sometimes easy to forget how dangerous it is. Life as a jockey is rarely safe and it usually involves a few broken bones. Once in a while, jockeys even die during a race.

Jill Cleveland spoke to jockey Vincent Dax in France. As a young man, Dax was one of the best jockeys of his generation. He knows the sport is dangerous, but he never worries. 'When the race starts, we forget about the danger. We know it's not like riding a bicycle or driving a car, but all we think about is winning.'

During his career, Dax has broken many bones, including both arms and one leg, and he once fell off his horse and was knocked unconscious. So why do jockeys risk their lives? 'We love racing. We love the speed and we love the money. Jockeys know the risks involved, but we are good at what we do. If we get hurt, we just get back on the horse. That's life.'

Lesson 4.3

9 A Student B: explain your problem. Then listen and respond to the advice.

Your friend would like a girlfriend. The problem is he works long hours and is too tired to go out in the evenings. He usually buys a take-away meal and falls asleep watching the TV. He doesn't have any hobbies and is getting fat. You know lots of single women, but you don't think they would be interested.

B Listen to another student's problem. Give the student some advice.

Lesson 5.1

3 Student C: read the text and make notes.

RABBIT-PROOF FENCE

It is Australia in 1931. Three Aborigine girls, Molly, fourteen, her sister Daisy, eight, and their cousin Gracie, ten, were taken from their home by government officials because of their race. They were sent to live in a camp far from home. Life at the camp was terrible, and they hated it.

One night when it was raining, the girls decided to escape. They knew that the rain would hide their footprints in the mud, so they began the long journey home. In the desert they had no food and nowhere to sleep.

They didn't have a map either, but while they were walking, they saw the 'rabbit-proof fence', one of the longest fences in the world. It was there to stop rabbits from entering farmland. The girls recognised the fence and walked next to it for 1,200 miles. After nine weeks they got home.

Many years later, Molly's daughter, Doris Pilkington Garimara, wrote a book about the journey and in 2002 the story was made into a film, *Rabbit-Proof Fence*.

Lesson 5.3

8 Student B: look at the map and ask Student A for directions to:
- The Quick Snack Café
- The Ferry Theatre
- the Concert Hall
- a bar called The Consultants' Rescue
- the Modern Art Gallery

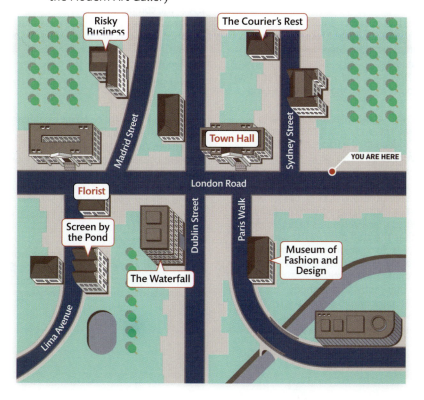

Lesson 6.3

6 A Student B: you are a patient seeing a doctor. Use the prompts to explain your problem.
- problem / two weeks
- pain / lower back
- hurts / walk
- accident / playing football

B Student B: now you are a doctor seeing a patient. Use the prompts to ask questions and make suggestions.
- how long?
- a temperature?
- feel ill?
- smoke cigarettes?
- have an X-ray
- give up smoking

Start like this:
Hello. What's the problem?

Lesson 4.3

9 A Student C: explain your problem. Then listen and respond to the advice.

Your flat-mate loves shopping. Every month she buys new clothes, shoes and designer bags using a credit card. Her room is full of clothes she never wears. She spends more money than she has and borrows money from you to pay her rent. She hasn't paid you back for two months.

B Listen to another student's problem. Give the student some advice.

AUDIO SCRIPTS

Lesson 1.1 Recording 1.1

1 How many people are in your family?
2 How often do you see your parents?
3 Do you enjoy spending time with your family?
4 When was your last family celebration?
5 Who do you live with?
6 How often do you eat out with friends?
7 Where does your best friend live?

Lesson 1.2 Recording 1.2

Story 1

My boyfriend and I were at a restaurant and I don't know how he did it, but he put the engagement ring in my salad. I didn't see it and I put it in my mouth. I think he panicked and tried to stop me. Anyway, luckily I felt something hard as I bit into my food and I didn't swallow it. I took it out, saw what it was and accepted! So that was how we got engaged. It was almost a disaster. We got married one month later.

Story 2

We decided to go on holiday in Egypt as we both liked diving. This was me and my girlfriend at the time. So we went on a dive and I proposed to her underwater. I didn't say anything. I just gave her the ring while we were, I don't know, ten feet under. Luckily, she smiled. We got back on the boat and she said yes.

Story 3

My husband and I are video artists. We met at art school and honestly we fell in love immediately. And what he did was he made a funny two-minute video, he put it on YouTube and sent a link to me. And it was him proposing. And in the video there was music and then all of our friends suddenly appeared, singing and dancing. It was amazing and such a surprise. I watched it and then I surprised him. I accepted his proposal, but I didn't tell him. Instead I made a video of me saying yes.

Lesson 1.3 Recording 1.5

Conversation 1

W = Woman   D = Davide   R = Rachel

W: Hi, Davide. This is my friend, Rachel.
D: Hi, Rachel. Pleased to meet you. Would you like a drink?
R: Sorry. What did you say?
D: Would you like a drink, Rachel?
R: Oh. I'd love a coffee, thank you.
D: So, do you work here?
R: No, I'm a student.
D: Are you here on holiday then?
R: Er … yes.
D: Where exactly do you come from?
R: I'm from Beckley, near Oxford.
D: OK, er, I'll just go and get the coffee.

Conversation 2

W = Woman   F = Felicia

W: Hi, Felicia. Nice day, isn't it?
F: Yes, it's lovely.
W: Did you have a good weekend?
F: Yes, it was OK. I didn't do much.
W: Did you watch the match last night?
F: Yes, it was terrible. We lost 3-0.
W: Oh no! I'm sorry to hear that.
F: That's OK. I'll see you later.
W: Yes, see you soon.

Lesson 1.4 Recording 1.7

I've known Michelle for a long time and we met when we were at school together. We were about eleven years old and I had to show her to her peg to hang up her coat and we've been mates ever since. Er … we get on really well. She's one of those people that if you haven't seen [them] for six months, six days, it's the same. It's like time hasn't passed. We've got lots of things in common. We play tennis together. The only problem with Michelle is that she's a bit competitive and we've fallen out over tennis. Sometimes if she wins, I haven't spoken to her … erm … and she's just one of those people you can rely on. She's sort of like number one in my phone book. Erm … and yes, she's a great person. We have a real laugh together.

Lesson 2.1 Recording 2.2

A: Today we're looking at how companies motivate their staff. Sarah, can you tell us more?
B: Absolutely. Internet companies are famous for this type of thing. At Yahoo there's a free bus ride to work for employees. There's also a dentist and a hairdresser at the office.
A: Makes life easier for employees …
B: Exactly. And, wait for it, one day a month the staff watch films together.
A: Great ideas.
B: Yep. Now at Google, lunch is free, and you can also get a cheap massage at the office.
A: Wow.
B: And other companies are bringing in new ideas, too. A company called Pontiflex in New York created a nap room, where employees could sleep for 15 minutes.
A: Nice idea.
B: At several companies we're hearing that the relationship between bosses and employees is changing. At one company, the boss writes thank you notes to employees. At another, the staff does a job swap two days a year. So a senior manager might clean floors for the day, and the cleaner can sit in an air-conditioned office.
A: Does that motivate everybody?
B: Well, it helps employees to see what everyone else is doing in the company, which I think is … very valuable and of course ….

Lesson 2.1 Recording 2.3

Conversation 1

M = Man   I = Interviewer

M: Hi. I work at Kinko's coffee shop across the street. But, er, at the moment I'm having a break here in the music shop.
I: And what are you doing on your break?
M: I'm choosing my free CD for the week.
I: Free CD? Can you tell us a bit more? Why are you doing this?
M: Sure. Kinko's, the coffee shop, has an agreement with the music shop. The employees at the music shop get free coffee at Kinko's. They all come in during their break. And we get one free CD a week from the music shop.
I: Great!
M: We all know each other and it works really well.

Conversation 2

W = Woman   I = Interviewer

W: So, this is the clothes shop. And this is the study area.
I: Right. So you have a study area?
W: Yeah. As you can see, David, over there, is studying. And these two are doing an online course.
I: And this is during company hours? Does the boss know about this?
W: It's the boss' idea. The company pays for employees to do courses. So during our breaks or after seven when the shop closes, we can stay on and study.
I: That's excellent. And are you studying at the moment?
W: Yeah, but I'm not studying anything connected with fashion.
I: What are you studying?
W: I'm studying history.
I: And the company pays?
W: The company pays. It pays for about six of us. I think six of us are doing online courses.
I: Brilliant.

Conversation 3

E = Employee   I = Interviewer

E: Hi there. I work for a software company.
I: And what are you doing now?
E: Well, I'm checking my emails at the moment because I need to see what work I have to do today.
I: At one o'clock?
E: Well, the company has flexible hours. You can arrive when you want and go home at any time.
I: That sounds good.
E: It's great. We get a salary for good work, not for the time we spend in the office. So, really, the important thing is to do your job well. That's what the boss says, anyway!

Lesson 2.3 Recording 2.5

I = Interviewer   M = Man

I: Can you tell us a little about what you do and what you like about your job?

M: Yes. I'm a marine biologist. I work mainly in the sea and also in the lab. One good thing about my job is that I like working outside.

I: I see.

M: In fact, I can't stand sitting at a desk all day. Um. What else?

I: Maybe you get to travel …

M: I travel a lot and I absolutely love travelling, particularly in South America and Australia.

I: Right. And what about your colleagues, people you work with?

M: Actually, most of my time is spent alone, which kind of suits me. I don't like working in a team. I prefer working alone.

I: Really? And what about the type of work?

M: It's interesting – there's a lot of lab work, but it's a very practical job. You're working with animals and plant life the whole time. And, y'know, I don't mind getting my hands dirty. That's important. Also, I'm keen on learning new things – and you do learn all the time in this job. You're always discovering new things.

I: That's great. It sounds wonderful.

M: I couldn't do an office job because I hate working under pressure. And I'm not very keen on working for a company. I just want to be my own boss.

I: So, you found the right job for you.

M: I found the right job for me, yes.

Lesson 2.4 Recording 2.8

A = Alistair   Z = Zeinab

A: Zeinab, can I ask you a few questions about your work/life balance?

Z: Of course.

A: OK. First question: how much time do you spend sleeping?

Z: Lots! Probably about eight or nine hours a night!

A: Really?!

Z: Yep.

A: OK. And what about studying?

Z: Well, I suppose usually about five or six hours a day, although it depends. I mean if I have an exam coming up or something, it's probably more.

A: And do you ever have a holiday?

Z: Oh yeah. Probably twice a year I try and go abroad and just completely relax.

A: OK. What about your weekends? Do you ever study at the weekend?

Z: Not usually, but once in a while I open a book!

A: Right. And do you think you have a good work/life balance?

Z: I think so, yeah. I'm not too stressed or anything.

A: Easy life being a student.

Z: Oh yeah!

Lesson 3.1 Recording 3.1

P = Presenter   R = Rafael   C = Carmen

P: You probably think there's nothing to do for free in New York, right? Well, New York may be one of the most expensive cities in the world, but if you look carefully, there are still lots of fun things to do that will cost you next to nothing, or may even be free. We sent two journalists, Rafael and Carmen, out onto the streets of New York with just $20 to spend. Their challenge was to organise a great day out, but not go over their budget. Let's listen to their plans. Rafael?

R: Yes.

P: Rafael, hi, can you tell us what you're planning to do with your $20?

R: Hi, yes, well, actually I'm going to start the day with a delicious bagel from a great bagel shop I've discovered on 3rd Avenue. They are really cheap and tasty. Then I'm going to spend the morning in Central Park. The park is filled with free events and street musicians, so I'm just going to listen to music and watch people. In the afternoon, I'm going to the Museum of American Finance. You have to pay to go in, but I'm really interested to find out about the history of American banking. After that, I'm taking the Staten Island Ferry. It's free, and it's a great way to see views of New York from the water. In the evening, I'm going to see some live music on 2nd Avenue. I'll need to buy one drink, but the music is free.

P: That sounds great, Rafael. Enjoy the day.

R: Thank you. I'm sure I will.

P: OK, so Rafael has chosen bagels, Central Park, the Finance Museum and live music in the evening. Let's hear about what Carmen is planning for her day. Carmen?

C: Hi.

P: Carmen, can you tell us what you've planned for your day in New York City?

C: Yes, of course. I'm really excited, because I'm going to the High Line to see some sculptures, and just walk around and see what's happening.

P: The High Line? What's that?

C: It's an old railway track. Now, it's used as a park, and there are lots of different activities and artists there. It's a really peaceful and beautiful place, right in the middle of the city. Lots of people go jogging there. I'm not going running, though. I'm going to see a free art exhibition. After that, I'm going to Times Square. It's such a famous place, and there are a lot of tourists there, but I really like the atmosphere, and there's an Italian restaurant that does the best cheesecake just nearby. So, I'm going to have something to eat, and then in the evening I'm meeting with a friend and we're going to a free hip-hop class. I'm going to learn to dance like a real New Yorker.

P: Wow, that sounds good. So, first you're going to eat cheesecake, and then you're going dancing. Right?

C: Exactly!

P: That sounds like a great plan. So, two great plans there. Which would you choose?

Lesson 3.3 Recording 3.4

Conversation 1

A: Como's Restaurant.

B: Hello, I'd like to book a table for four on Saturday night. Around eight thirty if possible.

A: Let me just have a look. This Saturday?

B: Yes.

A: Saturday the fifteenth. Sorry, we're completely full on Saturday. There's nothing at all.

B: Ah, what about Sunday?

A: Sunday, Sunday. Um … the best I can do is a table at nine o'clock.

B: Nine o'clock? You haven't got anything earlier?

A: Nothing at all, I'm afraid.

B: OK, let's go ahead. Nine o'clock.

A: Can I take your name, please?

B: The table is for Jack Hopper.

A: Jack … hang on … can you repeat that, please? Did you say Jack Hopper?

B: Yes. H-o-double p-e-r.

A: OK, that's all booked. Table for four, nine o'clock, Sunday.

B: Great. Thank you.

A: Thank you.

Conversation 2

A: RSA Theatre. Jenny speaking. How can I help you?

B: Hello, I was wondering if you could help me. I've booked tickets for the show on the tenth of June, but I'd like to change the date.

A: OK, one moment. Can I just check? What's the name, please?

B: The tickets are booked in the name of James King.

A: Sorry, I didn't catch that. Did you say King?

B: James King.

A: OK, yes. Two tickets for June the tenth. What date would you like to change to?

B: What dates do you still have seats for?

A: There's nothing on the twelfth or thirteenth. There are two seats for the eleventh, but they're separate. We have …

B: Sorry, can you slow down, please? Two seats for?

A: Sorry, two seats for the eleventh, but they aren't together. We can do you two seats together on the fourteenth of June.

B: Fourteenth of June. That's fine.

A: OK. I'll just go ahead and book that.

Conversation 3

A: Hello?

B: Hello, it's Mary here. … Hello? Can you hear me OK? It's Mary here.

A: Oh hi, Mary. How are you?

B: Very well, thanks. And you?

A: Yeah, fine.

B: Are you doing anything on Saturday? Because a few of us are going out for dinner.

A: Sorry, Mary, can you speak up, please? I'm at the station and I can't hear a thing.

B: D'you want to go for dinner on Saturday?

A: Oh, that sounds nice.

B: There's going to be a few of us, Mohammed and Clare, and Robin.

AUDIO SCRIPTS

A: That sounds like fun.

B: Are you free?

A: I think so.

B: Alright. Eight-thirty, Saturday. Pauly's.

A: OK. Pauly's on Saturday at eight-thirty.

B: That's right. Great. See you soon.

A: OK. Thanks for calling.

Conversation 4

A: Withertons. Who's calling?

B: Hello, this is Kim. Kim Brower. Can I speak to Alexandra Sanders, please?

A: I'm afraid she's not here at the moment.

B: Ah, do you know when she'll be back? I've tried her phone three or four times and left messages, but she hasn't called back.

A: She's visiting a customer. She should be back this evening. Can I take a message?

B: It's about dinner tonight. I've had to cancel because of work.

A: OK. I'll ask her to call you back.

B: Thanks.

A: Does she have your number?

B: It's 01823 2766.

A: Can you repeat that, please?

B: 01823 2766.

Lesson 3.4 Recording 3.8

OK. I'm going to tell you about how to go local in Pisa, Italy. I'm going to take you on a tour that only the locals would know about. First of all, we're starting the day with a coffee and a fresh pastry from a little bar near the Vettovaglie market. I love this place because it's where all the locals who are selling on the market go to have their coffee. And the coffee is delicious. We're going to spend the morning walking through the market and the old part of the city near the university. Afterwards, for lunch, we're going to one of the best restaurants I know. It's called Le Bandierine and they specialise in home-made spaghetti and seafood, and we're going to have a fantastic meal there. In the afternoon, we're planning to go a little outside Pisa to San Rossore park. It's a beautiful place to walk, but they also have horse races there, so we can have some fun watching the horses. In the evening, we're going back towards the Leaning Tower for an early evening drink to look at the Piazza dei Miracoli as the sun goes down, when all the tourists have gone home. We'll finish the evening with a wonderful pizza from a restaurant on the other side of the city. I'm sure you'll love it. It's going to be a day to remember.

Lesson 4.1 Recording 4.3

I = Interviewer   M = Mario

I: So Mario, can you tell us how you used your talent in your job?

M: Um, well, I've always enjoyed cooking. I come from a big Italian family and I learnt to cook by watching my mother in the kitchen.

I: But no one knew you could cook, right?

M: That's right, no one knew. I only cooked at home, but I did it well. Then in my twenties, I started to make meals for my friends. And, well, I was working in an office. And I brought food to office parties, that kind of thing.

I: Then you had an idea …

M: I had the idea to sell my food at work.

I: So your colleagues buy your food every day.

M: Yeah, I started selling it to friends and colleagues, and then to other people at work. I prepared all kinds of things: bread, pasta, cakes.

I: And then you made a decision.

M: Yeah, office work was OK, but I wanted to do something more interesting. So eventually, I asked the boss if I could open a café in the office.

I: And he was happy to …

M: He agreed. They gave me a room. Now I bring food there every day. We have chairs and tables. And now that's my job.

I: Have you ever thought, 'Oh, I prefer my old office job. This is too difficult.'?

M: Never. I've never thought that because this is what I love doing: cooking and preparing different menus. Really, it's the best decision I've ever made.

I: And have you thought about expanding the business, maybe opening a restaurant one day?

M: I've thought about it, but it's a long way away!

Lesson 4.3 Recording 4.6

G = Glynn   M = Magda

G: Magda, many of my students are too shy to speak in front of the class. They worry about making mistakes.

M: Yes, this is a common problem. Teachers should give students time to prepare. Tell them the question and give them a few minutes to think about what they'll say. They can take notes first.

G: That's a good idea.

M: Also, let them practise in groups before they speak in front of everyone. This'll give them confidence.

G: Yes, you're right. I do usually give them a chance to practise first. Now what about those students who have problems listening to English?

M: Problems listening. That's common, too.

G: Native speakers – for example people from the UK or Australia or the States – speak really fast and it's difficult to understand them.

M: Yes. Students should practise listening to native speakers. Fortunately, if they have the internet, there are lots of opportunities. They can listen to the news and to podcasts. But even better is to go on YouTube and watch film clips. When we can see the people speaking, it makes it easier. We can watch the mouth and the hands and the body language and it helps us to understand.

G: And using subtitles? Some teachers say we shouldn't use them. Ever!

M: I'm not sure that's a good idea. Subtitles can be a real help. Students can see the differences between the spelling and the pronunciation of words. They can see which words are swallowed …

G: I suppose so.

M: For me, students should use subtitles maybe the second time they watch.

G: OK, and what about … students' pronunciation. They have a lot of problems …

Lesson 4.4 Recording 4.7

A: OK, well, I think the most important invention is probably the internet. For me, it's number one.

B: Uhuh.

A: It's opened up the world and we can get lots of information for free now. And it joins people together from all different cultures and countries.

B: That's true, but I think there are more important inventions. Really simple things that are so common we forget about them.

A: Like what?

B: Well, things like aspirin. It's not really an invention, I suppose, but can you imagine life without aspirin?

A: Umm, not really.

B: And all the other medicines we use.

A: Antibiotics to cure illnesses. That's true actually. Painkillers.

B: And another invention that I see as really important is the car.

A: Oh yeah, definitely.

B: Before the car, travel was so slow it took days to get anywhere.

A: That's true. People went everywhere by horse, didn't they?

B: Yeah, and so the car opened up possibilities …

Lesson 5.2 Recording 5.3

1 These days, we always expect to hear English in tourist areas. Most people working in tourism speak it, but I always want to talk to local people and many of them don't speak English. So I try to learn a few words of the language, especially 'please' and 'thank you', and I always take a small dictionary.

2 I love walking when I go on holiday … 'cause I think … I think you see more, so I always take a really good pair of walking boots.

3 I think a good digital camera is important when you travel. I always take a lot of photos. And I also take binoculars.

4 When I'm not travelling for work, I usually spend my holidays in a warm place, so I always take a sun hat. But when I go somewhere during the winter or rainy season, I always take waterproof clothes.

5 I think it's a good idea to buy a really good suitcase. And when you pack, leave enough space for souvenirs. On the other hand, I enjoy travelling in wild places, so often I take a backpack not a suitcase. If you decide to go walking, a backpack is much easier to carry.

6 It's best to avoid carrying too much money because you don't want to look like a rich tourist! 'Cause of this, I always take a money belt on holiday.

7 I need to write things down to remember them so I take a notebook and pen.

Lesson 5.3 Recording 5.4

1 To get to Argentina, you wait at the corner for the bus. It takes you down Avenida das Cataratas and right into Avenida Mercosul. The bus goes straight on for about 25 minutes. Cross the bridge and you're in Argentina.

2 To see the Iguaçu Falls on the Brazilian side, you turn right and just go straight on down Avenida das Cataratas and Highway 469 and the Falls are in front of you. You can't miss them – they're the biggest in the world!

3 To get to Paraguay, you have to go left. You go along the main road through the park past the trees. Then you turn right and you're on Avenida Kubitschek. Let's see. From there you keep going until you reach Highway 277. Go left. The bridge is at the end of the highway. Cross the bridge and you're in Paraguay.

Lesson 5.3 Recording 5.5

Conversation 1

A: Excuse me. We're trying to get to the carnival. Is this the right bus stop?
B: Yes, but you don't need the bus. It's very close.
A: Oh! Can we walk?
B: Yes, it takes about ten minutes from here. Just go straight on. You'll hear the music!
A: OK. Thank you very much.

Conversation 2

A: Excuse me, can you help me? I'm looking for the Plaza Hotel. Is this the right way?
B: Um … Plaza Hotel, Plaza Hotel. Yes, keep going, past the cinema and take the first left.
A: OK.
B: Then keep going for about fifteen minutes until you reach the end of the road. And you'll see the sign for the hotel. You can't miss it.
A: OK. Can you show me on the map?
B: Sure.

Conversation 3

A: Excuse me, we want to get to The Grand Motel. Is it far?
B: Um … sorry, I've no idea. Jim, do you know?
C: What?
B: The Grand Motel?
C: The Grand Motel? Yeah, it's just over there. Just go to the end of this street. Go left and go past the … um … there's a restaurant. Go past the restaurant and it's on the left.
A: On the left. So I need to go to the end of the street, turn left, go past the restaurant and it's on the left.
C: Yeah, that's it.
A: Thanks a lot.

Lesson 5.4 Recording 5.8

OK, well, we would like to go to Easter Island. It is very isolated, very far from other places, and the nearest country is Chile, over two thousand miles away. We are going to travel there by plane and stay with different families and the trip is going to take three months. We want to experience the local culture, their music, food and way of life. So our plan is to speak to the local people about these things and to film them. We hope to find out about their traditions and to see what they think of their history. Well, finally, my husband and I always wanted to go to Easter Island. I read about it when I was a child and I saw pictures of these amazing stone heads on the island. So for us, this is the journey of our dreams.

Lesson 6.1 Recording 6.1

1 Do you live in a town, or by the sea?
2 How long have you lived there?
3 How long have you lived in the house you live in now?
4 What is the name of your best friend?
5 How long have you known him/her?
6 Do you work or study?
7 How long have you worked or studied where you are now?
8 What hobby do you enjoy?
9 How long have you done it for?
10 Do you have a bicycle or a car?
11 How long have you had it?

Lesson 6.2 Recording 6.3

I = Interviewer   S = Sue

I: Sue, what are the latest food trends?
S: We have lots of interesting developments, and even possible solutions for world problems related to food.
I: Great. So can you kind of …
S: Well, the key question is always what to eat, and here we may see some changes, things that you might not understand as food groups.
I: Can you give an example?
S: An example is insects.
I: As a food group?
S: Well, in Latin America, Asia and Africa, people have eaten insects for thousands of years, but it's only now that we in the West are seeing what a good food source they are. Insects are rich in protein, low in fat, and easy to farm.
I: So spiders and ants may be on the menu?
S: We might see them on menus in the West. Now, technology will also play a part in the future of food. Scientists have already found ways to create meat in the lab.
I: Right, but it tastes awful, doesn't it?
S: It tastes awful now, but maybe it won't in the future. And as well as meat made in a lab, we're also looking at ways to make proteins out of things like mud and wood and also seaweed.
I: It seems incredible that mud might be something we can eat.

S: Well, it's the same for seaweed, which again is easy to farm because it's everywhere. Um. Other developments on your kitchen table include an intelligent knife.
I: What's that?
S: An intelligent knife will tell you all about the food it's cutting. So, say you cut a slice of meat, the knife will tell you how much protein and fat is in the meat, where it's from, how old it is.
I: That's amazing.
S: Really giving people more information about their food.

Lesson 6.3 Recording 6.6

Conversation 1

D = Doctor   W = Woman

D: Hello. I'm Dr Andrews. Now, what's the matter?
W: Well, doctor, I feel terrible. I get these headaches and I feel sick.
D: Oh. How long have you had this problem?
W: A few weeks now. And I can't sleep at night because my head hurts.
D: You can't sleep?
W: That's right.
D: And are you very worried or under pressure at the moment?
W: No, I don't think so.
D: Do you have a healthy diet?
W: Hmm. Quite healthy.
D: Do you drink tea or coffee?
W: Yes, I do.
D: How much?
W: Tea? Probably about eight cups, or ten.
D: A day?
W: Yes.
D: I see. And has that changed in the last few weeks?
W: Not really.
D: OK. Well, the first thing is I think you should stop drinking so much tea and coffee. Try to drink just one small cup a day. I'll give you some painkillers for the headaches. Take two of these three times a day. I don't think it's anything to worry about, but if …

Conversation 2

D = Doctor   M = Man

D: Good morning. How can I help?
M: Well, I'm worried about my foot.
D: Your foot?
M: Yes. It hurts when I walk.
D: I see. Did you do anything to it? Did you have an accident?
M: Um. Well, sort of.
D: What happened?
M: I kicked a wall.
D: I see. When did you do that?
M: About a week ago.
D: OK. Did you go to hospital?
M: No.
D: Can I have a look?
M: Yes, of course.
D: Where does it hurt? Here?
M: Argh. Yes, there.

D: Can you move it?

M: Yes, a little, but it's very painful.

D: Hmm. I think it might be broken. It's nothing to worry about, but I think you should go to the hospital for an X-ray. I'll write you a note and if …

Lesson 6.4 Recording 6.8

To get healthy, you need a combination of things. You need the right diet. You need to exercise. You need to sleep seven or eight hours. Then there are other things related to lifestyle: how many friends you have, how happy your relationships are. These are really important and they affect your general health. In this person's case, there are some changes he can make. For example, he needs to do some exercise. I understand that his back gives him problems, which is quite common in someone of his age. But he could really help himself by doing more activity. He could try going for walks or cycling. Also, six hours of TV every day is too much. He should spend some of that time exercising or seeing his friends. He must lose weight, so maybe he could eat less meat, perhaps once a day instead of twice. Now, some of these changes are related to the people around him. For example, if it's his wife who does the cooking, she'll need to …

speakout 2ND EDITION

Pre-intermediate
Workbook

with key

Antonia Clare • JJ Wilson
Damian Williams

BBC

Pearson Education Limited
Edinburgh Gate
Harlow
Essex CM20 2JE
England
and Associated Companies throughout the world.

www.pearsonelt.com

First published 2015
This edition published 2016
ISBN: 978-1-292-14933-2

Set in Aptifer sans 10/12 pt

Photo acknowledgements
The publisher would like to thank the following for their kind permission to
reproduce their photographs:

(Key: b-bottom; c-centre; l-left; r-right; t-top)

123RF.com: 8, 9, Daniel Padavona 17/E; **Alamy Images:** AF archive 70/C, Carolyn
Clarke 15, Ian Dagnall Commercial Collection 17/F, Fotomaton 17/D, Lebrecht
Archive 17/A, Photoalto Sas 66, Pictorial Press Ltd 70/E, Alex Segre 17/C; **Corbis:**
Bettmann 24tc, Christopher Felver 72r, Peter M. Fisher 34, Gonzalo Fuentes /
Reuters 24tr, James Leynse 44cr, LGI Stock 70/B, David Moir / Reuters 43, Neal
Preston 45b, Steve Schapiro 44cl; **Fotolia.com:** Alfonso De Tomás 42/A, Kalani
42/D, Ldprod 64, Oleg 42/C, Saiko3p 60c, Touch 16, Maksym Yemelyanov 42/B,
69; **Getty Images:** Rafal Belzowski 51, Brand New Images 17/B, David Cannon
47t, Ezinigami 52, Jon Furniss 47l, Vitalii Gubin 33b, Jason LaVeris 47c, Ethan Miller
24tl, Mondadori 70/A, Han Myung-Gu 72l, Bertrand Rindoff Petroff 70/D, Jacom Stephens
6; **Imagestate Media:** John Foxx Collection. 55/3; **Reuters:** Miguel Vidal 65;
Shutterstock.com: Andrey Armyagov 42/F, Luis César Tejo 55/5, Steffen Foerster
62c, Forestpath 33c, Peter Gudella 55/6, Kamira 55/9, Michal Kowakski 68, Jakub
Krechowicz 62b, Raj Krish 55/2, Liza1979 42/E, Lucky Business 62t, Robert Palmer
55/8, David Persson 60b, Cheryl Savan 19, Smereka 55/4, Spirit Of America 59, Aleksandar
Todorovic 55/1, Mogens Trolle 55/7, Wallenrock 33t, WDG Photo 60t, Cedric Weber 18

All other images © Pearson Education

D.R. © 2008 por Pearson Educación de México, S.A. de C.V.

Avenida Antonio Dovalí Jaime #70
Torre B, Piso 6, Colonia Zedec Ed. Plaza Santa Fe
Delegación Álvaro Obregón, México, Ciudad de México, C. P. 01210

*La impresión y encuadernación se realizó en el mes de **julio del 2017**
enlos talleres de **DRUKO INTERNATIONAL S.A. de C.V.**
Calzada de chabacano #65-E, Col. Asturias, C.P. 06850, Del. Cuauhtémoc, CDdeMX.*

CONTENTS

VOCABULARY

FREE TIME

1 Match phrases 1–10 with pictures A–J.

1 go shopping _____
2 go on holiday _____
3 spend time with family _____
4 spend money _____
5 eat out _____
6 eat with friends _____
7 have time off _____
8 have a barbecue _____
9 play volleyball _____
10 play the guitar _____

A

B

C

D

E

F

G

H

I

J

GRAMMAR

QUESTION FORMS

2 Put the words in the correct order to make questions.

1 is / birthday / when / your?
When is your birthday?

2 English / time / lessons / your / start / what / do?
_____

3 friends / cook for / often / you / how / your / do?
_____

4 in / many / family / how / are / your / people?
_____

5 come / does / mother / where / your / from?
_____

6 sell / you / did / why / house / your?
_____

7 glasses / in / of / many / day / water / you / how / drink / a / do?
_____

8 is / where / the / classroom?
_____

9 your / best / see / did / friend / when / last / you?
_____

10 go / shopping / where / did / you?
_____

3 Write questions for the answers. Use the question words in the box.

~~where~~   what   why   when   who   how often
which   how many   what

1 A: *Where are you from* ?
B: I'm from Poland.

2 A: _____ ?
B: I'm a student.

3 A: _____ with?
B: I live with my friend Olga.

4 A: _____ ?
B: Only two people live in the house, Olga and me.

5 A: _____ ?
B: In our free time we like to go to the cinema or go out with friends. We both love reading, too.

6 A: _____ ?
B: We go to the cinema about once a week.

7 A: _____ ?
B: I'm studying English because I would like to work in this country.

8 A: _____ – 2A or 3A?
B: I'm in class 2A, Pre-intermediate.

9 A: _____ ?
B: I started learning English when I was at school.

READING

4 A Read the article and match headings A–F with paragraphs 1–6.

A Call a friend
B Just smile
C Do something nice for someone
D Be active
E Do that difficult job
F Plan for some future fun

MAKE YOURSELF HAPPY!

Six tips to make you happier in the next hour

You can make yourself happier starting now. In the next hour, do as many of these things as possible. Each thing you do will help you to feel happier.

1 _____ : stand up and walk around while you talk on the phone. Or go for a quick ten-minute walk outside. Doing exercise gives you energy and makes you feel better.

2 _____ : arrange to meet someone for lunch or send an email to a friend you haven't seen for a long time. Having good relationships with other people is one of the things that makes us happy, so stay in touch with your friends.

3 _____ : answer a difficult email or call to make that dentist's appointment. Do it now, don't wait. Cross something off your list of things to do, to give yourself energy.

4 _____ : order a book you want to read, plan a trip to a museum or a night out with friends. If you look forward to doing something fun in the future, it will make you feel happy right now.

5 _____ : buy someone flowers, carry their bag, tell them they look nice. Do good, feel good – this really works. If you do something nice for someone, it makes you feel better.

6 _____ : even when you don't feel happy, always try to smile. Put a smile on your face right now – it will make you feel better!

Tick things off the list when you do them. Do you feel happier yet?

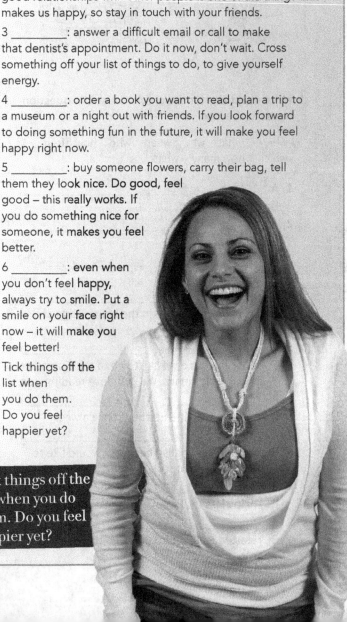

Tick things off the list when you do them. Do you feel happier yet?

B Read the article again. Are the sentences true (T) or false (F)?

1 Doing exercise makes you tired. _____
2 Having friends is an important part of being happy. _____
3 Doing a difficult job uses all your energy. _____
4 Planning fun things to do can make you feel happy. _____
5 If you do something to make someone else feel good, you will feel good yourself. _____
6 Smiling when you're not happy can make you feel bad. _____

C Read the article again and answer the questions.

1 What should you do when you talk on the phone?
_____

2 Why is it important to stay in touch with friends?
_____

3 What kinds of jobs are on a 'things to do' list?
_____

4 Why is it a good idea to organise something fun to do in the future?
_____

5 How will you feel if you buy someone flowers or carry their bag?
_____

6 What happens when you smile?
_____

D Complete the definitions with words from the article.

1 do _____ : do some kind of activity like walking or playing tennis
2 have good _____ with people: be friendly with people
3 stay in _____ with people: contact people regularly (by phone, email, etc.)
4 _____ something off a list: mark things on a list when you do them
5 look _____ to something: be excited about something which will happen in the future

VOCABULARY
RELATIONSHIPS

1 Look at the pictures and complete the story about when Harry met Sally. Use the words In the box.

| proposed   got engaged   ~~have a girlfriend~~   met |
| got married   accepted   got on well   fell in love |

1 Harry didn't
have a girlfriend.

2 He _____
Sally in a café.
They _____ .

3 They _____ .

4 He _____ to her
and she _____ .
They _____ .

5 They _____ .

GRAMMAR
PAST SIMPLE

2 A Mark the verbs in the box regular (R) or irregular (I).

| fall *I*   ask   decide   know   stop   like   go   say |
| see   spend   study   try   meet   walk   work   get |

B Write the past simple form of the irregular verbs in Exercise 2A.

3 Complete the story with the past simple form of the verbs in the box.

| become   decide   meet   send   get   propose |
| have   not tell   start   arrive   live   talk |

Many years ago, before it was fashionable to date on the internet, I [1]_____ a Swedish lady online. We [2]_____ on well from the first minute we [3]_____ chatting, and she soon [4]_____ my girlfriend. The only problem was that I [5]_____ in the UK and she was in Sweden. For a couple of years, we [6]_____ a long-distance relationship. We [7]_____ on the phone and [8]_____ emails to each other. We [9]_____ our friends how we met because we were embarrassed. After a while, I [10]_____ to leave England and move to Sweden. When I [11]_____, I [12]_____ to her and she said yes. Now, we are happily married and we have four children. I think online dating is fantastic. I met my wife because of it!

4 Complete the sentences with the past simple form of the verbs in brackets.

1 A: Where _____ (you/stay)?
B: We _____ (find) a hotel near the station.
2 We _____ (eat) in the hotel restaurant and the food _____ (be) delicious.
3 Mara and Steve _____ (not have) a barbecue on Sunday because it _____ (rain) all day.
4 We _____ (go) to the cinema, but I _____ (not like) the film. I _____ (think) it was really boring.
5 I _____ (spend) the weekend studying because I've got an exam tomorrow.
6 He _____ (be) really busy yesterday, so he _____ (not have) time to call you.
7 She _____ (write) a long letter explaining the problem, but her boyfriend still _____ (not understand).
8 They _____ (give) her some beautiful flowers for her birthday.
9 A: What time _____ (you/get) back home last night?
B: At about midnight.
10 I _____ (start) this job four years ago, when I _____ (move) to Rome.

5 A Say the words and circle the verb ending which sounds different.

1	played	stayed	tried	ended
2	asked	kissed	arrived	talked
3	finished	decided	pretended	wanted
4	studied	happened	invented	stayed
5	walked	helped	stopped	started

B ▶ 1.1 Listen and check.

LISTENING

6 A ▶ 1.2 Listen to Chris's story of how he met Amy. Number the sentences in the correct order.

a) Chris met Amy in Spain. _____

b) Chris met Amy in London. _____

c) Chris went on holiday with his friends. _____

d) They got married and had a son. _____

e) They decided to stop writing to each other. _____

f) They fell in love. _____

B Listen again and answer the questions.

1 How old was Chris when he met Amy?

_____

2 Where were they?

_____

3 What did they promise to do after the holiday?

_____

4 Why did they decide to stop writing to each other?

_____

5 When did they meet again?

_____

6 How did they feel when they saw each other?

_____

7 What's their son's name?

_____

C Read audio script 1.2 on page 41 and find words that match these meanings.

1 friends _____

2 lying in the sun _____

3 knew who somebody was when you saw them

_____

4 very surprised _____

5 spending time with someone

_____

WRITING

LINKING WORDS

7 Correct the linking words in *italics* in the sentences.

because

1 I didn't like the film ⁄ *so* it was scary.

2 We saw Pompeii *but* we thought it was wonderful.

3 She didn't like her job, *because* she decided to leave.

4 They couldn't get married *and* her father wouldn't allow it.

5 He started taekwondo lessons *but* he wanted to get fit.

6 They wanted to buy the house, *so* the bank didn't give them the money.

7 I wanted to go to the concert, *because* I couldn't find a ticket.

8 I didn't sleep very well, *but* I'm very tired today.

8 Join the sentences. Use *and, so, but* or *because*.

1 We decided to sell the car. We needed the money.

We decided to sell the car because we needed the money.

2 Jon met Ella in an online group. They got on really well.

_____

3 I didn't want to be late. I left home early.

_____

4 Matt proposed to Fiona. She said no.

_____

5 I like Clara. She can be a bit rude sometimes.

_____

6 We got married two years ago. We had a baby a year later.

_____

7 The film was terrible. They left early.

_____

8 I'm studying medicine. I want to be a doctor.

_____

VOCABULARY
CONVERSATION TOPICS

1 A Find six verbs in the puzzle.

G	O	S	S	I	P	T
D	F	A	S	N	R	K
W	E	Y	L	T	S	D
Q	H	R	T	E	L	L
W	J	E	E	R	G	T
T	T	S	A	R	I	I
H	A	V	E	U	O	U
H	L	V	G	P	S	T
R	K	S	U	T	I	L

B Complete the sentences with verbs from Exercise 1A. Use one of the verbs twice.

1 We often _____ interesting conversations in our English class.
2 You shouldn't _____ so much about people at work. It's not very nice.
3 You look sad. Shall I you _____ a joke?
4 What did your mum _____ when you got home late last night?
5 So, Judy, _____ me about your new job.
6 What did you _____ about with your sister last night?
7 Why do you always _____ me when I'm in the middle of a story? I hate that!

FUNCTION
MAKING CONVERSATION

2 Complete the conversations with the words and phrases in the box.

do you   work here   see you   did you
I'm sorry   my friend   isn't it   was terrible
would you   good weekend

1 A: Hi, Helen. This is _____ Joshua.
  B: Hi, Joshua. Pleased to meet you.
2 A: Did you have a _____?
  B: Yes, thanks. I didn't do much.
3 A: Nice day, _____?
  B: Yes, it's lovely.
4 A: So, do you _____?
  B: No, I'm just visiting.
5 A: _____ like a drink?
  B: Thanks. I'd love a glass of water.
6 A: _____ watch the film last night?
  B: Yes. It was brilliant.
7 A: Where exactly _____ come from?
  B: I'm from Bolton, near Manchester.
8 A: Sorry I'm late. I had some bad news at home.
  B: Oh, _____ to hear that.
9 A: Did you watch the match last night?
  B: Yes, it _____!
10 A: I'll see you later.
  B: Yes, _____ soon.

LEARN TO
SOUND NATURAL

3 ▶ 1.3 Listen and mark the linked words.

1 Do you like it here?
2 Where are you going?
3 I come from Italy.
4 It's a beautiful day.
5 I'm afraid I can't remember.
6 Where did you buy it?
7 I'm sorry, but I don't understand.

4 ▶ 1.4 Listen and write what you hear.

1 _____
2 _____
3 _____
4 _____
5 _____
6 _____

2)) WORK

VOCABULARY

WORK

1 Read the clues and complete the puzzle. What's the mystery word?

1 a business that makes or sells things or provides services
2 extra money a worker gets
3 everyone who works in a company
4 a job you have to do
5 a person who manages the workers
6 someone who works for a business
7 a place where many people work at desks
8 money you get regularly when you do a job

```
        1
        C  O  M  P  A  N  Y
     2
           3
           4
        5
        6
     7
        8
```

Mystery word: _____

GRAMMAR

PRESENT SIMPLE AND CONTINUOUS

2 Match the sentence halves.

1 a) I'm doing my homework, _____
   b) I do my homework _____
   i) on the bus most days.
   ii) so I can't come to the party with you.

2 a) I'm not enjoying this film – _____
   b) I don't enjoy films – _____
   i) can we watch the other DVD?
   ii) I prefer reading.

3 a) I'm looking for _____
   b) I look for _____
   i) new artists. It's an interesting job.
   ii) Maria. Have you seen her?

4 a) I'm standing _____
   b) I stand _____
   i) on the bridge every day and watch the boats.
   ii) on the bridge. I can see you!

5 a) The train is arriving _____
   b) The train arrives _____
   i) late sometimes.
   ii) in London now. See you in five minutes.

6 a) Are you using _____
   b) Do you use _____
   i) this pen? No? OK, I'll use it for a moment.
   ii) a pen and paper or do you do everything on the computer?

3 Complete the conversations with the present simple or present continuous form of the verbs in brackets.

1 A: Why _____ (you/smile)?
   B: Ahmed just told me a very funny joke!

2 A: How many people _____ (you/know) here?
   B: No one except you!

3 A: Did you hear that noise next door?
   B: Yes! What _____ they/do)?

4 A: What _____ (you/drink)?
   B: Apple juice. But I don't want any more, thanks.

5 A: _____ (he/be) an actor?
   B: No, that's his famous twin brother.

6 A: Which one is Sharon?
   B: _____ (she/wear) the blue dress.

4 A Complete the text with the present simple or present continuous form of the verbs in brackets.

❝ Here are some photos of my new friends. This is Amei. She ¹_____ (be) an artist, but at the moment she ²_____ (work) as a teacher. She ³_____ (not like) teaching very much! And this is Bruce, her husband. This is Hernan. He's from Santiago, Chile. He ⁴_____ (be) a maths teacher, but he ⁵_____ (do) his Master's in education in the USA at the moment. In the photo he ⁶_____ (smile) because he passed an exam that day! This is Julio from Colombia. He ⁷_____ (have) a job in an oil company. In the picture he ⁸_____ (play) his guitar – he's really good! The other picture is Natasha from Trinidad. She graduated last year and she ⁹_____ (look) for a job. Her parents ¹⁰_____ (visit) her at the moment. ❞

B Read the text again and label the people in the pictures.

1 _____

2 _____

3 _____

4 _____

5 _____

READING

5 A Read the article and choose the best summary.

1 how one company keeps its workers happy
2 things that companies do to motivate their workers
3 working for the world's best companies

FUN AT WORK

Are they great ideas or just crazy? Here are some ways that companies keep their employees happy.

1 **Sport can be a good way for busy workers to relax.** Wright, Newman & Fischer, a group of lawyers based in London, has a small golf course in the office. The first part of the course is on the fifth floor. When your ball drops down the ninth hole, the course continues on the fourth floor. An even more relaxing sport is bowling. Maybe this is why a company called Permatech has a complete bowling alley in the basement. The employees go bowling after work and really enjoy it.

2 **What about alternatives to boring suits and company uniforms?** One company has 'fancy-dress Fridays'. On the last Friday of every month, each department chooses a theme and the workers dress up accordingly. One department came as famous actors, with the boss dressed as Brad Pitt. Another department chose historical figures; there were three Julius Caesars and two Genghis Khans! And how about this idea from a company called LineHut, in Paris: they hold moustache-growing competitions for employees and customers! For men only, of course!

3 **Some companies like to take their employees out of the office.** Finchley Management takes its workers on a trip every year. The workers go to the airport, but they don't know what country they are flying to! Trips in the past have included Rio de Janeiro, Bangkok and the Bahamas. In another company, Wicked Shakes, the staff go on free skiing holidays. And if workers stay with the US-based Indulgence Swiss Chocolate Company for five years, they get a free trip to Switzerland to taste the chocolate!

B Read the text again and answer the questions.

1 Where exactly is the golf course at Wright, Newman & Fischer?

2 How can the employees at Permatech relax after work?

3 What are 'fancy-dress Fridays'?

4 What surprise do the employees of Finchley Management get every year?

C Find words in the article that match these meanings.

1 a place where you can go bowling (paragraph 1)

2 a room in a building that is below the level of the ground (paragraph 1)

3 other possibilities (paragraph 2)

4 clothes that everyone in a company or group wears (paragraph 2)

5 important or famous people from the past (paragraph 2)

6 a visit to a place (paragraph 3)

WRITING

AN EMAIL

6 A Underline the correct alternatives. Which email is formal? Which is informal?

> [1]*Dear/Hi* Mr Yevgeny,
> I am writing [2]*about/for* the advertisement for a hotel cleaner that I saw in Jobs Monthly. I have attached my CV.
> I look forward to [3]*hear/hearing* from you.
> [4]*Yours sincerely/Bye for now,*
> Milly Clapton

> [5]*Bye/Hi* Dave,
> [6]*It's/There's* about the party. Can you bring your laptop and some MP3s?
> [7]*See/Speak* you soon.
> [8]*Yours sincerely/Cheers,*
> Elena

B Your company has decided to have 'fancy-dress Fridays'. Write a formal email to your colleagues (50–100 words). Include the information below.

1 Say what you are writing about.
2 Explain what 'fancy-dress Fridays' are.
3 Invite ideas for fancy dress.

VOCABULARY

JOBS

1 Who's talking? Match the jobs in the box with what the people say.

~~motorcycle courier~~   sales rep   fashion designer foreign correspondent   personal trainer IT consultant   rescue worker

1 'The biggest problem in my job is the number of cars in the city.'   _motorcycle courier_

2 'I like my job because I travel the world and see important events.' _____

3 'We believe in making clothes for normal people, not only for beautiful models.' _____

4 'In my job, you need to love computers and technology.' _____

5 'In my team, we save about ten lives a year.' _____

6 'My job is easier when I like the product that I'm trying to sell.' _____

7 'I like helping people to get stronger and fitter.' _____

2 A Look at the jobs in Exercise 1 again. How many syllables does each job have? Write the job next to the number of syllables.

7 syllables: _____motorcycle courier_____

6 syllables: _____

5 syllables: _____, _____, _____

4 syllables: _____

2 syllables: _____

B Underline the stressed syllables in the words in Exercise 2A.

C ▷ 2.1 Listen and check.

3 Complete the job advertisements with the words in the box.

team   holidays   salary   ~~deal~~   with   pressure   risk

— IT CONSULTANT —

needed for six-month contract in Abu Dhabi. You will need to ¹ _deal_ with IT problems in the head office at Magran James Manufacturers. You must be good at working in a ² _____ and working under ³ _____.
Benefits: very good ⁴ _____ ($240,000, tax-free) and excellent conditions. House provided.

If you want a job with long ⁵ _____, come and speak to **Safari Travel Inc**. We are looking for qualified **safari guides**. You don't need to ⁶ _____ your life fighting lions and crocodiles, but you must know about outdoor living and be good at dealing ⁷ _____ customers.
Call the number below for more information.

0802 276 6671

GRAMMAR

ADVERBS OF FREQUENCY

4 A Underline the correct alternatives to complete the quotes.

1 'People who work sitting down _always_/never get paid more than people who work standing up.'

2 'The successful people are occasionally/usually the ones who listen more than they talk.'

3 'Politicians always/never believe what they say, so they are surprised when other people do.'

4 '_Once in a while_/Usually teachers will open a door, if you're lucky, but you have to enter alone.'

5 'Great artists like van Gogh rarely/sometimes live to see their success.'

6 'Doctors are the same as lawyers. The only difference is that lawyers rob you, but doctors rob you _and_ kill you occasionally/usually.'

7 'Find something you love doing and you'll sometimes/never have to work a day in your life.'

8 'The only place where success hardly ever/always comes before work is in the dictionary.'

B ▷ 2.2 Listen and check.

5 A What do these people think about accidents? Read the quotes and complete the sentences with the words in the box and *happen*.

~~hardly ever~~   never   rarely   often

1 'My job is really safe. In twenty years, I've only heard of one accident.' (estate agent)
Accidents _____hardly ever happen_____.

2 'Bad accidents happen once every two or three years.' (plumber)
Accidents _____.

3 'It's a very dangerous job. A lot of people die.' (fisherman)
Accidents _____.

4 'We have a completely safe job. The only danger is to your eyes from reading too much!' (university lecturer)
Accidents _____.

B What do these people think about accidents? Read the quotes and complete the sentences with the words in the box and *happen*.

once in a while   occasionally   always

1 'In ten years I've heard about one or two accidents when animals have attacked.' (vet)
Accidents _____.

2 'Danger is part of the job. When you work with guns, accidents happen every day.' (soldier)
Accidents _____.

3 'Three or four times a year there are serious accidents.' (electrician)
Accidents _____.

LISTENING

6 A Label the picture with the words in the box.

~~tour bus~~   safari guide   tourists   male elephant   pool

1 _____tour bus_____

2 _____

3 _____

4 _____

5 _____

B ▶ 2.3 Listen to two people talking about what happened in the picture. Answer the questions.

1 Who is speaking in each story?

_____

2 Why was it a frightening experience?

_____

3 What happened in the end? Was anyone injured?

_____

C Read the sentences. Are they from Story 1 or Story 2? Listen again to check.

1 I had a bus full of tourists. There were fifteen of them.   _____Story 1_____

2 There were twenty of us tourists.   _____Story 2_____

3 It was a beautiful, clear evening and about seven o'clock we saw some elephants.   _____

4 One evening, at about six o'clock, we went for a drive in the tour bus.   _____

5 I told the tourists to walk very slowly back to the bus.   _____

6 [He] told us to run back to the bus as fast as possible.   _____

D Circle the correct meaning for the phrases in bold.

1 They could **get off the bus**.
   a) stay on the bus
   b) leave the bus

2 The elephant **charged at us**.
   a) ran at us very fast
   b) looked at us and made a loud noise

3 The tourists were **screaming**.
   a) making a loud noise because they were frightened
   b) getting angry

4 I started driving **as fast as possible**.
   a) not very quickly
   b) very quickly

E Read audio script 2.3 on page 41 and check your answers.

13

FUNCTION

EXPRESSING LIKES/DISLIKES

1 A Complete the sentences with the words in the box.

don't	on	absolutely	can't
very	love	mind	keen

1 I'm very _____ on cooking and I _____ love great food.

2 I _____ riding my motorbike. I _____ stand sitting in an office all day.

3 I'm quite keen _____ technology and I don't _____ dealing with other people's computer problems.

4 I'm _____ keen on working with money and I _____ like people wasting it on stupid things.

B ▶ 2.4 Listen and check.

C Match jobs a)–d) with sentences 1–4 in Exercise 1A.

a) accountant _____
b) chef _____
c) IT consultant _____
d) motorcycle courier _____

2 A Put the words in the correct order to make sentences.

1 like / team / you / a / do / in / working?
_____

2 working / can't / pressure / I / stand / under
_____

3 my / not / I'm / very / on / boss / keen
_____

4 colleagues / don't / my / like / I
_____

5 dealing / don't / customers / I / mind / with
_____

6 keen / sport / you / on / are?
_____

B Match responses a)–f) with sentences 1–6 in Exercise 2A.

a) Why? What's wrong with her? _____
b) I'm not surprised. They don't seem very friendly. _____
c) That's good because it's important for a sales assistant. _____
d) I love it, especially football. _____
e) Why? Do you get stressed? _____
f) Yes, I do. Actually, I hate working alone. _____

VOCABULARY

TYPES OF WORK

3 Match sentences 1–8 with types of work A–H.

1 I deal with the money that goes in and out of the company.   _A_
2 I prepare fresh sandwiches for our customers. _____
3 I design clothes. _____
4 I teach teenagers maths and science. _____
5 I organise advertising for the company's products and speak to customers. _____
6 I show people all the best places to visit and things to do in my city. _____
7 I act in films and in the theatre. _____
8 I work in a shop, selling products to our customers. _____

A works in accounts   **B** works in retail

C works in education   **D** works in sales and marketing

E works in the fashion industry

F works in the entertainment industry

G works in the tourist industry

H works in the food industry

LEARN TO

RESPOND AND ASK MORE QUESTIONS

4 A Complete the words in the conversations.

Conversation 1

A: On Saturday I went to a conference about the Z-phone, this amazing new technology.

B: ¹R_ _ _lly? I read about that last week. It ²s_ _ _nds _nt_ _r_ _st_ng.

A: Well, everybody's talking about it.

B: ³_ _nd wh_t _ _b_ _ _t the cost?

A: Oh, I don't know. I had to leave before they discussed that.

Conversation 2

A: Today I was offered a job as a babysitter.

B: ⁴Th_t's gr_ _ _t!

A: Not really. They only offered me five pounds an hour.

B: Oh, I ⁵s_ _ _. So did you accept the job?

A: No. I'm going to look for something better.

B: ⁶R_ ght. What did you tell them?

A: I said, 'Dad, I know the baby is my sister, but I want a better salary!'

B ▶ 2.5 Listen and check.

C ▶ 2.6 Listen and repeat B's responses. Notice the intonation. Copy the intonation to sound interested.

VOCABULARY

TIME OUT

1 Complete the sentences with verbs.

1 I'm going to ___*see*___ a jazz band tonight. My sister says they're really good.

2 I usually _____ the bus to work because it's easy and it's cheap.

3 We like to _____ to a museum at the weekend. You can learn new things and it's better than watching television.

4 Did you _____ the photographic exhibition in the Sainsbury Centre? It was brilliant.

5 I'm really hungry. Can we stop and _____ a snack from this café?

6 We're going to _____ a drink in the bar later. Do you want to meet us there?

7 I really want to _____ dancing. I haven't been for ages!

8 Why don't we _____ sightseeing? We can spend the whole day walking around the city.

9 Where do you want to _____ dinner? There's a nice restaurant around the corner.

GRAMMAR

PRESENT CONTINUOUS/*BE GOING TO* FOR FUTURE

2 A Put the words in the correct order to make questions.

1 going / holiday / are / you / away / year / this / on?
_____

2 is / dinner / evening / who / your / cooking / this?
_____

3 are / going / to / dentist / when / the / you?
_____

4 weekend / are / this / doing / you / what?
_____

5 play / are / sport / you / to / this / any / going / week?
_____

6 you / marry / are / to / going / Roberto?
_____

7 what / meeting / you / time / your / are / sister?
_____

8 are / to / English / do / your / what / improve / going / you / to?
_____

9 you / a / the / are / party / at / weekend / having?
_____

10 gym / work / are / to / the / you / after / going?
_____

B Match answers a)–j) with questions 1–10 in Exercise 2A.

a) Nobody. I'm just going to eat some salad and fruit. ___*2*___

b) Six o'clock. We're going out for a meal. _____

c) Yes, we're getting married in the summer. _____

d) I'm going to read as much as possible in English. _____

e) Next Tuesday – in the morning. _____

f) No. I'm going to Greece next summer, but I'm not going anywhere this year. _____

g) Yes, I'm playing tennis with Jim on Friday. _____

h) Some friends are coming to stay, so we're taking them up to the mountains. _____

i) No, I'm going out for dinner. _____

j) Yes, do you want to come? _____

3 Complete the conversations with the phrases in the box.

are you coming   going to look for   are you going
'm speaking   are you doing   're going
are meeting   'm staying

1 A: Hi, Boris. What _____ later?
   B: Nothing much. I _____ at home tonight.

2 A: What are your plans for the summer?
   B: I'm _____ a job.

3 A: Have you seen Anita?
   B: No, but I _____ to her later.

4 A: When does your brother arrive?
   B: My parents _____ him at the station at 6.30p.m.

5 A: _____ to the party on Saturday?
   B: I'm not sure. I haven't been invited.

6 A: Where _____ for your holiday?
   B: We _____ cycling in the Netherlands.

THREE THINGS TO DO IN ... NEW YORK

There are so many things to see and do in New York, sometimes it's difficult to know where to start. In this week's guide, we look at three things you can't miss when you visit the city.

Start by spending some time in Central Park. With over 25,000 trees and lots of different types of birds, it's easy to forget you're in a big city. Relax and enjoy the fresh air or go for a tour in a horse and carriage. In summer you can go out on the lake in a boat or kayak, and in winter you can go ice-skating! After all that activity you'll be hungry, so have lunch at the famous Tavern on the Green. Great concerts take place in Central Park, too. Every year the New York Philharmonic Orchestra gives a free open-air concert and there's also the New York Shakespeare Festival at the theatre in the park.

They say that Paris has the Eiffel Tower, London has the London Eye and New York has the Empire State Building. But many people think the best views of the city are from the 'Top of the Rock' – the top floor of the GE (General Electric) building, a skyscraper in the middle of the city. At 260 metres high, it's the fourteenth tallest building in New York, and from the top you can have a fantastic view of the city.

Many people visit the famous Statue of Liberty by ferry, but also on the way is the Immigration Museum on Ellis Island. This was the place where people first arrived from 1892 to 1954, many after a long and difficult journey from other countries. Most of the island is closed to the general public, but you can visit the museum and find out about the many people who arrived here. You can also go on a tour with a guide to visit some of the old, unused buildings on the island. A very interesting day out for everyone.

READING

4 A Read the article and complete the sentences with a name or a number.

1 There are more than _____ trees in Central Park.

2 The famous restaurant in Central Park is called the _____.

3 Every year, the New York _____ Festival has plays in the park.

4 The top floor of the GE building is called the '_____'.

5 On Ellis island you can visit the _____ Museum.

6 People from other countries started arriving on Ellis Island in _____.

B Read the article again and answer the questions.

1 Why is it 'easy to forget you're in a big city' when you visit Central Park?

_____

2 What can you do in Central Park in winter?

_____

3 What is the GE building?

_____

4 How do you get to Ellis Island and the Statue of Liberty?

_____

5 What else, apart from the museum, can you visit on Ellis island?

_____

WRITING

INVITATIONS

5 Find and correct eight grammatical mistakes in the messages.

> Hi Mike,
> *I'm playing*
> ~~I play~~ football later with a few of the boys from work. Would you like to coming?
> Dan

> Dan,
> I'm sorry, but I busy tonight. I take Leila out for a meal. Wish me luck!
> Thanks anyway.
> Mike

> Hi guys,
> A few of us is going out for a curry on Friday night. Do you want come with us? We're meet at the Indian Tree at 8p.m.
> Emma

> Hi Emma,
> I love to. See you there.
> Jan

6 A Complete the invitations using the prompts.

> 1 _____
> (I / have / party) at my house on Saturday.
> 2 _____
> (you / want / come)?
> 3 _____
> (we / go / have / music) and plenty of food. Bring your friends too. Just let me know.
> Kristoph

> 4 _____
> (Julie / get / tickets / for / theatre) next Wednesday.
> 5 _____
> (we go / see / Shakespeare's *Hamlet*).
> 6 _____
> (would / like / come)? The tickets are £17.50.
> Becca

B Write your own answers to the emails in Exercise 6A, explaining why you would like to/can't come. Write 50–100 words.

VOCABULARY

PLACES TO VISIT

1 A Match 1–8 with a)–h) to make compound nouns. Then write them in the spaces below. Which compound nouns are two words? Which are one word?

1 night	a) field
2 shopping	b) front
3 water	c) hall
4 nature	d) club
5 concert	e) trail
6 street	f) side
7 sports	g) market
8 country	h) mall

1 _____   5 _____

2 _____   6 _____

3 _____   7 _____

4 _____   8 _____

B Match the photos with words from Exercise 1A.

LISTENING

2 A Look at the picture. What do you think the other man says?

What do you think, Terry?

B ▶ 3.1 Listen to the conversation. Are the sentences true (T) or false (F)?

1 Terry doesn't like the painting. _____

2 The painting is black and white. _____

3 David thinks you don't always have to understand art. _____

4 The painting was expensive. _____

5 Terry thinks he can paint it in five days. _____

6 Mary will be back in five minutes. _____

C Listen again. What are the answers to Terry's questions?

1 How much did the painting cost?

_____

2 Has Mary seen the painting?

_____

3 Does Mary like modern art?

_____

D Read audio script 3.1 on page 42 and find words that match these meanings.

1 very bad

_____

2 everywhere (2 words)

_____

3 an idea in a film, painting, etc. that someone is trying to tell people about

_____

4 a person who paints pictures

_____

5 not here

_____

6 something you don't expect

_____

GRAMMAR
QUESTIONS WITHOUT AUXILIARIES

3 A Complete the questions with the phrases in the box.

Who invented	Who earned	How many	Who uses
Which French	Which city	Who spends	
What country	Which painting	Which Caribbean	

1 _____ makes the most films every year?

2 _____ the World Wide Web?

3 _____ by van Gogh cost more: *Sunflowers* or *Portrait of Dr Gachet*?

4 _____ country invented the modern version of the dance called salsa?

5 _____ museum appears in the novel *The Da Vinci Code*?

6 _____ more time outdoors: people in New Zealand or people in Canada?

7 _____ people visit the Eiffel Tower every year?

8 _____ the internet more: Canadians or Americans?

9 _____ $1 million for each episode of *The Big Bang Theory* in 2014?

10 _____ has the most famous carnival every year?

B Match answers a)–j) with questions 1–10 in Exercise 3A.

a) the Louvre _____

b) Canadians _____

c) *Portrait of Dr Gachet* _____

d) Cuba _____

e) nearly seven million _____

f) Jim Parsons, for his role as Sheldon Cooper _____

g) Tim Berners-Lee _____

h) people in New Zealand _____

i) India _____

j) Rio de Janeiro _____

4 Write questions for the underlined answers. Start with *who*, *what*, *whose* or *how many*.

1 <u>Larry Page and Sergey Brin</u> started Google in the late 1990s.
   Who started Google in the late 1990s?

2 <u>Dr James Naismith</u> invented basketball in 1891.
   _____
   _____

3 Canadians spend <u>over forty hours</u> a month online.
   _____
   _____

4 <u>Charles Miller</u> brought football to Brazil from England in the nineteenth century.
   _____
   _____

5 <u>Jerry Seinfeld's</u> sitcom is one of the most successful TV shows of all time.
   _____
   _____

6 <u>Iepe Rubingh</u> first developed the sport of chess boxing in the 1990s.
   _____
   _____

7 <u>Germany</u> won the World Cup in 2014.
   _____
   _____

8 <u>The Carcross Desert</u> in Canada is the smallest desert in the world.
   _____
   _____

9 <u>Elvis Presley's</u> daughter is called Lisa Marie.
   _____
   _____

10 <u>Nearly seven million people</u> visit the British Museum every year.
   _____
   _____

VOCABULARY
COLLOCATIONS

1 A Find seven verbs in the puzzle.

A	R	R	A	N	G	E	V
C	A	N	C	E	L	M	O
H	B	Y	H	A	V	E	D
A	O	E	E	I	G	P	I
N	O	S	C	L	F	N	T
G	K	T	K	P	E	L	A
E	R	O	O	C	T	K	L
T	M	F	A	E	S	R	K

B There is a verb missing in each sentence. Complete the sentences with verbs from Exercise 1A.

arrange

1 Did you ⱦ to meet friends? If you didn't, we can meet later.
2 She called me because she wanted to a chat.
3 Please a table for us at the Blue Fin Restaurant tonight.
4 There's been a problem and I can't attend, so I'm calling to my reservation.
5 Don't forget to the train times before you leave for the station.
6 I'd like to come to the 4.30 performance, not the 6.30 one, and I'm calling to my ticket.
7 The manager of Triad Books is on the phone. He wants to business.

FUNCTION
MAKING A PHONE CALL

2 Match the sentence halves.

1 Who's
2 Hello, this
3 Can I speak
4 Can I
5 I'm afraid she's
6 I'll ask her
7 Thanks for

a) calling.
b) to call you back.
c) leave a message?
d) is John.
e) calling?
f) not here at the moment.
g) to Alexandra, please?

3 Find and correct four mistakes in the conversation.

A: Hello. I'm Jim. Is Trudy there?
B: I'm afraid but she's not here at the moment.
A: Oh really? Can I leave the message?
B: Of course.
A: Can you tell her that we need to discuss the party on Friday?
B: Yes, I will. I'll ask her for calling you back.
A: Thanks a lot.
B: You're welcome. Bye.
A: Bye.

4 Number the sentences in the correct order to make a phone conversation.

a) Yes. I'm going to be twenty minutes late. ____
b) Thank you very much. See you soon. ____
c) One moment. Who's calling please? ____
d) Hello. Can I speak to Kim? ____
e) Thanks for calling. Bye. ____
f) Good morning. Craven Beauty Parlour. Beverley speaking. ____
g) No problem. I'll tell her. ____
h) It's Liz Holder here. ____
i) Hi, Liz. Oh, I'm afraid Kim's at lunch. Is it about today's appointment? ____
j) Bye. _10_

LEARN TO
MANAGE PHONE PROBLEMS

5 Put the words in the correct order to complete the questions.

1 **A:** Hi, I'm waiting for a delivery of fifteen chocolate rabbits. Have you sent them yet?
   B: One moment. _____? (name, / the / please / what's)
2 **A:** Hello, this is Hillary Kenton, calling from Newark.
   B: Sorry, _____. (catch / that / didn't / I) Did you say Hillary Clinton from New York?
3 **A:** Hello, my name is Aloysius Venoziak Menkovsky.
   B: _____? (repeat / you / can / that)
4 **A:** Hi, um … I'm … um … waiting for a … er … a package from Dublin.
   B: Sorry, _____? (speak / you / up, / can / please)
5 **A:** Hello. I'd like to order two Pentium Bidmark 6.40 large photocopiers, three Ribdale Energy Star fax machines, five Rubicon Jump Drives, and …
   B: Sorry, _____? (down, / slow / you / can / please)

LISTENING

6 ▶ 3.2 Listen to three phone conversations and complete the notes.

1 Pauline calling. No _____ for the concert. Call back tonight _____

2 Elise called. Meet her at the _____ at _____

3 Roundhouse Bar and Grill doesn't take _____ Come before _____

GRAMMAR QUESTION FORMS

1 A Complete the questions with a question word or an auxiliary verb.

1 When _____does_____ the film start?
2 _____ often do you see your grandmother?
3 _____ are my keys? I can't find them.
4 _____ you enjoy watching films?
5 _____ you know Sabina? She's my best friend.
6 _____ do you usually go on holiday?
7 _____ many hours do you work?
8 _____ time did you get here? I'm sorry I'm late.

B Match answers a)–h) with questions 1–8 in Exercise 1A.

a) About five minutes ago. Don't worry, it's no problem. _____
b) No, I don't. Hi, Sabina. _____
c) Once or twice a year. _____
d) We usually go to Spain. My aunt has a house there. _____
e) Here they are. They were on the television! _____
f) Yes, I do. But I don't like horror films. _____
g) Usually about thirty-five hours a week. _____
h) In half an hour. _____

VOCABULARY PHRASES WITH GET, GO, HAVE, SPEND

2 A Write the words in the box in the correct column.

married children money on clothes a barbecue
time off work the bus time with family on well
on holiday to the cinema sightseeing

get	go	have	spend
married			

B Which phrases from Exercise 2A would you use for situations 1–7?

1 You meet someone you like and want to spend your life together. _____get married_____
2 You travel home on public transport.
_____
3 You visit your mother every day.
_____
4 You do this to watch a film.
_____
5 You eat in the garden and the food is cooked over a fire. _____
6 You have a good relationship with someone.
_____
7 You visit the places tourists see in a city.
_____

GRAMMAR PAST SIMPLE

3 Complete the article with the past simple form of the verbs in brackets.

ANGRY MOTHER PUNISHES SIXTY-ONE-YEAR-OLD SON

An angry mother [1] _____ (take) the house keys and money away from her sixty-one-year-old son because he [2] _____ (stay) out late at night and [3] _____ (not tell) her where he planned to go when he [4] _____ (go out). The mother, who is eighty-one years old, even went to the police in Caltagione, Italy, the town where she lives. She [5] _____ (ask) the police to tell her son that he should 'grow up' and behave in a better way towards his mother.

The son [6] _____ (complain) that it was his mother who [7] _____ (be) the problem. 'It's not my fault,' he [8] _____ (tell) reporters. 'She always treats me badly. And her cooking is really awful!'

A policeman [9] _____ (talk) to the mother and the son, and they finally [10] _____ (decide) to go home together.

FUNCTION MAKING CONVERSATION

4 A Complete the words in the conversations.

1 **A:** Hello. My name's Felipe. It's n _i c e_ to meet you.
  B: Hi, I'm Magda. Nice to meet you, t__ __.
2 **A:** Nice day, i__ __'t it?
  B: Yes, it's l_v_ly.
3 **A:** S__, where exactly do you c__m__ from?
  B: Zaragoza. It's a small c__ty in Northern Spain.
4 **A:** Did you have a g__ __d w__ __k__ __d?
  B: Yes, it was OK. I didn't d__ m__ch.
5 **A:** So, w__ __ __ __d you l_k__ a dr__ __k?
  B: Yes, I'd l_v_ a glass of w_t_r.
6 **A:** I'll s__ __ you l_t_r.
  B: S__ __ you s__ __ n.

B ▶ R1.1 Listen and check.

GRAMMAR PRESENT SIMPLE AND CONTINUOUS

5 Find and correct the mistakes in the sentences.

don't like
1 I ∧ am not liking fish.
2 I stay with some friends for a few days so I can look for somewhere to live.
3 I'm not knowing what time the lesson starts.
4 They spend time with their family in Germany at the moment.
5 We're usually going out for a pizza about once a week.
6 I'm not understanding where Ian is. He never arrives late.
7 Do you watch this programme, or can I watch the football on the other channel?

GRAMMAR ADVERBS OF FREQUENCY

6 The words in bold are in the wrong place in the sentences. Correct the sentences.

1 We come (always) here. It's the best club in the area.
2 **Hardly ever** I see her because she works for a different company.
3 My **occasionally** parents help us when we're busy.
4 I get up at **usually** about 6.30a.m.
5 Sal's very upset – she wants to see him **never** again.
6 We go to **once in a while** Scotland.
7 **Rarely** I have the chance to spend time with my sister.
8 I take the children **every day** to school.

FUNCTION LIKES/DISLIKES

7 Complete the second sentence so that it has the same meaning as the first sentence. Use the words in brackets.

1 I don't enjoy getting up early. (not very keen)
   I _____'m not very keen on_____ getting up early.
2 I like punk music very much. (absolutely)
   I _____ punk music.
3 I hate sales reps who try to sell me products on the telephone (stand)
   I _____ sales reps who try to sell me products on the telephone.
4 Marjorie isn't very keen on doing housework. (like)
   Marjorie _____ doing housework.
5 I'm quite happy to do physical jobs. (mind)
   I _____ doing physical jobs.
6 John really doesn't like eating spicy food. (hate)
   John _____ eating spicy food.
7 I'm happy working in a team. (like)
   I _____ in a team.
8 I enjoy walking in the countryside. (keen)
   I _____ walking in the countryside.

GRAMMAR PRESENT CONTINUOUS/*BE GOING TO* FOR FUTURE

8 Underline the correct alternatives.

1 *I'm going/I going to go* shopping later. Do you want to come?
2 My sister *is/is going to* having a party on Friday, but I don't know what to wear.
3 He *starting/'s going to start* karate lessons in January.
4 So, *are you/are you going to* staying with your parents for the weekend?
5 I'm not *coming/going to coming* to the lesson this evening.
6 *We're/We're going to* flying to Italy on 19 December.

VOCABULARY WORK; TIME OUT

9 Complete the words in the sentences.

1 Pete gets a good s__l__ry, but he doesn't like his b__ss.
2 I love going s__ghts__ _ _ __ng when I'm on holiday.
3 We w__rk under a lot of pr__ss__re in the busy months.
4 There were some wonderful photographs in the exh__b__t__ __n.
5 The best thing about the job is that I g__t very l__ng h__l__d__ys.
6 We bought this painting from that new __rt g__ll__r__ in West Street.
7 I love their music and I really wanted to go to their c__nc__rt, but I didn't have enough money for the t__ck__t.
8 I enjoy my job because I can always find an interesting t__sk to do.

GRAMMAR QUESTIONS WITH/WITHOUT AUXILIARIES

10 A The auxiliary verb is missing in eight of the questions. Add the missing auxiliary where necessary.

       is
1 Who ⋀ your teacher?
2 Where you come from?
3 Who forgot to bring the keys?
4 Why David leave his job?
5 How often you play football?
6 How much it cost to fly to Russia?
7 Which class won the competition?
8 Who wrote *The Jungle Book*?
9 When you last go to a concert?
10 Whose bag is that?
11 Why you learning English?
12 Where you buy that coat?

B Match answers a)–l) with questions 1–12 in Exercise 10A.

a) Our class did. We won the competition! _____
b) About €300. _____
c) It's mine. Sorry, I left it there. _____
d) I come from Argentina. _____
e) I want to study in the USA. _____
f) Zavier. He always forgets things. _____
g) I play once or twice a week. _____
h) He didn't like his boss. _____
i) Two months ago. I saw a really good jazz trio. _____
j) Rudyard Kipling. _____
k) I bought it in Toronto last year. _____
l) Her name's Mrs Taylor. _____

CHECK

Circle the correct option to complete the sentences.

1 What _____ the time?
   a) be **b)** 's **c)** are

2 When _____ start work?
   a) do you **b)** are you **c)** you do

3 They _____ married in 2013.
   a) get **b)** are getting **c)** got

4 I _____ €100 on these boots and they're broken.
   a) spend **b)** spent **c)** paid

5 Why _____ you sad? Is there a problem?
   a) do **b)** is **c)** are

6 We _____ in love the first time we saw each other.
   a) fell **b)** felt **c)** fall

7 When _____ to the UK?
   a) moved you **b)** did you move **c)** did you moved

8 She _____ and walked away.
   a) smile **b)** smiled **c)** smiles

9 When I _____ college, I started looking for a job.
   a) leave **b)** am leaving **c)** left

10 Did you _____ a good weekend?
   a) have **b)** get **c)** like

11 Where _____ do you come from?
   a) absolutely **b)** really **c)** exactly

12 I usually _____ to Helen when I have a problem.
   a) am talking **b)** talk **c)** talked

13 We like to keep our prices low. This makes our _____ happy.
   a) customers **b)** employee **c)** staff

14 I'm looking for a job with a higher _____.
   a) boss **b)** salary **c)** task

15 At the moment I _____ a book about a young boy in Afghanistan.
   a) 'm reading **b)** read **c)** going to read

16 I can't _____ computer games. I really hate them.
   a) hate **b)** stand **c)** keen

17 It's important to _____ good relationships with the other employees.
   a) get **b)** make **c)** have

18 I look forward to _____ from you.
   a) hearing **b)** heard **c)** hear

19 It's a dangerous job: you _____ your life every day.
   a) work **b)** deal with **c)** risk

20 We _____ a lot of different problems.
   a) work **b)** deal with **c)** risk

21 I'm not very keen _____ violent films.
   a) of **b)** about **c)** on

22 Eve _____ to Australia next month.
   a) is going **b)** went **c)** go

23 I _____ dinner tonight. I'm just going to have a snack.
   a) don't have **b)** 'm not having **c)** don't having

24 _____ to come out on Saturday night?
   a) Do you like **b)** Would you like **c)** Are you liking

25 I'm afraid Ella isn't here at the moment. Can I _____ a message?
   a) make **b)** give **c)** take

26 I bought these souvenirs at a _____ market in Greece.
   a) street **b)** shopping **c)** nature

27 We can't go to the restaurant, so we'll have to _____ our reservation.
   a) arrange **b)** book **c)** cancel

28 Hello. Petra _____. Can I help you?
   a) is speaking **b)** speaking **c)** I'm speaking

29 Hi, Mike. Pleased _____ you. I'm Nia.
   a) of meeting **b)** I met **c)** to meet

30 What are your plans for the weekend? _____ anything nice?
   a) Are you doing **b)** Did you do **c)** Do you do

RESULT _____ /30

VOCABULARY:
MAKE AND DO

1 A Complete the phrases with *make* or *do*.

1 _____ a speech
2 _____ well/badly
3 _____ a project
4 _____ a phone call
5 _____ business
6 _____ a decision
7 _____ my homework
8 _____ a meal

B Write answers beginning with *I made* or *I did*. Use the words in brackets.

1 How did you lose weight? (decision)
I made a decision to start eating healthily.

2 How did you contact her? (phone)
_____

3 How do you know Ben Garmin? (business)
_____

4 I heard the restaurant was closed, so what did you do? (meal)
_____

5 What type of work did you do at school today? (project)
_____

6 What did you do in the library after school? (homework)
_____

7 How did the Public Speaking conference finish? (speech)
_____

8 How was the singing competition? (well)
_____

GRAMMAR:
PRESENT PERFECT + *EVER/NEVER*

2 Complete the sentences with the present perfect form of the verbs in brackets.

1 I _____*'ve never been*_____ (never / be) on TV.
2 _____ (you / ever / sing) to an audience?
3 Sheena and Rick _____ (never / travel) by train.
4 My granddad _____ (never / use) a computer.
5 _____ (she / ever / make) a speech?
6 _____ (you / ever / lie) to your best friend?
8 Lisa _____ (never / eat) octopus.
7 _____ (you / ever / win) a competition?

3 Circle the correct sentence in each pair.

1 a) I've first played the guitar when I was a teenager.
  b) I first played the guitar when I was a teenager.
2 a) When you worked in Hollywood, have you ever met anyone famous?
  b) When you worked in Hollywood, did you ever meet anyone famous?
3 a) Have you ever eaten sushi? Try some!
  b) Did you ever eat sushi? Try some!
4 a) Last night I read until 2a.m.
  b) Last night I've read until 2a.m.
5 a) Did you ever see the film *No Country for Old Men*? I have the DVD.
  b) Have you ever seen the film *No Country for Old Men*? I have the DVD.
6 a) In 1989 the government did something that changed the world.
  b) In 1989 the government has done something that changed the world.
7 a) She has never been to the theatre.
  b) She has ever been to the theatre.
8 a) I've ever worked in retail in my life.
  b) I've never worked in retail in my life.

4 Underline the correct alternatives.

Hi Janine,

I [1]*was/'ve been* here for a week now and already I [2]*made/'ve made* lots of friends. I share a room with a man called Don. Yesterday he asked me, [3]'*Did you ever spend/Have you ever spent* time in a place like this?' I told him, 'I [4]*went/have been* camping when I was ten.' He [5]*laughed/has laughed*! He [6]*spent/has spent* half his life here!

There are lots of things to do: there's a gym, a cinema, a library and a few clubs. I [7]*didn't have/haven't had* time to join any clubs yet, but this afternoon we [8]*watched/have watched* a film in the cinema.

The only bad thing is the food. I [9]*didn't ever eat/'ve never eaten* such terrible food before in my whole life!

Best wishes,

Bob

MORE THAN A HOBBY

Gordon Ramsay   Winston Churchill   Woody Allen

1 When Wallace Stevens walked into his office every morning, his colleagues didn't know about his secret: Stevens lived a double life. By day he worked for an insurance company. The rest of his life was spent becoming one of the greatest American poets of the twentieth century.

2 Secret talent is more common than we think, even with people who are already famous in one area. Take Luciano Pavarotti, who was one of the world's greatest classical singers. Not many people know that before he became a singer, he was an outstanding football player. The same is true of TV chef Gordon Ramsay, who is now well-known for his brilliant cooking and his bad language. Ramsay played professional football for Glasgow Rangers, one of Scotland's best teams.

3 A number of politicians first made their name in other jobs. Most people know that Arnold Schwarzenegger had a very successful acting career before becoming Governor of California. Winston Churchill, prime minister of Great Britain, also had another talent: he wrote great history books. Churchill's books won him the Nobel Prize in Literature in 1953. Václav Havel, who was the first president of the Czech Republic, was also a great writer.

4 There are also musicians and actors who have secret talents. Paul McCartney and David Bowie are both painters, Paul Newman was a racing car driver and actor Colin Farrell is a professional line dancer. And only those who go to a little hotel bar in New York City every Monday would know that one of the best clarinet players in town is actor and film director Woody Allen. He certainly plays the clarinet better than Bill Clinton plays the saxophone!

READING

5 A Do you recognise any of the people in the photos? Why are they famous? What else are/were they good at? Read the article to find out.

B Read the article again. Are the sentences true (T) or false (F)?

1 The people in the text are famous for one thing, but also good at another thing. _____
2 Wallace Stevens' colleagues didn't know he was a poet. _____
3 Gordon Ramsay was a chef before he became a famous footballer. _____
4 Churchill and Havel were both actors and politicians. _____
5 Woody Allen plays the clarinet and the saxophone. _____

C Circle the correct meaning for the words and phrases from the text.

1 lived a double life (paragraph 1)
   a) had two very different lifestyles
   b) had a difficult life
2 the same is true of (paragraph 2)
   a) this situation is very different from
   b) this situation is very similar to
3 bad language (paragraph 2)
   a) speaking badly about another person
   b) saying bad words
4 made their name (paragraph 3)
   a) became famous
   b) learnt to do something

WRITING

CORRECTING MISTAKES

6 Find and correct nine mistakes in the text: three grammar (gr), three spelling (sp) and three punctuation (p).

THE GREATEST MIND IN FICTION

belong (gr)

Most of fiction's great minds ~~belongs~~ ⟨ either to criminals or to the men and women who catch them. A greatest of these is probably Sherlock Holmes. The Holmes stories were written by Sir Arthur Conan Doyle a docter from edinburgh, Scotland. Conan Doyle knew a lot about the human body and pollice work, and he has used this information in his books. Very quickly, Conan Doyle's hero beccame popular. When Holmes was killed in one story, thousands of readers protested. Conan Doyle changed his mind, and Holmes appeared in another story

VOCABULARY
EDUCATION

1 Read the clues and complete the crossword.

Crossword grid with 1 ACROSS answer **MAKE** filled in.

Across

1 One of the best things about going to university is that you ___make___ a lot of new friends.

4 On Friday, we have to do a _____, so I need to learn the vocabulary.

7 I'd love to play the _____, but our flat is too small to have one – so I play the guitar instead!

8 At my school we play a lot of _____. It keeps us fit.

10 I don't study _____ very often because I don't have internet access at home.

11 I have to _____ an exam at the end of the year.

Down

1 I don't like speaking French because I make a lot of _____.

2 At the end of the year all the students give a _____.

3 When you _____ art, you learn about painters like Picasso and Salvador Dalí.

5 I'd like to study foreign _____ like Russian and Spanish.

6 At school we didn't have to wear a _____. We wore our own clothes.

9 Every week we _____ games like tennis or netball.

GRAMMAR
CAN, HAVE TO, MUST

2 Read the advertisements and complete the conversations with *can, can't, have to* or *don't have to*.

> ### LEARN TO PLAY MUSIC – BEGINNERS' CLASS
> Always wanted to play the drums? Or the guitar? Want to try the piano? Come and join us for fun music lessons. Try any instrument you want, and we'll help you learn to play. No previous experience necessary. We supply the instruments, so you don't need to bring your own. Children and adults welcome.

Conversation 1

Susan: Hi. I'd like to come to the beginners' music class. Do I [1] ___have to___ be able to play an instrument?

Teacher: No, you [2] _____ play an instrument. You [3] _____ choose your instrument here, and we'll help you to learn.

Susan: [4] _____ I come to a lesson first to see if I like it?

Teacher: Well, I'm afraid you [5] _____ come to the lessons unless you sign up for the whole course.

Susan: OK.[6] _____ I bring children?

Teacher: Yes, you [7] _____. Children love it.

Susan: Do I [8] _____ bring my own instrument?

Teacher: No, we have instruments here you [9] _____ use.

> ### Join our Arabic language and culture course
> Full price: £180   Reduced rates for students: £130
> Just come along to the first class. No need to register first, just bring an enrolment form with you. Pay after the class if you wish to enrol.

Conversation 2

Student: I'm a student. How much do I [1] _____ pay?

Secretary: It's a reduced rate, so you only [2] _____ pay £130.

Student: Do I [3] _____ register first?

Secretary: No, you [4] _____ to register. You [5] _____ come along to the first class. If you like the class, you [6] _____ complete the form at the end of the lesson.

Student: [7] _____ I pay by cheque?

Secretary: Yes, you [8] _____ pay by card or cheque on the night.

3 A ▶ 4.1 Listen and complete the sentences.

1 How much _____ pay?

2 _____ park here?

3 _____ visit her before we leave.

4 _____ stay in this hotel.

5 _____ wear that!

6 _____ tell anyone.

B Practise saying the sentences.

4 A Rewrite the sentences. Replace the underlined words with phrases with *can/can't*.

1 You <u>are not allowed to</u> have your mobile phone switched on.
2 You have to register before <u>it's possible to</u> use the site.
3 I'm afraid <u>it isn't possible for her to</u> speak to you at the moment.
4 <u>It's OK to</u> use my computer if you want to.

B Rewrite the sentences. Replace the underlined words with phrases with *have to/don't have to* or *must/mustn't*. There may be more than one possible answer.

1 <u>It's necessary to</u> be good at foreign languages if you want to learn Mandarin.
2 <u>It's important to</u> be there on time or they won't let us in.
3 <u>It isn't necessary for us to</u> have a licence to fish here.
4 <u>It's important that you don't</u> tell him I'm here.

5 Look at the exam rules and complete the conversation with *can/can't, have to/don't have to* or *must/mustn't*. There may be more than one possible answer.

EXAM RULES

mobile phones	✗
talk to other students	✗
arrive on time	✓
eat/drink in the examination room	✗ (but water OK)
have a dictionary	✓

Teacher: Are there any questions?
Dan: Yes. ¹____*Can*____ we bring our mobile phones into the room?
Teacher: No, you ²_____. You ³_____ turn them off and leave them outside in your bag.
Julie: Is it OK to eat during the exam?
Teacher: No. You ⁴_____ have a bottle of water, but you ⁵_____ have anything else to eat or drink.
Marco: Do we ⁶_____ leave our dictionaries in our bags?
Teacher: No, you ⁷_____ bring dictionaries into the examination.
Dan: What happens if we arrive late?
Teacher: You ⁸_____ arrive on time or you ⁹_____ come into the examination room.
Julie: ¹⁰_____ we talk to other students?
Teacher: No. You ¹¹_____ talk at all during the examination. Now, does everybody understand? Is everything clear?

LISTENING

6 A ▶ 4.2 Listen to the first part of an interview about different types of learner. Match the pictures with the types of learner.

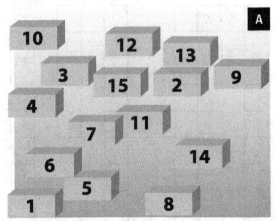

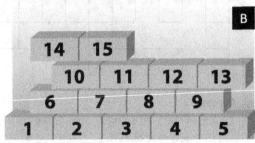

1 Picture _____: holist – learns lots of information about a topic, but in no particular order
2 Picture _____: serialist – learns things in sequence from the bottom up

B ▶ 4.3 Listen to the second part of the interview. Are the sentences about serialists (S) or holists (H)?

1 This learner likes to understand detail. _____
2 This learner reads instructions before using a new piece of equipment. _____
3 This learner might read a chapter from the middle of a book first. _____
4 This learner makes a careful plan before writing. _____
5 This learner reads around the topic and makes lots of notes before writing. _____

C Circle the correct option to complete the statements.

1 Students
   a) are always either serialists or holists.
   b) often use both serialist and holist approaches.
2 Serialists like to learn things
   a) in the correct order.
   b) in any order.
3 A holist likes to have an idea of the 'big picture' and
   a) doesn't worry about detail.
   b) thinks that the detail is very important.

VOCABULARY
LANGUAGE LEARNING

1 Complete the words in the sentences.

1 I find remembering new words very difficult, so I try to m_ _ _ _ise five to ten words a day. I write each word in a sentence and then say the sentence again and again in my head.

2 If I don't understand the meaning of a word, I l_ _k it u_ in a dictionary.

3 Sometimes I rer_ _ _d an article for a second time, looking for new words and phrases.

4 I like to ch_ _ on the internet. I speak to other learners from all over the world.

5 I like watching films in English, especially ones with su_ _ _ _ _ _ _s.

6 It's a good idea to g_ on_ _ _ _ to read websites in English.

7 I always n_ _ _ _ d_ _ _ _ any new words or phrases in my vocabulary notebook, then look back at them later and try to use them.

FUNCTION
GIVING ADVICE

2 Read the questions asking for advice. Put the words in the correct order to complete the answers.

> I'm thinking about changing my hairstyle. Any ideas?

1 _____ (think / don't / you / I / should) change it. It looks great.

2 _____ (try / why / you / don't) red and black stripes? It's cool.

> I don't know what to buy my husband for his birthday. His only interest is watching sport.

3 _____ (should / think / I / get / you) him a pair of trainers and tell him to do some sport instead of watching it all day!

4 _____ (you / don't / why / buy) him some tickets to a football match?

> I'm going to babysit for my nephew (3) and niece (6). I've never done this before. Can anyone help?

5 _____ (try / think / I / should / you) to make a simple recipe, like chocolate biscuits or a cake. They'll enjoy helping you.

6 _____ (idea / it's / think / a / to / good) about the things you enjoyed doing as a child: colouring, making things, singing songs, etc.

3 Read the problems and complete the advice using the words in brackets.

> I'm 29 years old and I work in a bank. I love my job, I have good friends and a boyfriend who loves me. I don't understand why I'm not happy. I'm always so stressed. Why can't I just be happy?

1 _____ (think / should) sit down and work out what is making you feel unhappy.

2 _____ (why not) write a list of the things that you are happy about in your life, and a list of the things that are not right?

3 _____ (try / talk) about your problems with your boyfriend. Does he understand?

> I have my end of university exams next month. I'm so frightened that I'm not going to pass them that I'm thinking of leaving university, and not going to the exams. I've studied hard but now I feel like I don't know anything.

4 _____ (not think / good idea) leave the university. If you've studied hard, you probably have nothing to worry about.

5 _____ (why / you / try) talking to your university professor? He/She can probably help.

6 _____ (think / should) try some relaxation techniques to help you with the exam stress.

LEARN TO
RESPOND TO ADVICE

4 A Match advice 1–6 with responses a)–f). Then complete the responses.

1 Why don't we go to the cinema tonight?
2 I don't think you should buy that car.
3 I think we should organise a party.
4 Maybe you should say sorry.
5 You shouldn't play so many computer games.
6 I think you should study more.

a) I _____ so. I'll call Louise later.
b) _____ right. I need to get out more.
c) That's _____ idea. Do you know what's on?
d) I suppose _____. I want to do well in the exam.
e) I'm not _____ a good idea. We're too busy.
f) You're _____. It's too expensive.

B ▶ 4.4 Listen and check.

C ▶ 4.5 Listen to the advice again. Say the responses.

5)) TRAVEL

VOCABULARY

TRANSPORT

1 A Find fourteen types of transport in the word snake.

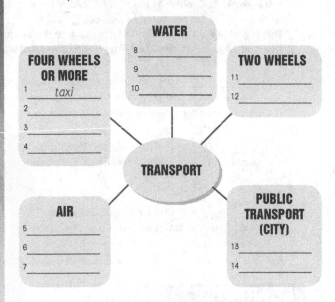

taxi ship motorbike tram moped aeroplane lorry speedboat helicopter coach ferry hot air balloon underground minibus

B Complete the word web with the types of transport in Exercise 1A.

WATER
8 _____
9 _____
10 _____

FOUR WHEELS OR MORE
1 _____taxi_____
2 _____
3 _____
4 _____

TWO WHEELS
11 _____
12 _____

TRANSPORT

AIR
5 _____
6 _____
7 _____

PUBLIC TRANSPORT (CITY)
13 _____
14 _____

C What types of transport are the people talking about?

1 'I always call one to get home at night.'
_____taxi_____

2 'I use it every morning to get to work. The roads are full of cars, so it's the quickest way to travel.'
_____

3 'It's my dream to travel in one of these, to feel the wind in my face and look down at the world below.' _____

4 'We enjoy touring foreign cities in them. They are perfect for groups of thirty or forty people.'
_____

5 'I drive it for twelve hours a day. It's my job. I transport products for food companies across the country.' _____

6 'I can take you to your house. It's big enough for two people and I have two helmets.' _____

7 'It's the fastest way to travel on water. I use mine for waterskiing.' _____

8 'In the past, everyone used these to visit other continents. It took three weeks to get to the USA! Now this type of travel is only for rich people.'
_____

GRAMMAR

PAST SIMPLE AND PAST CONTINUOUS

2 Match the sentence halves.

1 The last time they spoke to Marina _____
2 The teacher explained the exercise to us, but _____
3 Were there any calls for me _____
4 It started to rain _____
5 My mobile phone rang while _____
6 I fell asleep while I _____
7 Were you doing something important _____
8 I didn't go out last night _____

a) while we were playing football.
b) when I phoned you?
c) while I was shopping?
d) I was cooking.
e) because I was studying.
f) we weren't listening.
g) she was working in a bar.
h) was watching TV.

3 Complete the conversations with the past simple or past continuous form of the verbs in brackets.

Conversation 1

A: I came to see you yesterday, but you weren't at home. What [1] _____were you doing_____ (you/do)?

B: I was here, but I [2] _____ (play) with my son in the garden, so I [3] _____ (not hear) the doorbell.

Conversation 2

A: I heard you broke your leg. How [4] _____ (it/happen)?

B: It happened when I [5] _____ (climb) a mountain two weeks ago. I fell and I [6] _____ (land) badly.

Conversation 3

A: Wendy told me you [7] _____ (see) Jim last week.

B: Yes. I [8] _____ (study) in the library and he [9] _____ (say) 'hello'.

Conversation 4

A: I hear you crashed the car again. [10] _____ (you/drive) too fast?

B: No! It wasn't my fault! I [11] _____ (go) at thirty miles an hour when this other car suddenly [12] _____ (come) out of a side street.

Conversation 5

A: I [13] _____ (see) you on your bicycle yesterday. Where [14] _____ (you/go)?

B: I [15] _____ (go) to the shops, but I [16] _____ (drop) my wallet on the way!

4 A Match the phrases in the box with the pictures.

drop his ticket   try to sleep
decide to use his mobile phone   go for a walk
go through security   pay the taxi driver

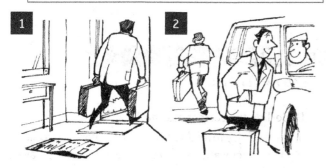

B Complete the story with the past simple or past continuous form of the phrases in Exercise 4A.

This is the story of Tim Bobo's first trip in an aeroplane. He was very excited, but as he was going out of the house, he ¹ _dropped his ticket_ on the floor. He took a taxi to the airport, but while he ² _____, someone took his bag. Luckily, there was nothing important in the bag. He checked in, but while he ³ _____, he found some keys in his pocket. Soon he was on the aeroplane. When it was taking off, he ⁴ _____ around the plane! The flight attendant told him to sit down immediately. Then soon after this he noticed that everyone seemed unhappy, so he started singing. Unfortunately, the other passengers ⁵ _____ and they told him to be quiet. A few hours later, he made one more mistake: while the plane was landing, he ⁶ _____ his mobile phone!

5 A ▶ 5.1 Listen to the pronunciation of *was* and *were* in the sentences. Then listen again and repeat.

B Read audio script 5.1 on page 43. Listen again, read and repeat.

LISTENING

6 A ▶ 5.2 Listen to a story about a German tourist. Choose the map which shows his journey.

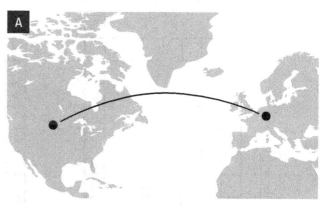

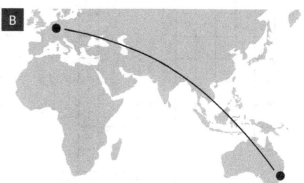

B Listen again. Are the sentences true (T) or false (F)?

1 A German man wanted to visit his girlfriend in Sydney, Australia.   _____
2 When he was booking his ticket, he made a mistake.   _____
3 His flight took him to the wrong town in Australia.   _____
4 He was wearing summer clothes because the weather in Montana was hot.   _____
5 His parents and friends sent him warm clothes.   _____
6 After a few days, he bought a ticket to Australia.   _____

7 A Read the sentences from the recording. Can you remember the rest of the second sentence?

1 A twenty-one-year-old German tourist called Tobi Gutt wanted to visit his girlfriend in Sydney, Australia. Unfortunately, _____ _____.
2 When he looked at the plane to Sidney, he became confused. Strangely, _____ _____.
3 A few friendly people helped him with food and drink until eventually, _____ _____.

B ▶ 5.3 Listen, check and complete the sentences.

VOCABULARY
TRAVEL ITEMS

1 A Read the clues and complete the crossword.

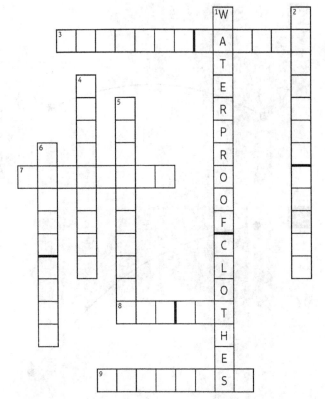

Across

3 You use this to take photos and put them on your computer.

7 You write names, addresses and ideas in this.

8 You put this on your head when the sun is very hot.

9 You pack your clothes in this. It is hard and sometimes has wheels.

Down

1 You wear these when it rains.

2 You wear these on your feet when you climb a mountain or go for a long walk.

4 You buy these to remember the places you visited.

5 You use these to look at birds and animals that are far away.

6 You carry important documents and money in this so they are safe.

B Complete the sentences with the words in Exercise 1A.

1 I wrote her phone number in my ___notebook___.

2 Before we leave for the airport, I'd like to buy some _____ for my friends.

3 It's very hot. You'll need to wear a _____ _____.

4 These _____ _____ are new and my feet are really hurting.

5 It's raining. We'll have to wear some _____ _____.

6 Can you see that beautiful bird? Have a look through the _____.

7 My passport was in my _____ _____, but I took it off when I went swimming.

8 Thirty kilos. I'm afraid your _____ is too heavy. You'll need to pay extra.

9 I wanted to take some photos, but I left my _____ _____ at home.

GRAMMAR
VERB PATTERNS

2 Underline the correct alternatives.

1 I really enjoy *to read/reading* in bed before I go to sleep.

2 My brother wants *to see/seeing* you before he leaves.

3 We chose *to get/getting* married in Venice because that's where we first met.

4 My parents love *spend/spending* time with their grandchildren.

5 It always seems *to rain/raining* when I come to stay.

6 The company decided *to refund/refunding* the money we paid for the tickets.

7 We should avoid *to travel/travelling* when there is too much traffic.

8 The builders need *to finish/finishing* their work before we can paint the house.

9 We hope *to see/seeing* you again soon.

10 I must finish *to write/writing* this letter.

11 Just imagine *to live/living* in a place as beautiful as this!

12 I hate *to go/going* to the supermarket.

3 Write sentences using the prompts.

1 the children / love / play / on beach / in sun
   The children love playing on the beach in the sun.

2 I / expect / hear from / travel agent / later today
   _____

3 we / want / go / on holiday / but / we / too busy
   _____

4 we / seem / go back / same place / every year
   _____

5 Alan / chose / stay / in hotel
   _____

6 we / enjoy / walk / and look at / beautiful countryside
   _____

7 I / decided / travel / on my own
   _____

8 we / avoid / visit / tourist resorts / in summer
   _____

9 we / need / book / our flights / before / prices / go up
   _____

READING

4 A Read the article and match topics a)–d) with paragraphs 1–4.

a) dealing with problems _____

b) having the best experience _____

c) doing something different _____

d) preparing for your trip _____

My top travel tips

Sandy Graves is an experienced travel writer who regularly travels all over the world. Here she shares some of her top tips.

1 When you start packing, leave your suitcase open somewhere. As you think of something you need to take, pack it. Don't leave it until later or you might forget. Make photocopies of all your important documents and put them in your suitcase, too. If you lose your passport, having a copy will make it easier to get a new one. Pack earplugs. They're great for long flights and noisy hostels, when you really need to sleep.

2 While you're travelling, be patient. Everybody wants to leave on time, but it doesn't always happen. Buses can be late, you can have problems with your documents or your card might not work in the ATM. Don't worry, there's always a way to get there. Smile and enjoy it – you won't have another chance to!

3 If you want more than just a holiday, try volunteering, spending some time learning new skills and meeting new people. You can travel anywhere in the world to do all kinds of different jobs, from building in Tanzania to looking after elephants in Thailand. Just think what you could do.

4 Do your best to try everything around you. Try the local food, buy the terrible, cheap souvenirs (they won't feel terrible when you're back home) and take lots of photos. And talk to local people – you can get so much more out of your trip if you do. Keep an open mind, and don't criticise the local culture. You might see or experience things which seem strange to you, but are normal there.

B Read the article again. Are the statements true (T) or false (F)?

1 Try to pack things at the same time as you think of them. _____

2 It's a good idea to take earplugs for when you want to go swimming. _____

3 It's best not to worry when you have problems. _____

4 There aren't many opportunities to do anything different when you travel. _____

5 Don't buy souvenirs if they're not good. _____

6 Try to accept things which seem strange to you. _____

C Find words in the article that match these meanings.

1 things you put in your ears to keep out noise (paragraph 1): _____

2 places where you can eat and sleep cheaply for a short time (paragraph 1): _____

3 able to wait calmly (paragraph 2): _____

4 a machine where you can get money from your bank (paragraph 2): _____

5 abilities; things you can do (paragraph 3): _____

6 from the place where you are (paragraph 4): _____

WRITING

USING SEQUENCERS

5 A Look at the pictures of two stories. Put sentences a)–i) in the correct order to tell the stories.

a) We had a great night out.

b) First, we met in a bar in town.

c) Finally, when we arrived, the hotel didn't have our reservation.

d) After the meal, we went dancing.

e) Then, our taxi broke down on the way to the hotel.

f) First, the flight was cancelled.

g) The holiday was a disaster.

h) Then we went out for a pizza.

i) We waited, and after a while we had to fly to a different airport.

Story 1

__*a*__ , _____ , _____ , _____

Story 2

__*g*__ , _____ , _____ , _____ , _____

B Write about a time when you went on holiday or had a good night out. Write 50–100 words. Use the sequencers in the box.

first   then   after that/after a while   finally

VOCABULARY

TOURISM

1 Match the sentence halves.

1 There were a lot of _____
2 I always wanted to be a tour _____
3 We went on a guided _____
4 They saw a lot of tourist attractions, including _____
5 I really enjoyed the boat trip _____
6 The best thing about Corsica is the scenery, which _____
7 Our boat took us under a _____

a) the History Museum and the National Art Gallery.
b) guide because I love showing people my city.
c) tour around the churches of Rome.
d) includes mountains, beaches and forests.
e) waterfall, which was fifty metres high.
f) down the River Nile.
g) tourists in our hotel.

FUNCTION

ASKING FOR/GIVING DIRECTIONS

2 Underline the correct alternatives. Where no word is necessary, choose (-).

1 For the police station, go straight *in/over/ on* and you can't miss it.
2 Go *(-)/for/along* the main road until you see the sports field.
3 To reach the train station, you need to go *up/through/in* the centre of town.
4 Keep going *(-)/on/by* until you reach the corner of King's Road.
5 You'll find the bar *up/at/of* the corner.
6 Walk for two minutes and you'll see the school in front *of/by/to* you.
7 Take *to/(-)/on* the second left after the library and you'll see my house.
8 For the post office, go *past/through/on* the turning for the station.

3 A ▶ 5.4 Look at the map and listen to the directions. Where is the man trying to go?

1 *restaurant* _____
2 _____
3 _____
4 _____
5 _____
6 _____

B Read audio script 5.4 on page 43 to check your answers.

LEARN TO

SHOW/CHECK UNDERSTANDING

4 A Put the words in the correct order to complete the conversations.

Conversation 1

A: Excuse me. ¹_____?
(help / you / me / can) I'm looking for the Science Museum.
B: Go straight on. ²_____.
(can't / you / it / miss)

A: OK, so it's easy! ³_____?
(map / you / the / me / on / can / show)
B: Yes, of course.

Conversation 2

A: Excuse me. I'm trying to find the internet café.
⁴_____? (the / this / way / right / is)
B: Yes. Keep going. ⁵_____.
(it / see / of / front / in / you / you'll)

A: ⁶_____? (walk / I / can)
B: Yes, you can. ⁷_____.
(about / minutes / it / ten / takes)

Conversation 3

A: ⁸_____ to the tube? (far / it / is)
B: No. It's about two minutes' walk.

A: OK. ⁹_____?
(to / need / left / so / the / go / at / I / cinema)
B: That's right. It's easy!

B ▶ 5.5 Listen and check.

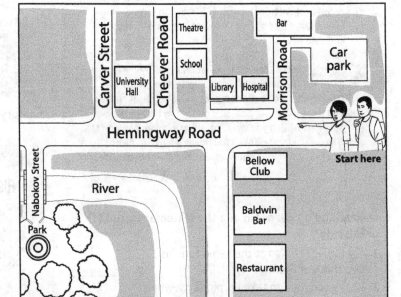

VOCABULARY
HEALTH

1 Complete the texts with the words in the box.

running fresh caffeine junk worrying fizzy
vitamins alcohol relaxing exercise

I have a healthy life, I think. I buy lots of ¹_____ fruit and vegetables and use these to cook with. I don't like to eat ²_____ food like hamburgers or crisps and I never drink ³_____ – not even beer or wine.

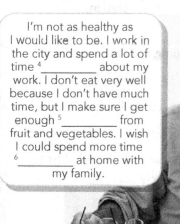

I'm not as healthy as I would like to be. I work in the city and spend a lot of time ⁴_____ about my work. I don't eat very well because I don't have much time, but I make sure I get enough ⁵_____ from fruit and vegetables. I wish I could spend more time ⁶_____ at home with my family.

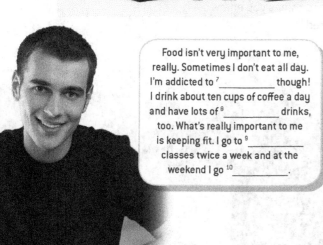

Food isn't very important to me, really. Sometimes I don't eat all day. I'm addicted to ⁷_____ though! I drink about ten cups of coffee a day and have lots of ⁸_____ drinks, too. What's really important to me is keeping fit. I go to ⁹_____ classes twice a week and at the weekend I go ¹⁰_____.

GRAMMAR
PRESENT PERFECT + *FOR/SINCE*

2 Complete the conversations with the present perfect form of the verbs in brackets.

1 **A:** How long _has Carlos worked_ here? (Carlos/work)
   B: About four years. He _____ here for four years. (be)

2 **A:** Did you see that comedy film last night?
   B: Yes, it was the funniest film I _____! (ever/watch)

3 **A:** Do you know where Morris _____? (go)
   B: No. I _____ him all day. (not see)

4 **A:** _____ your homework? (you/finish)
   B: No. I _____ it yet. (not start)

5 **A:** Do you know if my parcel _____? (arrive)
   B: Just a minute. I'll have a look for you.

6 **A:** _____ your watch? (you/find)
   B: Yes, it was under the sofa.

7 **A:** How long _____ Marissa? (you/know)
   B: Not very long. We _____ friends for long at all. (not be)

8 **A:** _____ my news? (you/hear)
   B: No. _____ to leave your job? (you/decide)

3 Write sentences using the prompts. Use the present perfect with *for/since*.

1 I / know / Imelda / ages
   I've known Imelda for ages.

2 he / work / for that company / six months
   _____

3 we / live / Turkey / 2013
   _____

4 I / not be / to the cinema / a long time
   _____

5 they / be here / two months now
   _____

6 I / not clean / the house / last Monday
   _____

7 she / not listen to / that music / she was a teenager
   _____

8 we / not hear / from him / he left
   _____

9 Bob / be a builder / more than forty years
   _____

10 the phone / not ring / 10 o'clock
   _____

11 I / want / to climb a mountain / I was a child
   _____

4 Underline the correct alternatives.

I = Interviewer **J** = Joy

I: So, Joy, you ¹*have started/started* the Laugh to Live organisation in 2012.

J: That's right.

I: Why ²*did you start/have you started* it? What ³*did you want/have you wanted* to do?

J: I ⁴*started/have started* Laugh to Live because I ⁵*felt/have felt* I had something I wanted to share with people. In my life I ⁶*have lived/lived* and worked in four different countries, in four different continents, so ⁷*I've had/I had* a lot of experience and ⁸*I've worked/I worked* with people from all over the world.

I: And what have you learnt from these experiences?

J: I think I've learnt something very important in life. Most people just want to live a simple, happy life. But they don't know where to look for happiness. Years ago, when I ⁹*travelled/have travelled* to Africa, I ¹⁰*met/have met* poor children in the jungle who had nothing. But they had the biggest smiles ¹¹*I have ever seen/ I saw*. This taught me that happiness and laughter are inside us all. I have a few techniques which I ¹²*have used/used* to help people learn to laugh more often, especially when things are difficult in their lives. And because they now laugh more, they ¹³*have become/became* happier people.

I: Thank you, Joy. And good luck with your work.

5 A ▶ 6.1 Listen and tick (✓) the sentence you hear.

1 **a)** I've known her for ages.
  b) She's known it for ages.
2 **a)** They travelled a lot.
  b) They've travelled a lot.
3 **a)** He's never seen it before.
  b) He's never been here before.
4 **a)** Nothing has changed.
  b) Nothing changed.
5 **a)** I've worked in other countries.
  b) I worked in other countries.

B Listen again and repeat.

LISTENING

6 A ▶ 6.2 Listen to the first part of a news report and circle the correct option.

1 The reporter went to a table tennis centre for people aged _____.
  a) under fifteen **b)** under fifty **c)** over fifty
2 People should eat _____ portion(s) of fruit and vegetables a day.
  a) five **b)** one **c)** eight
3 Living a healthy life can add _____ years to your life.
  a) four **b)** fourteen **c)** forty

B ▶ 6.3 Listen to the whole report. Are the statements true (T) or false (F)?

1 The people at the centre play table tennis four times a week. _____
2 The first woman says playing table tennis gives her a great feeling. _____
3 Scientists studied 20,000 people for fifteen years. _____
4 They found that people who don't smoke, exercise regularly and eat lots of fruit and vegetables every day live longer. _____
5 Doctors say that only big changes to your lifestyle can help improve your health. _____
6 The second woman says she always eats five portions of fruit and vegetables a day. _____

C Read the sentences from the recording. Match the words in bold 1–5 with meanings a)–e).

1 I feel **fabulous**.
2 Scientists have now **worked out** that you can live longer if you have a healthy lifestyle.
3 They **did** some **research**.
4 People who don't smoke, who do **regular** exercise and who eat lots of fresh fruit and vegetables every day …
5 It's **part of the fun**.

a) happening once a week/once a month, etc.
b) studied something carefully to find out information
c) very good, wonderful
d) one of the things you enjoy
e) calculated

VOCABULARY

FOOD

1 Find seven types of fruit using these letters. You can use the letters more than once.

2 Complete the words in the menu and the recipe.

THE TERRACE
BISTRO MENU

CHEF'S CHOICE

Tender baby [1]ch__ck__n grilled in a [2]l__m__n
and herb sauce.
Served with rice and [3]br__cc__l__.

MEAT-EATER'S DELIGHT

[4]B____fst____k marinaded in a cream
and [5]sp__n__ch sauce.
Served with [6]p__t__t__es.

KING'S FEAST

Roasted [7]l__g __f l__mb with rice, [8]c__bb__gc
and freshly steamed [9]c____rg__tt__s.

Pasta Atlantica

- Fry 50g of [10]shr__mps in a pan with a little butter.

- Add [11]__n____ns and [12]g__rl__c to the pan.

- Boil 50g of [13]m__ss__ls.

- Cook the pasta.

- Mix the pasta and seafood and put in a tray.

- Add a layer of [14]ch____ s__ on top and cook in the oven for twenty minutes until brown.

GRAMMAR

MAY, MIGHT, WILL

3 Circle the correct option to complete the sentences.

1 **A:** What are you doing this weekend?
   B: I'm not sure. We _____ go to the seafood restaurant.
   a) may   **b)** will   **c)** won't

2 **A:** Will that café on Wardour Street be open tomorrow?
   B: I don't know. It _____ be.
   a) will   **b)** won't   **c)** might

3 **A:** I've cooked little Johnny some vegetables for tonight's dinner.
   B: Thanks, but he _____ eat them.
   a) might   **b)** will   **c)** won't

4 **A:** Can I try your food?
   B: Be careful. It _____ be too hot for you.
   a) may   **b)** won't   **c)** may not

5 **A:** Do we need to buy any ingredients for this recipe?
   B: Maybe. We _____ have enough garlic. Can you check?
   a) won't   **b)** might not   **c)** will

6 **A:** You know Melissa's a vegetarian, don't you?
   B: OK, I _____ cook meat.
   a) won't   **b)** will   **c)** may

7 **A:** Are you going to that new bar before you leave town?
   B: I don't know. I hope so, but we _____ have time.
   a) won't   **b)** will   **c)** may not

8 **A:** What are your predictions for food in the future?
   B: The good news is I think it _____ be more healthy.
   a) won't   **b)** will   **c)** might not

4 Put the words in the correct order to make six predictions about food.

1 more / eat / know / people / what / about / will / they
   People will know more about what they eat.

2 future / we / animals / the / eat / won't / in
   _____

3 eat / food / we / more / organic / may
   _____

4 might / illegal / junk / become / food
   _____

5 fatter / people / West / will / the / get / in
   _____

6 the / left / may / there / sea / not / be / in / fish / any
   _____

READING

5 A Read the text and match pictures A–D with paragraphs 1–4.

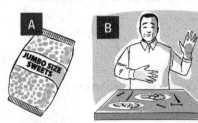

How to eat less

*Brian Wansink of Cornell University did some **experiments** to show why we eat too much. Here are some of the results.*

1 Wansink invited a group of people to lunch. He told half of them they were eating something expensive and delicious: Royal Italian Bolognese with haricots verts. He told the other half they were eating cheap food from a can. In fact, both groups ate the same food. He secretly watched them. The ones who thought they were eating expensive food ate much more than the others.

CONCLUSION: If people think the food sounds good and is expensive, they think it tastes better.

2 Wansink did an experiment at a cinema in Chicago. He gave everyone a free bag of popcorn, but the popcorn was old and tasted bad. Most people noticed this, but they still ate almost all of it.

CONCLUSION: How much we eat depends on: where we are (in the cinema); what we are doing (**concentrating** on a film, not on food); what other people are doing (eating popcorn). These things may be more important than the taste of the food.

3 Wansink went to a sports bar and gave the customers free chicken. The waiters cleaned half the tables every few minutes and took away the chicken bones. No one cleaned the other tables. The people with clean tables ate seven pieces of chicken **on average**. The others ate five.

CONCLUSION: When we see how much we're eating, we eat less. When we can't see how much we're eating, we eat more.

4 Wansink invited people to watch a video. He gave them each a bag of sweets to eat during the film. Half the bags had sweets with seven different colours. The other bags had sweets with ten different colours. The people whose sweets had more colours ate forty-three more sweets than the others.

CONCLUSION: When there is a big **variety**, people want to try everything, so they eat more.

B Read the text again and circle the correct option.

1 Why did Wansink do the experiments?
   a) to improve the food we eat
   b) to discover why people eat more than they need

2 How did Wansink do his experiments?
   a) He asked questions about what people ate.
   b) He gave free food to people and then watched them.

3 Who ate more?
   a) the people who thought their food was expensive
   b) the people who thought their food was cheap

4 What was interesting about the popcorn experiment?
   a) The popcorn didn't taste good.
   b) The popcorn had different colours.

5 Who ate more chicken?
   a) the people with messy tables
   b) the people with clean tables

6 Who ate more sweets?
   a) the people whose sweets had seven colours
   b) the people whose sweets had ten colours

C Match the words in bold in the text with these meanings.

1 giving your attention to something _____
2 many different types of things _____
3 scientific tests to find information _____
4 based on a calculation of what
   most people do _____

WRITING

SENTENCE STRUCTURE

6 A Join the sentences with *and*, *but* or *when*. Use each word twice.

1 I have always liked cooking. I cook every day.
   _____

2 I was very young. I cooked my first meal.
   _____

3 I don't eat much meat. I eat a lot of fish.
   _____

4 I was working as a chef in a horrible hotel. I decided to open my own restaurant.
   _____

5 I don't drink alcohol. I use a little wine in some of the dishes I prepare.
   _____

6 I like meeting customers at my restaurant. I ask them about the food.
   _____

B Put the words *and* and *also* in the correct place in the sentences.

1 My favourite types of food are pasta fresh fish. I like fruit.

2 Every morning I buy vegetables herbs from the market. I buy meat there.

3 I find that the food in the market is fresher better quality. It's cheaper.

VOCABULARY

ILLNESS

1 Read the clues and complete the crossword.

Across

5 It's very painful. I'm taking _____.

7 She fell down the stairs and she's _____ her leg.

9 The doctor's given me some _____ to stop the infection.

10 My arm hurts. I think I need to go to the hospital for an _____.

Down

1 We've got some _____ for your cough.

2 I don't feel well. I think I've caught a _____.

3 I'm tired. I need to get some _____.

4 He feels hot. He's got a high _____.

6 My head hurts. I've got a _____.

8 I can't speak. I've got a _____ throat

FUNCTION

SEEING THE DOCTOR

2 Match the sentence halves.

Doctor

1 What's the	**a)**	hurt?
2 How long have you	**b)**	pills/antibiotics/medicine.
3 Where does it	**c)**	had this problem?
4 Can I have a	**d)**	worry about.
5 It's nothing to	**e)**	matter?
6 I'll give you some	**f)**	look?

Patient

7 I feel	**g)**	about my leg.
8 It	**h)**	very painful.
9 It's	**i)**	sleep.
10 I'm worried	**j)**	hurts when I walk.
11 I can't	**k)**	sick/terrible.

3 A Some of the lines in the conversations have words missing. Write the missing word, or put a tick if the sentence is correct.

D = Doctor   P = Patient

Conversation 1

D: Good morning. How can I help? ✓

P: I'm worried my leg.

D: Your leg? What's matter with it?

P: Well, very painful. It hurts when I walk.

D: I see. How long have you the problem?

P: Since yesterday.

D: Can I a look?

P: Yes, of course.

Conversation 2

D: Hello. What's matter, Mr Smith?

P: I feel terrible.

D: All right. Where does hurt?

P: Everywhere. And I can't sleep.

D: Ah. Have you got temperature?

P: I don't know.

D: OK. Can I have look?

P: Yes, of course.

D: That's fine. It's nothing worry about.

P: But I feel terrible!

B ▶ 6.4 Listen and check.

LEARN TO

PREDICT INFORMATION

4 A Predict what the doctor says using the words in brackets.

D = Doctor   P = Patient

Conversation 1

D: Good afternoon. [1]_____ (matter)?

P: I've got a sore throat and a headache.

D: I see. [2]_____ (long)?

P: About two weeks.

D: [3]_____ (temperature)?

P: Yes. It's 38.5, so I've taken some aspirin.

D: I see. I think [4]_____ (cold). You need [5]_____ (rest) and [6]_____ (drinks).

Conversation 2

P: I think I've broken my arm.

D: Oh dear. [1]_____ (look)?

P: Yes. Here you are.

D: So, [2]_____ (where/hurt)?

P: Here, and here.

D: [3]_____ (how/do)?

P: I fell over.

D: I think you should [4]_____ (go/hospital/X-ray).

B ▶ 6.5 Listen and check.

GRAMMAR PRESENT PERFECT + EVER/NEVER OR PAST SIMPLE

1 Complete the sentences with the correct past simple or present perfect form of the verbs in brackets.

1 He ____*has never travelled*____ (never/travel) abroad.

2 I _____ (never/visit) Amsterdam, but I'd like to go in the future.

3 My grandparents _____ (come) to this country in 1956.

4 So far on this trip, we _____ (be) to ten countries.

5 Jane _____ (get) her exam results yesterday.

6 When you lived in Germany, _____ (you/go) to Frankfurt?

7 I hear Lindsay's girlfriend is very nice, but I _____ (not meet) her yet.

8 I _____ (not hear) you come in last night.

9 That girl started playing tennis three years ago, but she _____ (never/win) a match!

10 I know your mother likes foreign food, but _____ (she/ever/eat) snails?

GRAMMAR CAN, HAVE TO, MUST

2 Circle the correct options to complete the text.

> To enter the university library, everyone ¹ _____ show a current student or staff ID. No exceptions. To borrow books, you ² _____ take the books to the front desk and show your ID. You ³ _____ take out a maximum of eight books. There are some books that you ⁴ _____ take out. These are marked *Reference Only*. There is a late fee of 20p per day, but you ⁵ _____ renew the books online for an extra week. If you have renewed the books before the due date, you ⁶ _____ pay the fee. To order books that are not in the library, you ⁷ _____ fill in the form at the front desk, marked *Special Orders*. You ⁸ _____ write the full title of the book, the author and the ISBN. We ⁹ _____ guarantee a date for the arrival of these books. You ¹⁰ _____ write in the books; anyone who is caught doing this will pay a fine.

1 a) must   b) have to   c) can
2 a) doesn't have to b) has to   c) have to
3 a) can't   b) mustn't   c) can
4 a) don't have to b) can't   c) have to
5 a) can   b) has to   c) don't have to
6 a) don't have to b) must   c) can't
7 a) has to   b) don't have to c) have to
8 a) can't   b) must   c) don't have to
9 a) doesn't have to b) can't   c) has to
10 a) don't have to b) has to   c) mustn't

FUNCTION GIVING ADVICE

3 Complete the conversations with words in the box.

> ~~should~~ think why suppose
> shouldn't sure should

Ella: What do you think I ¹ ___*should*___ wear to the interview? ² _____ I wear jeans?

Beth: No, you ³ _____! You have to try and look smart.

Ella: I ⁴ _____ so. What about this? This dress will be OK, won't it?

Beth: I'm not ⁵ _____ that's a good idea. It's a bit short.

Ella: Oh yes, maybe you're right.

Beth: I ⁶ _____ you should wear trousers and a jacket.

Ella: A jacket? I haven't worn a jacket since I was at school!

Beth: I've got a nice jacket. Here. ⁷ _____ don't you try this on?

GRAMMAR PAST SIMPLE AND PAST CONTINUOUS

4 Underline the correct alternatives.

This story ¹*happened/was happening* while Guillermo Diaz ²*studied/was studying* English at a community college in the USA. Diaz was a very bad student who never attended classes. One evening when he ³*sat/was sitting* in a bar, he ⁴*saw/was seeing* another student, Arturo, who told him about an exam the next day. Arturo said the exam was in Room 52, but Diaz thought he said Room 62. The next day, when Diaz was doing the exam, he ⁵*realised/was realising* that he didn't know any of the answers. He tried to ask another student for the answers while the professor ⁶*didn't look/wasn't looking*, but the other student ⁷*didn't help/wasn't helping* him. The exam ⁸*had/was having* multiple-choice questions, so Diaz guessed all of the answers. A week later, while Diaz ⁹*watched/was watching* TV at home, he ¹⁰*received/was receiving* his results by post. He scored 100 percent in the exam … on American history!

GRAMMAR VERB PATTERNS

5 Each sentence has a verb missing. Complete the sentences with the infinitive or *-ing* form of the verbs in the box.

> ~~be~~ drive cook lose get up clean write shop
>   *to be*

1 We expect ∧ home by 2.30.

2 I want a great book so I can become famous!

3 I need early tomorrow, so I'm going to bed now.

4 We usually avoid at this time because of all the traffic.

5 Do you enjoy meals for large groups of people?

6 They decided the whole house after the party.

7 She loves for clothes.

8 I always seem something when I travel – usually my plane ticket!

FUNCTION   ASKING FOR AND GIVING DIRECTIONS

6 Match the sentence halves.

1	The restaurant is in	a)	bridge.
2	Go along	b)	through the centre of town.
3	Take the	c)	second right.
4	Keep going until	d)	the main road.
5	You'll see the bar	e)	you reach the cinema.
6	Go	f)	at the corner.
7	Cross the	g)	front of you.

GRAMMAR   PRESENT PERFECT + FOR/SINCE

7 Cross out the incorrect alternative in each sentence.

1 They've been waiting here *since the office opened/for hours/since ten minutes*.
2 I've played the guitar *since 2012/for six years/since months*.
3 They haven't visited us *since last Christmas/for January/for several weeks*.
4 Have you known Sourav *since you were at school/for a long time/since years*?
5 I haven't eaten *for the last meal/for hours/since last night*.
6 We've lived in the USA *for a very long time/since the government changed/for now*.
7 My team hasn't won a game *for three years/since months/since they won the cup last year*.

GRAMMAR   MAY, MIGHT, WILL

8 Find and correct the mistakes in the sentences.

1 I don't will go to the cinema tonight because I'm busy.
2 I may to send her an email.
3 We not might have time to go to the museum.
4 The weather report on TV said there might to be storms.
5 Joshua may not be go to the game.
6 I'm might be late to class tonight.

FUNCTION   SEEING THE DOCTOR

9 A Who says phrases a)–f), the doctor (D) or the patient (P)?

a) How long have you had this problem? _____
b) It's very painful. _____
c) What's the problem? _____
d) But I'm worried about missing work. _____
e) Doctor, I feel terrible. _____
f) Where does it hurt? _____

B Complete the conversation with phrases a)–f) from Exercise 9A.

D = Doctor   P = Patient

D: Good morning. ¹_____
P: ²_____ I have a backache all the time and it hurts when I walk.
D: I see. ³_____
P: About two weeks.
D: Can I have a look? ⁴_____
P: Here. ⁵_____ Sometimes I can't sleep because of the pain.
D: OK, I'll give you some medicine for it. And you shouldn't do any heavy work for a few weeks.
P: ⁶_____ I'm a builder.
D: I'll write a note. OK?
P: OK. Thanks, Doctor.

C ▶ R2.1 Listen and check.

VOCABULARY   REVISION

10 Write a word from Units 4–6 to match these meanings. The first letter of each word is given.

1 a_____: a school subject which involves painting and drawing
2 b_____: you look through these to see things far away
3 c_____: it's in coffee and tea and it makes you feel active
4 d_____: you make this when you decide to do something
5 e_____: a formal test
6 f_____ drink: a drink with gas
7 g_____: we play these (e.g. football, tennis)
8 h_____: students do this after school for their teacher
9 i_____ t_____: the subject of computers; what *IT* stands for
10 j_____ f_____: food that isn't healthy because it has lots of fat or sugar
11 first aid k_____: a bag of medicines, bandages, etc., to treat ill/injured people
12 l_____: books, poems, plays
13 m_____: a fast form of transport with two wheels
14 n_____: it's got empty pages and you write notes in it
15 o_____: connected to the internet
16 p_____: a small round piece of medicine that you put in your mouth and swallow
17 r_____: a sport for which you have to wear special boots with wheels
18 s_____: a large boat that carries people or things across the sea
19 t_____: an electric street train
20 u_____: special clothes that students have to wear at school
21 v_____: potatoes, carrots, onions and peas are this type of food
22 w_____: clothes that don't allow water to enter are this
23 y_____: an activity that helps relax the body and mind

CHECK

Circle the correct option to complete the sentences.

1 Everyone likes that film, but I _____ it.
   a) saw   **b)** don't see   **c)** haven't seen

2 I started writing ten years ago, but I _____ anything.
   a) have never published   **b)** don't publish
   c) didn't publish

3 He _____ his girlfriend in 2014.
   a) did meet   **b)** met   **c)** has met

4 You _____ have a passport to get into the country.
   a) has to   **b)** have to   **c)** can

5 She _____ do any homework tonight so she can come with us.
   a) doesn't have to   **b)** can   **c)** has to

6 You _____ see the dentist about that tooth.
   a) should   **b)** try   **c)** don't

7 _____ don't you ask your friend to help you with this?
   a) How   **b)** Should   **c)** Why

8 She has to _____ an appointment with a dentist.
   a) start   **b)** do   **c)** make

9 He _____ too many mistakes and failed the exam.
   a) made   **b)** did   **c)** wrote

10 I usually _____ new words in a dictionary.
   a) study up   **b)** look up   **c)** take up

11 I _____ along the street when I met Dave.
   a) walked   **b)** am walking   **c)** was walking

12 The radio was on, but nobody _____.
   a) did listen   **b)** was listening   **c)** listened

13 She _____ her arm while she was skiing.
   a) was broke   **b)** broke   **c)** was breaking

14 They expect _____ this game easily.
   a) win   **b)** winning   **c)** to win

15 Try to avoid _____ a lot of noise because your brother is sleeping.
   a) making   **b)** to make   **c)** make

16 I've decided _____ law.
   a) studying   **b)** study   **c)** to study

17 Keep walking until you _____ the river.
   a) at   **b)** reach   **c)** get

18 The bar is in front _____ you.
   a) to   **b)** by   **c)** of

19 Did you travel _____ train?
   a) on   **b)** by   **c)** the

20 You look tired – you should _____ some rest.
   a) catch   **b)** make   **c)** get

21 I've known Rami _____ my first year at college.
   a) since   **b)** for   **c)** because

22 She has worked with us _____ three years.
   a) since   **b)** by   **c)** for

23 They haven't been here _____ 1987.
   a) for   **b)** since   **c)** until

24 You _____ need a special visa, but I'm not sure.
   a) will   **b)** have   **c)** might

25 In the future, cars _____ use oil because it will be too expensive.
   a) will   **b)** can't   **c)** won't

26 I _____ come to the lesson because I have to work late.
   a) may not   **b)** am not   **c)** will

27 You've caught a _____.
   a) backache   **b)** cold   **c)** cough

28 Where does it _____?
   a) sore   **b)** hurt   **c)** pain

29 I _____ yoga twice a week.
   a) do   **b)** play   **c)** exercise

30 We try to _____ some exercise every day.
   a) make   **b)** play   **c)** do

RESULT /30

UNIT 1 Recording 1

1 played, stayed, tried, ended
2 asked, kissed, arrived, talked
3 finished, decided, pretended, wanted
4 studied, happened, invented, stayed
5 walked, helped, stopped, started

UNIT 1 Recording 2

When I was eighteen, I went on holiday with a group of mates to Spain. We had a great time. Every day we went sunbathing on the beach and at night we went out dancing. On the last night, I met an American girl called Amy and we got on really well. We went to a 24-hour café and talked all night. Soon it was morning and we both had to go.

We promised to write to each other when we got home, and at first we did. But after a few months we decided that it was too difficult because we lived in different countries, so we stopped. I started university and forgot about her.

Ten years later, I started a new job in London. On the first day, I walked into the office and who do you think I saw? It was Amy! I recognised her immediately – she still looked the same. Of course, we were both really shocked to see each other. She explained that she now lived alone in London because of her job with the company. Well, of course, we got on really well again and we started hanging out with each other. I showed her round London and we went to museums, concerts and restaurants. It wasn't long until we fell in love! It felt right, so I proposed to her and she accepted! We got married soon after and had our son, Jamie. We're very happy together!

UNIT 1 Recording 3

1 Do you like it here?
2 Where are you going?
3 I come from Italy.
4 It's a beautiful day.
5 I'm afraid I can't remember.
6 Where did you buy it?
7 I'm sorry, but I don't understand.

UNIT 1 Recording 4

1 Did you have a nice weekend?
2 Where did you go?
3 Would you like a drink?
4 So, do you like it here?
5 It was nice to meet you.
6 Let's keep in touch.

UNIT 2 Recording 1

7 syllables: motorcycle courier
6 syllables: foreign correspondent
5 syllables: fashion designer, IT consultant, personal trainer
4 syllables: rescue worker
2 syllables: sales rep

UNIT 2 Recording 2

1 People who work sitting down always get paid more than people who work standing up.
2 The successful people are usually the ones who listen more than they talk.
3 Politicians never believe what they say, so they are surprised when other people do.
4 Once in a while, teachers will open a door, if you're lucky, but you have to enter alone.
5 Great artists like van Gogh rarely live to see their success.
6 Doctors are the same as lawyers. The only difference is that lawyers rob you, but doctors rob you *and* kill you occasionally.
7 Find something you love doing and you'll never have to work a day in your life.
8 The only place where success always comes before work is in the dictionary.

UNIT 2 Recording 3

1 I work on a safari as a guide. I take tourists to see the animals. Everyone thinks my job is dangerous, but I don't think so. Well, I didn't think so until last month. So, what happened? Well, I had a bus full of tourists. There were fifteen of them. It was a beautiful, clear evening and about seven o'clock we saw some elephants. Everyone wanted to take photos, so I told them they could get off the bus for a few minutes. So there we were – these tourists taking photos of the elephants. Then suddenly, the male elephant turned. It looked at us. And I could see that it was angry. So I told everyone to stand still. 'Don't move!' Well, the elephant continued looking at us and I thought that it was going to charge, you know, to run at us. I told the tourists to walk very slowly back to the bus. Then the elephant charged at us. I jumped into the bus and started driving as fast as possible. The elephant came very close and the tourists were all shouting and screaming. But it was OK in the end. We escaped.

2 I was on a safari holiday. It was a really beautiful place, very quiet. One evening, at about six o'clock, we went for a drive in the tour bus. There were twenty of us tourists. Well, we soon saw some elephants. They were drinking at a pool. So we got out of the bus to take photos. Anyway, suddenly, this large male elephant started looking very angry. Then it walked towards us. The guide told us to run back to the bus as fast as possible. So we did. This was a really bad idea because the elephant followed us. Then the guide got into the bus and drove away very fast. We were really quiet and calm because we didn't want to frighten the elephant. But it wasn't a nice experience and we were happy to get back to the hotel that night.

UNIT 2 Recording 4

1 I'm very keen on cooking and I absolutely love great food.
2 I love riding my motorbike. I can't stand sitting in an office all day.
3 I'm quite keen on technology and I don't mind dealing with other people's computer problems.
4 I'm very keen on working with money and I don't like people wasting it on stupid things.

UNIT 2 Recordings 5/6

1
A: On Saturday I went to a conference about the Z-phone, this amazing new technology.
B: Really? I read about that last week. It sounds interesting.
A: Well, everybody's talking about it.
B: And what about the cost?
A: Oh, I don't know. I had to leave before they discussed that.

2
A: Today I was offered a job as a babysitter.
B: That's great!
A: Not really. They only offered me five pounds an hour.
B: Oh, I see. So did you accept the job?
A: No. I'm going to look for something better.
B: Right. What did you tell them?
A: I said, 'Dad, I know the baby is my sister, but I want a better salary!'

AUDIO SCRIPTS

UNIT 3   Recording 1

D = David   T = Terry

D: So what do you think, Terry? I put it on this wall because of the light.

T: Um. It's … it's … well, I want to say I like it. But I don't.

D: You don't like it?

T: No, David, I don't. It's terrible.

D: What?

T: It's just black. All over. It's black on black. It looks like a painting of a black bird flying over a black building on a black night.

D: It's modern art, Terry.

T: I know, I know. But it doesn't say anything.

D: What do you mean, it doesn't say anything? It's art. It doesn't talk.

T: You know what I mean. It has no message. I don't understand it.

D: You don't have to understand it, Terry. It's art. It just exists. It's not there to be understood.

T: So why is it all black? Why not white? Or white and black? Or red, white and black?

D: Why don't you ask the artist?

T: How much did it cost?

D: I'm not telling you.

T: How much did it cost?

D: Why?

T: I want to know.

D: It was expensive.

T: What does that mean? What's expensive? Fifty dollars? Fifty thousand dollars?

D: Nearer fifty thousand.

T: Nearer fifty thousand dollars than fifty?

D: Yes. Forty-five thousand. Forty-five thousand dollars.

T: I can't believe it! You bought a black painting … you spent forty-five thousand dollars …

D: I liked it. I like it. No, I love it.

T: It's black, David. Black on black. I could paint it for you in five minutes.

D: But you didn't.

T: You didn't ask me to.

D: I didn't want you to.

T: Has Mary seen it?

D: Not yet. She's away. She'll be back on Friday.

T: Does she know you bought it?

D: No. It's a surprise.

T: Oh yes, it will be. A big surprise! Does Mary even like modern art?

D: Yes. She'll like this.

T: How do you know?

D: I know.

T: How?

D: Because I know what Mary likes and what Mary doesn't like. And she'll like this.

T: I hope so. Because if she doesn't, you're dead.

UNIT 3   Recording 2

1

A: You've reached Danny's voicemail. Please leave a message.

B: Hi, Danny. It's Pauline here. I'm calling about tomorrow night. Unfortunately, there are no more tickets for the concert. I called them at about two o'clock, but they were already sold out. So, I don't know what you want to do. Anyway, give me a call tonight after six. Bye.

2

A: Hi, is Tricia there, please?

B: No, I'm afraid she isn't. Who's speaking?

A: It's Elise here.

B: Hi, Elise. No, I'm afraid Tricia is out at the moment. Do you want to leave a message?

A: Yes, can you tell her I'll be at the station at eight. She's going to meet me there.

B: Sorry, can you repeat that?

A: Yes. I'll be at the station at eight.

B: Oh, OK. At eight. I'll tell her that.

A: Thanks. Oh, and can you tell her that her mobile isn't working?

B: Yes, OK. I think she needs to recharge it.

A: Thanks. Bye.

B: Bye.

3

A: Roundhouse Bar and Grill. How can I help you?

B: Oh hello there. I'd like to book a table for three people for Wednesday evening.

A: Oh, we don't take bookings, actually.

B: Oh really?

A: Yeah, if you just show up at the door, that'll be fine.

B: OK.

A: Around eight is usually our busiest time, between eight and nine thirty. So if you come a bit before that …

B: Great. Thanks very much for your help.

A: You're welcome.

R1   Recording 1

1

A: Hello. My name's Felipe. It's nice to meet you.

B: Hi, I'm Magda. Nice to meet you, too.

2

A: Nice day, isn't it?

B: Yes, it's lovely.

3

A: So, where exactly do you come from?

B: Zaragoza. It's a small city in Northern Spain.

4

A: Did you have a good weekend?

B: Yes, it was OK. I didn't do much.

5

A: So, would you like a drink?

B: Yes, I'd love a glass of water.

6

A: I'll see you later.

B: See you soon.

UNIT 4   Recording 1

1 How much do I have to pay?

2 Can I park here?

3 We must visit her before we leave.

4 We don't have to stay in this hotel.

5 She can't wear that!

6 You mustn't tell anyone.

UNIT 4   Recording 2

I = Interviewer   P = Professor

I: Professor Morris, we're looking at learning and the different ways in which people like to learn, and one of the things we can look at is the type of learner. Is that right?

P: Yes, research has shown that there may be many different types of learner. But one way we can look at this is to divide people into two groups: holists and serialists. Now, most people will probably use both approaches, but often we find people are quite strongly one or the other.

I: Holists and serialists. So, what's the difference between the two?

P: Well, students who are serialists like to study taking one step at a time. They look at a subject or topic and work through the different parts of the topic in order.

I: And holistic learners? How are they different?

P: The holists are very different. They like to have a general understanding of the whole topic. And they find it easier to study and learn if they have an idea of the 'big picture'. They don't worry so much about the detail.

I: Oh. That's me. I think I'm more of a holist.

P: Are you? Well, you see …

UNIT 4   Recording 3

I = Interviewer   P = Professor

I: So, tell me a little bit more about the serialist. You said that they like to learn things in sequence, in order.

P: That's right. So, they start at the beginning, and when they feel they've fully understood one part, then they are ready to move on to the next part. But it's very important to them that they understand the detail.

I: OK. These are the kind of people who always read the instructions before they try a new piece of equipment or machinery.

P: That's right.

I: And what about the holistic learners?

P: OK. Well, a holist never starts learning about a topic at the beginning. They jump around and get lots of information. So, they might pick up a book about the topic and choose a chapter in the middle and start reading there.

I: That's like me. I choose the bit I'm most interested in.

P: Exactly. But a serialist learner will start at the beginning and read each chapter in order.

I: That's very interesting. What about writing? Is there a difference there too?

P: Yes, absolutely. A serialist will make a careful plan of everything they have to write and then begin to research each area. But a holist will read about a lot of different things and have lots of bits of paper with notes. Then they will try to put the different pieces together when they begin writing.

I: That's very true. There is paper everywhere. I think my tutors at university would like me to be more serialist.

P: Yes, that's probably true …

UNIT 4 Recordings 4/5

1

A: Why don't we go to the cinema tonight?

B: That's a good idea. Do you know what's on?

2

A: I don't think you should buy that car.

B: You're right. It's too expensive.

3

A: I think we should organise a party.

B: I'm not sure that's a good idea. We're too busy.

4

A: Maybe you should say sorry.

B: I suppose so. I'll call Louise later.

5

A: You shouldn't play so many computer games.

B: You're right. I need to get out more.

6

A: I think you should study more.

B: I suppose so. I want to do well in the exam.

UNIT 5 Recording 1

1 We were open. We were opening the shop.

2 I was fine. I was finding it difficult.

3 They were right. They were writing a book.

4 It was you. It was using too much gas.

5 She was clean. She was cleaning the house.

6 Where were you? Where were you going?

UNIT 5 Recording 2

A twenty-one-year-old German tourist called Tobi Gutt wanted to visit his girlfriend in Sydney, Australia. Unfortunately, he typed the wrong destination on a travel website. He landed near Sidney, Montana, in the United States, 13,000 kilometres away. This is his story.

Tobi left Germany for a four-week holiday. He was wearing a T-shirt and shorts, perfect clothes for the Australian summer. But the plane didn't land in Australia. It landed in freezing-cold Montana in the United States.

He had to take a connecting flight, but when he looked at the plane to Sidney, he became confused. Strangely, it was very small. And then he realised his mistake. Sidney, Montana, was an oil town of about 5,000 people. It was also in the United States, not Australia.

Tobi then spent three days waiting in the airport. He had only a thin jacket in the middle of winter, and no money. A few friendly people helped him with food and drink until eventually, his parents and friends from Germany sent him some money. He bought a ticket to Australia, where, finally, he saw his girlfriend.

UNIT 5 Recording 3

1 A twenty-one-year-old German tourist called Tobi Gutt wanted to visit his girlfriend in Sydney, Australia. Unfortunately, he typed the wrong destination on a travel website.

2 When he looked at the plane to Sidney, he became confused. Strangely, it was very small.

3 A few friendly people helped him with food and drink until eventually, his parents and friends from Germany sent him some money.

UNIT 5 Recording 4

1 Go along Hemingway Road. Go past The Bellow Club and take the first left. It's next to the Baldwin Bar.

2 Go along Hemingway Road, then take the first right. You'll be on Morrison Road. Go along Morrison Road for about five minutes, past the turning for the car park. It's in front of you.

3 Go along Hemingway Road. Keep going until you reach Carver Street. Turn right on Carver Street and it's the first building on your right.

4 Go straight along Hemingway Road. Take the second right. You'll be on Cheever Road. Go along Cheever Road. Go past the school. It's on your right.

5 Go straight along Hemingway Road. Keep going until you reach Nabokov Street. Turn left on Nabokov Street. Go straight on. There's a river, the Faulkner River. Cross the bridge and it's in front of you.

6 Go along Hemingway Road. Take the first right on Morrison Road. Then take the first left. There's a hospital. It's next to the hospital.

UNIT 5 Recording 5

1

A: Excuse me. Can you help me? I'm looking for the Science Museum.

B: Go straight on. You can't miss it.

A: OK, so it's easy! Can you show me on the map?

B: Yes, of course.

2

A: Excuse me. I'm trying to find the internet café. Is this the right way?

B: Yes. Keep going. You'll see it in front of you.

A: Can I walk?

B: Yes, you can. It takes about ten minutes.

3

A: Is it far to the tube?

B: No. It's about two minutes' walk.

A: OK. So I need to go left at the cinema?

B: That's right. It's easy!

UNIT 6 Recording 1

1 I've known her for ages.

2 They've travelled a lot.

3 He's never seen it before.

4 Nothing has changed.

5 I've worked in other countries.

UNIT 6 Recordings 2/3

P = Presenter	W1 = Woman 1
W2 = Woman 2	W3 = Woman 3
M = Man	

Part 1

P: We're in Manchester, and this is table tennis for the over-fifties. The people who play here play three times a week, so you don't need to tell them about how exercise makes you feel better.

W1: It gives you a great feeling. You feel fabulous. Any type of exercise is good for you, especially when you're my age. It just makes you feel good.

P: Scientists have now worked out that you can live longer if you have a healthy lifestyle. They did some research. They followed 20,000 people for more than ten years, and they looked at the different lifestyles they had. The results are interesting. They showed that people who don't smoke, who do regular exercise and who eat five portions of fresh fruit and vegetables every day actually live longer. These people actually live about fourteen years longer than the people who didn't have such healthy lifestyles. They lived longer and they didn't have so many health problems. Doctors say that even making a small change to your lifestyle can make a big difference to your health. Also, don't worry if you've got bad habits now. It's never too late to start. So, does everyone agree that it's a good idea to give up smoking, eat healthily, and do exercise in order to live longer? We asked people on the street to tell us what they think.

Part 2

W2: I don't know. I don't think it's that important. I mean, I don't eat five portions of fruit and vegetables every day. I don't like them, so I'm not going to do that.

W3: If I go out with my friends in the evening, then I'm going to smoke. Having a cigarette is social. It's part of the fun.

M: Absolutely. I think it's a great idea. Do exercise, eat well, stop smoking. And live a long and happy life. Everyone should do it.

P: The message is clear: scientists are telling us that if we want to live a long and healthy life, we need to look at how we live. So, I'm going to have a game of table tennis.

UNIT 6 Recording 4

D = Doctorv   P = Patient

1

D: Good morning. How can I help?

P: I'm worried about my leg.

D: Your leg? What's the matter with it?

P: Well, it's very painful. It hurts when I walk.

D: I see. How long have you had the problem?

P: Since yesterday.

D: Can I have a look?

P: Yes, of course.

2

D: Hello. What's the matter, Mr Smith?

P: I feel terrible.

D: All right. Where does it hurt?

P: Everywhere. And I can't sleep.

D: Ah. Have you got a temperature?

P: I don't know.

D: OK. Can I have a look?

P: Yes, of course.

D: That's fine. It's nothing to worry about.

P: But I feel terrible!

UNIT 6 Recording 5

D = Doctor   P = Patient

1

D: Good afternoon. What's the matter?

P: I've got a sore throat and a headache.

D: I see. How long have you had the problem?

P: About two weeks.

D: Have you got a temperature?

P: Yes. It's 38.5, so I've taken some aspirin.

D: I see. I think you've got a cold. You need plenty of rest and hot drinks.

2

P: I think I've broken my arm.

D: Oh dear. Can I have a look?

P: Yes. Here you are.

D: So, where does it hurt?

P: Here and here.

D: How did you do it?

P: I fell over.

D: I think you should go to hospital for an X-ray.

R2 Recording 1

D = Doctor   P = Patient

D: Good morning. What's the problem?

P: Doctor, I feel terrible. I have a backache all the time and it hurts when I walk.

D: I see. How long have you had this problem?

P: About two weeks.

D: Can I have a look? Where does it hurt?

P: Here. It's very painful. Sometimes I can't sleep because of the pain.

D: OK, I'll give you some medicine for it. And you shouldn't do any heavy work for a few weeks.

P: But I'm worried about missing work. I'm a builder.

D: I'll write a note. OK?

P: OK. Thanks, Doctor.

UNIT 1

1.1

1

1 B 2 E 3 G 4 J 5 H
6 D 7 F 8 A 9 I 10 C

2

2 What time do your English lessons start?
3 How often do you cook for your friends?
4 How many people are in your family?
5 Where does your mother come from?
6 Why did you sell your house?
7 How many glasses of water do you drink in a day?
8 Where is the classroom?
9 When did you last see your best friend?
10 Where did you go shopping?

3

2 What do you do
3 Who do you live
4 How many people live with you/in the house/in your house
5 What do you do/like to do in your free time
6 How often do you go to the cinema
7 Why are you studying English
8 Which class are you in
9 When did you start learning English

4A

1 D 2 A 3 E 4 F 5 C 6 B

B

1 F 2 T 3 F 4 T 5 T 6 F

C

1 You should stand up and walk around.
2 Having good relationships makes you happy.
3 Things like answering a difficult email and making a dentist's appointment.
4 You will feel happy now because you will look forward to the special thing.
5 You will feel good/better.
6 When you smile, you feel better.

D

1 exercise 2 relationships
3 touch 4 cross 5 forward

1.2

1

2 met, got on well 3 fell in love
4 proposed, accepted, got engaged
5 got married

2A

ask R decide R know I stop R
like R go I say I see I spend I
study R try R meet I walk R
work R get I

B

fall – fell know – knew go – went
say – said see – saw spend – spent
meet – met get – got

3

1 met 2 got 3 started 4 became
5 lived 6 had 7 talked 8 sent
9 didn't tell 10 decided 11 arrived
12 proposed

4

1 did you stay, found
2 ate, was
3 didn't have, rained
4 went, didn't like, thought
5 spent
6 was, didn't have
7 wrote, didn't understand
8 gave
9 did you get
10 started, moved

5A

1 ended (ends in /ɪd/, the others end in /d/)
2 arrived (ends in /d/, the others end in /t/)
3 finished (ends in /t/, the others end in /ɪd/)
4 invented (ends in /ɪd/, the others end in /d/)
5 started (ends in /ɪd/, the others end in /t/)

6A

a 2 b 4 c 1 d 6 e 3 f 5

B

1 He was eighteen (years old).
2 They were in Spain.
3 They promised to write to each other.
4 They decided to stop because it was too difficult.
5 They met again ten years later.
6 They felt (really) shocked.
7 Their son's name is Jamie.

C

1 mates 2 sunbathing 3 recognised
4 shocked 6 hanging out (with each other)

7

2 We saw Pompeii **and** we thought it was wonderful.
3 She didn't like her job, **so** she decided to leave.
4 They couldn't get married **because** her father wouldn't allow it.
5 He started taekwondo lessons **because** he wanted to get fit.
6 They wanted to buy the house, **but** the bank didn't give them the money.
7 I wanted to go to the concert, **but** I couldn't find a ticket.
8 I didn't sleep very well, **so** I'm very tired today.

8

2 Jon met Ella in an online group and they got on really well.
3 I didn't want to be late, so I left home early.
4 Matt proposed to Fiona, but/and she said no.
5 I like Clara, but she can be a bit rude sometimes.
6 We got married two years ago and we had a baby a year later.
7 The film was terrible, so they left early.
8 I'm studying medicine because I want to be a doctor.

1.3

1A

G	O	S	S	I	P	T
D	F	A	S	N	R	K
W	E	Y	L	T	S	D
Q	H	R	T	E	L	L
W	J	E	E	R	G	T
T	T	S	A	R	I	I
H	A	V	E	U	O	U
H	L	V	G	P	S	T
R	K	S	U	T	I	L

B

1 have 2 gossip 3 tell
4 say 5 tell 6 talk 7 interrupt

2

1 my friend 2 good weekend 3 isn't it
4 work here 5 Would you 6 Did you
7 do you 8 I'm sorry 9 was terrible
10 see you

3

2 Where‿are‿you going?
3 I come from‿Italy.
4 It's‿a beautiful day.
5 I'm‿afraid‿I can't remember.
6 Where did‿you buy‿it?
7 I'm sorry, but‿I don't‿understand.

4

1 Did you have a nice weekend?
2 Where did you go?
3 Would you like a drink?
4 So, do you like it here?
5 It was nice to meet you.
6 Let's keep in touch.

UNIT 2

2.1

1

1 company 2 bonus 3 staff 4 task
5 boss 6 employee 7 office 8 salary
Mystery word: customer

2

1 a ii, b i   2 a i, b ii   3 a ii, b i   4 a ii, b i
5 a ii, b i   6 a i, b ii

3

1 are you smiling   2 do you know
3 are they doing   4 are you drinking
5 Is he   6 She's wearing

4A

1 is   2 's/is working   3 doesn't like
4 's/is   5 's/is doing   6 's/is smiling
7 has   8 's/is playing   9 's/is looking
10 are visiting

B

1 Julio   2 Bruce   3 Natasha   4 Amei
5 Hernan

5A

2

B

1 It is in the office (on the fourth and
  fifth floors).
2 They can go bowling.
3 On the last Friday of every month,
  each department chooses a theme
  and the workers dress up accordingly.
4 They get a surprise trip.

C

1 (bowling) alley   2 basement
3 alternatives   4 uniforms
5 historical figures   6 trip

6A

1 Dear   2 about   3 hearing
4 Yours sincerely   5 Hi   6 It's   7 See
8 Cheers

The first email is formal. The second one
is informal.

2.2

1

2 foreign correspondent
3 fashion designer   4 IT consultant
5 rescue worker   6 sales rep
7 personal trainer

2A/B

6 syllables: foreign correspondent
5 syllables: fashion designer, IT
  consultant, personal trainer
4 syllables: rescue worker
2 syllables: sales rep

3

2 team   3 pressure   4 salary
5 holidays   6 risk   7 with

4A

2 usually   3 never   4 Once in a while
5 rarely   6 occasionally   7 never
8 always

5A

2 rarely happen   3 often happen
4 never happen

B

1 happen once in a while/occasionally
  happen
2 always happen
3 happen once in a while/occasionally
  happen

6A

2 safari guide   3 male elephant   4 pool
5 tourists

B

1 Story 1: a safari guide
  Story 2: a tourist
2 Because an elephant charged at them.
3 They escaped in the bus. No one was
  injured.

C

3 Story 1   4 Story 2   5 Story 1   6 Story 2

D

1 b   2 a   3 a   4 b

2.3

1A

1 keen, absolutely   2 love, can't
3 on, mind   4 very, don't

C

a 4   b 1   c 3   d 2

2A

1 Do you like working in a team?
2 I can't stand working under pressure.
3 I'm not very keen on my boss.
4 I don't like my colleagues.
5 I don't mind dealing with customers.
6 Are you keen on sport?

B

a 3   b 4   c 5   d 6   e 2   f 1

3

2 H   3 E   4 C   5 D   6 G   7 F   8 B

4A

1 Really   2 sounds interesting
3 And what about   4 That's great
5 see   6 Right

UNIT 3

3.1

1

2 get   3 go   4 see   5 get   6 have
7 go   8 go   9 have

2A

1 Are you going away on holiday this
  year?
2 Who is cooking your dinner this
  evening?
3 When are you going to the dentist?
4 What are you doing this weekend?
5 Are you going to play any sport this
  week?
6 Are you going to marry Roberto?
7 What time are you meeting your sister?
8 What are you going to do to improve
  your English?
9 Are you having a party at the weekend?
10 Are you going to the gym after work?

B

b 7   c 6   d 8   e 3   f 1   g 5   h 4
i 10   j 9

3

1 are you doing, 'm staying
2 going to look for   3 'm speaking
4 are meeting   5 Are you coming
6 are you going, 're going

4A

1 25,000   2 Tavern on the Green
3 Shakespeare   4 Top of the Rock
5 Immigration   6 1892

B

1 Because there are over 25,000 trees
  and many different types of birds.
2 You can go ice-skating.
3 It's a skyscraper (in the middle of the
  city).
4 By ferry.
5 (Some of the) old, unused buildings
  (on the island).

5

Hi Mike,
I'm playing football later with a few of
the boys from work. Would you like to
come?
Dan

Dan,
I'm sorry, but **I'm busy** tonight. **I'm taking**
Leila out for a meal. Wish me luck!
Thanks anyway.
Mike

Hi guys,
A few of us **are** going out for a curry on
Friday night. Do you want **to** come with
us? We're **meeting** at the Indian Tree at
8p.m.
Emma

Hi Emma,
I'd love to. See you there.
Jan

6A

1 I'm having a party
2 Do you want to come
3 We're going to have music
4 Julie is getting tickets for the theatre
5 We're going to see Shakespeare's *Hamlet*
6 Would you like to come

3.2

1A

1 d nightclub   2 h shopping mall
3 b waterfront   4 e nature trail
5 c concert hall   6 g street market
7 a sports field   8 f countryside

B

A concert hall   B nightclub
C shopping mall   D waterfront
E sports field   F street market

2B

1 T   2 F   3 T   4 T   5 F   6 F

C

1 45,000 dollars   2 no   3 yes

D

1 terrible   2 all over   3 message
4 artist   5 away   6 surprise

3A

1 What country   2 Who invented
3 Which painting   4 Which Caribbean
5 Which French   6 Who spends
7 How many   8 Who uses
9 Who earned   10 Which city

B

a 5   b 8   c 3   d 4   e 7   f 9   g 2
h 6   i 1   j 10

4

2 Who invented basketball in 1891?
3 How many hours a month do Canadians spend online?
4 Who brought football to Brazil from England in the nineteenth century?
5 Whose sitcom is one of the most successful TV shows of all time?
6 Who first developed the sport of chess boxing in the 1990s?
7 What/Which country won the World Cup in 2014?
8 What is the smallest desert in the world?
9 Whose daughter is called Lisa Marie?
10 How many people visit the British Museum every year?

3.3

1A

A	R	R	A	N	G	E	V
C	A	N	C	E	L	M	O
H	B	Y	H	A	V	E	D
A	O	E	E	I	G	P	I
N	O	S	C	L	F	N	T
G	K	T	K	P	E	L	A
E	R	O	O	C	T	K	L
T	M	F	A	E	S	R	K

B

2 She called me because she wanted to **have** a chat.
3 Please **book** a table for us at the Blue Fin Restaurant tonight.
4 There's been a problem and I can't attend, so I'm calling to **cancel** my reservation.
5 Don't forget to **check** the train times before you leave for the station.
6 I'd like to come to the 4.30 performance, not the 6.30, and I'm calling to **change** my ticket.
7 The manager of Triad Books is on the phone. He wants to **talk** business.

2

2 d   3 g   4 c   5 f   6 b   7 a

3

A: Hello. ~~I'm~~ **It's/This is** Jim. Is Trudy there?
B: I'm afraid ~~but~~ she's not here at the moment.
A: Oh really? Can I leave ~~the~~ **a** message?
B: Of course.
A: Can you tell her that we need to discuss the party on Friday?
B: Yes, I will. I'll ask her ~~for calling~~ **to call** you back.
A: Thanks a lot.
B: You're welcome. Bye.
A: Bye.

4

a 6   b 8   c 3   d 2   e 9   f 1   g 7
h 4   i 5   j 10

5

1 What's the name, please
2 I didn't catch that
3 Can you repeat that
4 can you speak up, please
5 can you slow down, please

6

1 tickets, after six/6/6.00
2 station, eight/8/8.00
3 bookings, eight/8/8.00

1A

2 How   3 Where   4 Do   5 Do
6 Where   7 How   8 What

B

a 8   b 5   c 2   d 6   e 3   f 4   g 7   h 1

2A

get: the bus, on well
go: on holiday, to the cinema, sightseeing
have: children, a barbecue, time off work
spend: money on clothes, time with family

B

2 get the bus   3 spend time with family
4 go to the cinema   5 have a barbecue
6 get on well   7 go sightseeing

3

1 took   2 stayed   3 didn't tell
4 went out   5 asked   6 complained
7 was   8 told   9 talked   10 decided

4A

1 too   2 isn't, lovely   3 So, come, city
4 good, weekend, do, much
5 would, like, drink, love, water
6 see, later, See, soon

5

2 I ~~stay~~ **'m/am staying** with some friends for a few days so I can look for somewhere to live.
3 I'm not knowing **don't know** what time the lesson starts.
4 They ~~spend~~ **'re spending** time with their family in Germany at the moment.
5 ~~We're~~ usually ~~going~~ **We** usually **go** out for a pizza about once a week.
6 I'm not understanding **don't understand** where Ian is. He never arrives late.
7 ~~Do you watch~~ **Are you watching** this programme, or can I watch the football on the other channel?

6

2 I hardly ever see her because she works for a different company.
3 My parents occasionally help us when we're busy.
4 I usually get up at about 6.30a.m.
5 Sal's very upset – she never wants to see him again.
6 Once in a while we go to Scotland./We go to Scotland once in a while.
7 I rarely have the chance to spend time with my sister.
8 I take the children to school every day./Every day I take the children to school.

7

2 absolutely love   **3** can't stand
4 doesn't like   **5** don't mind   **6** hates
7 like working   **8** 'm/am keen on

8

1 I'm going   **2** is   **3** 's going to start
4 are you   **5** coming   **6** We're

9

1 salary, boss   **2** sightseeing
3 work, pressure   **4** exhibition
5 get, long, holidays   **6** art gallery
7 concert, ticket   **8** task

10A

2 Where **do** you come from?
3 ✓
4 Why **did** David leave his job?
5 How often **do** you play football?
6 How much **does** it cost to fly to Russia?
7 ✓
8 ✓
9 When **did** you last go to a concert?
10 ✓
11 Why **are** you learning English?
12 Where **did** you buy that coat?

B

a 7   **b** 6   **c** 10   **d** 2   **e** 11   **f** 3   **g** 5
h 4   **i** 9   **j** 8   **k** 12   **l** 1

CHECK 1

1 b   **2** a   **3** c   **4** b   **5** c   **6** a   **7** b
8 b   **9** c   **10** a   **11** c   **12** b   **13** a
14 b   **15** a   **16** b   **17** c   **18** a   **19** c
20 b   **21** c   **22** a   **23** b   **24** b   **25** c
26 a   **27** c   **28** b   **29** c   **30** a

UNIT 4

4.1

1A

1 make   **2** do   **3** do   **4** make   **5** do
6 make   **7** do   **8** make

B

2 I made a phone call.
3 I did business with him.
4 I made a meal.
5 I did a project.
6 I did my homework.
7 I made a speech.
8 I did (really) well.

2

2 Have you ever sung
3 have never travelled
4 has never used
5 Has she ever made
6 Have you ever lied
7 has never eaten
8 Have you ever won

3

1 b   **2** b   **3** a   **4** a
5 b   **6** a   **7** a   **8** b

4

1 've been   **2** 've made
3 Have you ever spent
4 went   **5** laughed   **6** has spent
7 haven't had   **8** watched
9 've never eaten

5B

1 T   **2** T   **3** F   **4** F   **5** F

C

1 a   **2** b   **3** b   **4** a

6

The Greatest Mind in Fiction
Most of fiction's great minds ~~belongs~~ **belong (gr)** either to criminals or to the men and women who catch them. ~~A~~ **The (gr)** greatest of these is probably Sherlock Holmes. The Holmes stories were written by Sir Arthur Conan Doyle, **(p)** a ~~docter~~ **doctor (sp)** from ~~edinburgh~~ **Edinburgh (p)**, Scotland. Conan Doyle knew a lot about the human body and ~~pollice~~ **police (sp)** work, and he ~~has~~ **(gr)** used this information in his books. Very quickly, Conan Doyle's hero ~~beccame~~ **became (sp)** popular. When Holmes was killed in one story, thousands of readers protested. Conan Doyle changed his mind, and Holmes appeared in another story. **(p)**

4.2

1

Across: 4 test   **7** piano   **8** sport
10 online   **11** take
Down: 1 mistakes   **2** performance
3 study   **5** languages   **6** uniform
9 play

2

Conversation 1: 2 don't have to   **3** can
4 Can   **5** can't   **6** Can   **7** can
8 have to   **9** can
Conversation 2: 1 have to   **2** have to
3 have to   **4** don't have to   **5** can
6 can   **7** Can   **8** can

3

1 do I have to   **2** Can I   **3** We must
4 We don't have to   **5** She can't
6 You mustn't

4A

1 You **can't** have your mobile phone switched on.
2 You have to register before **you can** use the site.
3 I'm afraid **she can't** speak to you at the moment.
4 **You can** use my computer if you want to.

B

1 **You have to/must** be good at foreign languages if you want to learn Mandarin.
2 **We have to/must** be there on time, or they won't let us in.
3 **We don't have to** have a licence to fish here.
4 **You mustn't** tell him I'm here.

5

2 can't   **3** must/have to   **4** can
5 can't/mustn't   **6** have to   **7** can
8 must/have to   **9** can't   **10** Can
11 can't/mustn't

6A

1 A   **2** B

B

1 S   **2** S   **3** H   **4** S   **5** H

C

1 b   **2** a   **3** a

4.3

1

1 memorise   **2** look, up   **3** reread
4 chat   **5** subtitles   **6** go online
7 note down

2

1 I don't think you should
2 Why don't you try
3 I think you should get
4 Why don't you buy
5 I think you should try
6 It's a good idea to think

3

1 I think you should
2 Why don't you/Why not
3 Try talking
4 I don't think it's a good idea to
5 Why don't you try
6 I think you should

4A

1 c   **2** f   **3** e   **4** a   **5** b   **6** d
a suppose   **b** You're   **c** a good   **d** so
e sure that's   **f** right

UNIT 5

5.1

1A

ship, motorbike, tram, moped, aeroplane, lorry, speedboat, helicopter, coach, ferry, hot air balloon, underground, minibus

B

four wheels or more: taxi, lorry, coach, minibus
air: aeroplane, helicopter, hot air balloon
water: ship, speedboat, ferry
two wheels: motorbike, moped
public transport (city): tram, underground

C

2 underground   3 hot air balloon
4 coach   5 lorry   6 motorbike/moped
7 speedboat   8 ship

2

1 g   2 f   3 c   4 a   5 d   6 h   7 b   8 e

3

2 was playing   3 didn't hear
4 did it happen   5 was climbing
6 landed   7 saw   8 was studying
9 said   10 Were you driving
11 was going   12 came   13 saw
14 were you going   15 was going
16 dropped

4A

1 drop his ticket   2 pay the taxi driver
3 go through security   4 go for a walk
5 try to sleep   6 decide to use his mobile phone

B

2 was paying the taxi driver
3 was going through security
4 went for a walk   5 were trying to sleep
6 decided to use

6A

A

B

1 T   2 T   3 F   4 F   5 F   6 T

7

1 he typed the wrong destination on a travel website
2 it was very small
3 his parents and friends from Germany sent him some money

5.2

1A

Across: 3 digital camera   **7** notebook
8 sun hat   **9** suitcase
Down: 1 waterproof clothes
2 walking boots   **4** souvenirs
5 binoculars   **6** money belt

B

2 souvenirs   3 sun hat   4 walking boots
5 waterproof clothes   6 binoculars
7 money belt   8 suitcase
9 digital camera

2

1 reading   2 to see   3 to get
4 spending   5 to rain   6 to refund
7 travelling   8 to finish   9 to see
10 writing   11 living   12 going

3

2 I expect to hear from the travel agent later today.
3 We want to go on holiday, but we're too busy.
4 We seem to go back to the same place every year.
5 Alan chose to stay in a hotel.
6 We enjoy walking and looking at (the) beautiful countryside.
7 I decided to travel on my own.
8 We avoid visiting tourist resorts in (the) summer.
9 We need to book our flights before (the) prices go up.

4A

a 2   b 4   c 3   d 1

B

1 T   2 F   3 T   4 F   5 F   6 T

C

1 earplugs   2 hostels   3 patient
4 ATM   5 skills   6 local

5A

Story 1: b, h, d
Story 2: f, i, e, c

5.3

1

1 g   2 b   3 c   4 a   5 f   6 d   7 e

2

1 on   2 along   3 through   4 –   5 at
6 of   7 –   8 past

3A

2 bar   3 university hall   4 theatre
5 park   6 library

4A

1 Can you help me
2 You can't miss it
3 Can you show me on the map
4 Is this the right way
5 You'll see it in front of you
6 Can I walk
7 It takes about ten minutes
8 Is it far
9 So I need to go left at the cinema

UNIT 6

6.1

1

1 fresh   2 junk   3 alcohol   4 worrying
5 vitamins   6 relaxing   7 caffeine
8 fizzy   9 exercise   10 running

2

1 has been   2 have ever watched
3 has gone, haven't seen
4 Have you finished, haven't started
5 has arrived   6 Have you found
7 have you known, haven't been
8 Have you heard, Have you decided

3

2 He's worked for that company for six months.
3 We've lived in Turkey since 2013.
4 I haven't been to the cinema for a long time.
5 They've been here for two months now.
6 I haven't cleaned the house since last Monday.
7 She hasn't listened to that music since she was a teenager.
8 We haven't heard from him since he left.
9 Bob has been a builder for more than forty years.
10 The phone hasn't rung since 10 o'clock.
11 I've wanted to climb a mountain since I was a child.

4

2 did you start   3 did you want
4 started   5 felt   6 have lived
7 I've had   8 I've worked   9 travelled
10 met   11 I have ever seen
12 have used   13 have become

5A

1 a   2 b   3 a   4 a   5 a

6A

1 c   2 a   3 b

B

1 F   2 T   3 F   4 T   5 F   6 F

C

1 c   2 e   3 b   4 a   5 d

6.2

1

In any order: mango, plum, grape, apple, orange, lemon, melon
(NB: *Pear* is also possible, but it does not appear in the Students' Book.)

2

1 chicken 2 lemon 3 broccoli
4 Beefsteak 5 spinach 6 potatoes
7 leg of lamb 8 cabbage 9 courgettes
10 shrimps 11 onions 12 garlic
13 mussels 14 cheese

3

1 a 2 c 3 c 4 a 5 b 6 a 7 c 8 b

4

2 We won't eat animals in the future.
3 We may eat more organic food.
4 Junk food might become illegal.
5 People in the West will get fatter./
  People will get fatter in the West.
6 There may not be any fish left in the
  sea.

5A

1 C 2 D 3 B 4 A

B

1 b 2 b 3 a 4 a 5 b 6 b

C

1 concentrating 2 variety
3 experiments 4 on average

6A

1 I have always liked cooking **and** I cook
  every day.
2 I was very young **when** I cooked my
  first meal.
3 I don't eat much meat, **but** I eat a lot
  of fish.
4 I was working as a chef in a horrible
  hotel **when** I decided to open my own
  restaurant.
5 I don't drink alcohol, **but** I use a little
  wine in some of the dishes I prepare.
6 I like meeting customers at my
  restaurant **and** I ask them about the
  food.

B

1 My favourite types of food are pasta
  and fresh fish. I **also** like fruit.
2 Every morning I buy vegetables **and**
  herbs from the market. I **also** buy
  meat there.
3 I find that the food in the market is
  fresher **and** better quality. It's **also**
  cheaper.

6.3

1

Across: 5 painkillers **7** broken
9 antibiotics **10** X-ray
Down: 2 cold **3** rest **4** temperature
6 headache **8** sore

2

Doctor: 1 e **2** c **3** a **4** f **5** d **6** b
Patient: 7 k **8** j **9** h **10** g **11** i

3A

1
P: I'm worried **about** my leg.
D: Your leg? What's **the** matter with it?
P: Well, **it's** very painful. It hurts when I
   walk.
D: I see. How long have **had** you the
   problem?
P: Since yesterday. ✓
D: Can I **have** a look?
P: Yes, of course. ✓

2
D: Hello. What's **the** matter, Mr Smith?
P: I feel terrible. ✓
D: All right. Where does **it** hurt?
P: Everywhere. And I **can't** sleep.
D: Ah. Have you got **a** temperature?
P: I don't know. ✓
D: OK. Can I have **a** look?
P: Yes, of course. ✓
D: That's fine. It's nothing **to** worry about.
P: But I feel terrible! ✓

4A

1
1 What's the matter
2 How long have you had the problem
3 Have you got/Do you have a
  temperature
4 you've got a cold
5 plenty of rest
6 hot drinks

2
1 Can I have a look
2 Where does it hurt
3 How did you do it
4 go to hospital for an X-ray

REVIEW 2

1

2 've/have never visited 3 came
4 've/have been 5 got 6 did you go
7 haven't met 8 didn't hear
9 's/has never won
10 has she ever eaten

2

1 a 2 c 3 c 4 b 5 a 6 a 7 c
8 b 9 b 10 c

3

2 Should 3 shouldn't 4 suppose
5 sure 6 think 7 Why

4

1 happened 2 was studying
3 was sitting 4 saw 5 realised
6 wasn't looking 7 didn't help 8 had
9 was watching 10 received

5

2 I want **to write** a great book so I can
  become famous!
3 I need **to get up** early tomorrow, so
  I'm going to bed now.
4 We usually avoid **driving** at this time
  because of all the traffic.
5 Do you enjoy **cooking** meals for large
  groups of people?
6 They decided **to clean** the whole
  house after the party.
7 She loves **shopping** for clothes.
8 I always seem **to lose** something
  when I travel – usually my plane
  ticket!

6

1 g 2 d 3 c 4 e 5 f 6 b 7 a

7

2 since months 3 for January
4 since years 5 for the last meal
6 for now 7 since months

8

1 I ~~don't will~~ **won't** go to the cinema
  tonight because I'm busy.
2 I may ~~to~~ send her an email.
3 We ~~not might~~ **might not** have time to
  go to the museum.
4 The weather report on TV said there
  might ~~to~~ be storms.
5 Joshua may not ~~be~~ go to the game.
6 I~~'m~~ might be late to class tonight.

9A

a D b P c D d P e P f D

B

1 c 2 e 3 a 4 f 5 b 6 d

10

1 art 2 binoculars 3 caffeine
4 decision 5 exam 6 fizzy 7 games
8 homework 9 information technology
10 junk food **11** kit 12 literature
13 motorbike/moped 14 notebook
15 online 16 pill 17 rollerblading
18 ship 19 tram 20 uniform
21 vegetables 22 waterproof 23 yoga

CHECK 2

1 c 2 a 3 b 4 b 5 a 6 a 7 c
8 c 9 a 10 b 11 c 12 b 13 b
14 c 15 a 16 c 17 b 18 c 19 b
20 c 21 a 22 c 23 b 24 c 25 c
26 a 27 b 28 b 29 a 30 c